THE BOOK OF
HUMAN
EMPOWERMENT

CREATED BY

MULTI #1 INTERNATIONAL BESTSELLING AUTHOR & AWARD WINNING SPEAKER

ERIK SWANSON

PURPOSE & MINDSET

THE BOOK OF HUMAN EMPOWERMENT

PURPOSE & MINDSET

FEATURING

ERIK SWANSON ~ BRIAN SMITH
DORIA CORDOVA ~ LUCAS FOSTER

FOREWORD BY BRIAN TRACY

Hardback ISBN: 978-1-964330-09-9
Paperback ISBN: 978-1-964330-06-8

Global Speakers Mastermind & Habitude Warrior Masterminds

Join us and become a member of our tribe! Our Global Speakers Mastermind is a virtual group of amazing thinkers and leaders who meet twice a month. Sessions are designed to be 'to the point' and focused while sharing fantastic techniques to grow your mindset as well as your pocketbooks. We also include famous guest speaker spots for our private Masterclasses. We also designate certain sessions for our members to mastermind with each other & and counsel on the topics discussed in our previous Masterclasses. It's time for you to join a tribe who truly cares about **YOU** and your future and start surrounding yourself with the famous leaders and mentors of our time. It is time for you to up-level your life, businesses, and relationships.

For more information to check out our Masterminds:
Team@HabitudeWarrior.com
www.DecideToBeAwesome.com

PURPOSE & MINDSET

BECOME AN INTERNATIONAL
#1 BESTSELLING AUTHOR & SPEAKER

Habitude Warrior International has been highlighting award-winning Speakers and #1 Bestselling Authors for over 25 years. They know what it takes to become #1 in your field and how to get the best exposure around the world. If you have ever considered giving yourself the GIFT of becoming a well-known Speaker and a fantastically well known #1 Best-Selling Author, then you should email their team right away to find out more information in how you can become involved. They have the best of the best when it comes to resources in achieving the bestselling status in your particular field. Start surrounding yourself with the N.Y. Times Bestsellers of our time and start seeing your dreams become reality!

For more information to become a #1 Bestselling Author & Speaker on our Habitude Warrior Conferences Please text the word AUTHORS to 619-304-6268 And also go to: www.DecideToBeAwesome.com

Contents

Prologue

THE BOOK OF HUMAN EMPOWERMENT

Empowerment is more than a feeling or experience—it's a global movement. I'm thrilled to introduce you to *The Book of Human Empowerment* book series, a transformative collection that brings together 33+ remarkable co-authors and a select lineup of celebrity contributors, each sharing their personal stories, insights, and experiences on what it means to create, design, and live an empowered life. Our series is designed to ignite the power within you, one action at a time.

Volume 1: Purpose & Mindset

Living on purpose is the foundation for a meaningful life. We often find ourselves drifting without clear direction in today's fast-paced world. But in this first volume, our authors teach you how to take control, live with intention, and align your daily actions with your deepest values and goals. It's about waking up daily with purpose, embracing your passions, and sharing your unique talents with the world. You'll learn practical strategies for setting goals, being present, and making decisions that move you closer to the life you truly want to live.

Volume 2: Trust & Integrity

In this volume, we explore the bedrock of very successful relationships —whether personal, professional or even your relationship with yourself. Trust starts from within. It's the confidence in who you are, the values you stand for, and the authenticity you bring to the table. Allow our co-authors to walk you through personal journeys in building trust, maintaining integrity, and staying true to your moral compass, even in challenging times. As you read this volume, you'll discover that integrity isn't just a word; it's a way of life that leads to lasting success and deep, meaningful connections.

Volume 3: Community & Alignment

Community & Alignment teaches us that no one succeeds alone. True empowerment comes from when we align ourselves with others—finding common ground, working together, and supporting one another toward shared goals. This volume is packed with stories and strategies from people who have built strong, thriving communities by understanding the importance of connection and collaboration. Our co-authors emphasize that going further with a team is far better than struggling alone. When we align our purpose with those of others, the potential for growth, productivity, and fulfillment is limitless.

This series is a guide to help all of us unlock our full potential and live the life we were meant to live. Take this journey with us, dive deep into each pillar of success, and empower yourself to rise to new heights. I invite you to join all of us in this journey of human empowerment as we strive to bring awesomeness to the world together!

Erik Swanson ~ Multi #1 International Bestselling Author & Award-Winning Speaker

Introduction

DON GREEN

Human empowerment simply means that people have the power to control their own lives. Empowerment fosters equality and allows people to be respected in their communities and confident in their abilities. Empowerment also gives people the tools to be stronger or more successful. A true leader knows how to create an atmosphere that is conducive to developing empowerment in others. A true leader does not say that he or she empowers others. Rather, they create an environment and atmosphere that empowers others.

In high school, one of my earliest business ventures was operating a small zoo on the side of US Highway 23. At the time, it was a major highway and most people traveling from north to south used this road. Today, it is still a busy road and will take travelers from Mackinaw City, Michigan to Jacksonville, Florida.

My little zoo was called Indian Mountain Reptile Garden and one of the biggest attractions was the snake pit. The snake pit contained several varieties of snakes, such as rattlesnakes and copperheads, that were native to my local area. The admission price was $0.25 for adults and $0.10 for children. I advertised for the business by nailing Royal Crown Cola signs to trees along US 23. The bottom of the sign said, "Indian Mountain Reptile Garden straight ahead."

With a good income and very little expenses, I was able to add exhibits to my zoo. One of my prized animals was a black bear that I named Sammy. Black bears were rare at this time, so it was a treat for customers to see him. I also had monkeys, one bobcat, one skunk, several exotic birds, and a few smaller animals. Business was very good and my Dad helped me build a souvenir stand, which greatly added to my income. I purchased items, such as ashtrays, for $0.25, placed an Indian Mountain Reptile Garden sticker on them, and resold the items for $1.00. Not a bad markup.

When I first started the zoo, the sole exhibit was the snake pit. At the time, I showed visitors the snakes and gave a little description of each one. However, the souvenir stand added an extra source of income.

In the 1950s, many locals in my area traveled north or south to seek employment in other industries. Often, during summer vacations, these same people would travel home to visit with friends and family and many of these people would stop at my zoo. On good days, the zoo brought in more than $100.

If I had regular customers, I would often let them take visitors around the zoo, showing the animals, while I worked in the souvenir stand. The person who showed the animals felt empowered. Notice, I did not empower the person but allowed them to be in a position of empowerment.

When I started high school, a new highway was completed that bypassed my zoo. As you might guess, business slowed and I decided to work for a consumer loan company, making $1.15 an hour. My duty was to try to collect past due funds. Most of the time, the people who were behind on their loans had suffered harassment from collectors and were unlikely to cooperate. I was given a route that contained twenty or more delinquent accounts.

Many people would not answer the door when I came to their house. I knew I needed to handle the accounts differently if I wanted to be successful, so I learned to help those who were behind on their loans. I wanted to work with people and would often help them develop a payment plan.

Additionally, my manager and I would allow customers to borrow additional amounts, perhaps with a co-signer or a new loan. These techniques created an atmosphere of empowerment and led my customers to feel empowered, instead of harassed or threatened. As a result, they were more likely to work with me and pay their future bills on time.

I worked long, hard hours for the consumer loan company and climbed the ladder until I became manager and had my own office. At the time, I was one of the youngest managers in the company's history. My office was located in Indiana and upper management periodically offered incentives to employees. One of the incentive programs was to award offices with points for such objectives as increasing loans, and controlling past due debts. These points could then be used to purchase items from a gift catalog that was provided by the company. The catalogs contained hundreds of items and contained gifts that would appeal to everyone.

However, the points went straight to the office manager to distribute to the employees. In other words, employees did not individually earn points—the entire office earned points. Many branch managers would collect 50% of the points earned and distribute the rest to the employees. I wanted to promote an atmosphere of empowerment, so I decided that all of the employees of my branch would receive the same percentage of points. We were all working towards the same goal.

My office ended up winning the most points of the other branches at least five times. When the contest was over, I attended a managers' meeting and the President of the Company asked me to come forward. He asked me how I had achieved the results. I pointed out that it was not me— instead, it was a group effort that allowed us to have great results.

A few years later, I started working in a newly formed bank. I worked for that bank for eight years and then I took a job with another bank. This bank was in bad financial shape with only $35,000 in capital. It had lost about $1,500,000 by the time I started working there. The first year after I came, the bank made a profit of $90,000 and during my eighteen-year career, the bank made millions of dollars and was later sold.

At that point, I started working as the Executive Director of the Napoleon Hill Foundation, a position that I have held for twenty-four years. Throughout my career, I diligently tried to create an environment that allowed others to feel empowered. I believe this was one of the keys to my success. My success was directly tied to those who worked with me.

DON GREEN

Don Green is an American business entrepreneur, having built a successful savings bank, a real estate enterprise, and a host of other small and successful businesses in southwestern Virginia prior to his latest career with the Napoleon Hill Foundation.

As CEO of the Napoleon Hill Foundation, Don Green has energized the works of the famed author with a host of new books by noted authors, demonstrating how the principles of the late Mr. Hill work to advance the individual in network with others around the globe. He has demonstrated unique determination to expand knowledge of Mr. Hill's motivational work the world over.

Moreover, Don is a new global social entrepreneur. He has become one of the leading evangelists of entrepreneurial self-help through properly utilizing Mr. Hill's *Keys to Success* and *Think and Grow Rich.* He accepts nontraditional ideas, change, and foresight, which are tempered and bounded only by positive action. He is a realist with a visionary outlook.

Don is a goal-setter. He calibrates his goals and objectives carefully but routinely works with sound methodology with a dedicated fever to achieve success. Don takes great pride in working with younger adults who seek to better understand the principles of business entrepreneurialism and work ethic. Each year, he devotes an extended period of his time to assisting Central Appalachian college students through scholarships.

Don Green, a resident of Wise, Virginia, the birthplace of Napoleon Hill, brings nearly 45 years of banking, finance, and entrepreneurship experience to his role as Executive Director of the Napoleon Hill Foundation. His first youthful business venture was charging admission to see his pet bear—yes, the living, growling kind! Since 2000, Green has traveled worldwide and used his finance skills to grow the Foundation's funds to continue the Foundation's educational outreach to prisons.

Green has modeled leadership skills as a CEO and taught them through the PMA Science of Success course at the University of Virginia's College at Wise. Don specializes in discussing his personal experiences in leadership and providing audiences with proven methods of applying Dr. Hill's success philosophy to business. Dr. Peter Yun recently featured him in a presentation on the Importance of Entrepreneurship in a National Economy at a United Nations Forum.

Don M. Green is executive director of the Napoleon Hill Foundation and president of the foundation board at the University of Virginia-Wise. He became CEO of Black Diamond Savings Bank at 41 and studied under personal development master W. Clement Stone. He travels extensively, lecturing worldwide for the Foundation. Most recently, Mr. Green was featured in a United Nations forum on the importance of entrepreneurship within the national economy.

www.NapHill.org

PURPOSE & MINDSET

Foreword

BRIAN TRACY

As someone who has spent more than five decades teaching, coaching, and empowering individuals worldwide, I have witnessed firsthand how a powerful mindset can truly transform lives.

I am particularly grateful to Erik Swanson for the opportunities to contribute to many of his book series. Erik has been a dear friend and mentee for over twenty-five years, and his journey as a speaker and leader has been remarkable. Watching him grow into the influential figure he is today has been immensely rewarding. Erik has embodied the principles that I have shared with countless others, and I am proud of the impact he continues to have on so many. It is with great respect that I contribute my thoughts here, as Erik's invitation to share these ideas comes from a place of mutual respect and a shared passion for empowering others.

There are more than eight million millionaires in the United States today. Most of them are self-made. They started with nothing and earned all their money within one generation. The ten wealthiest multi-billionaires in the U.S. all started with nothing and earned their fortunes within their lifetimes. As I've learned and taught, the path to success is accessible to all.

Fully 80% of self-made millionaires are entrepreneurs or salespeople. Starting and building your own business has always been the high road to wealth in the U.S. Today, the country remains one of the most entrepreneurial nations in the world. Remarkably, 70% of Americans dream of starting their own business, and 1/12th of Americans currently work in startups.

Entrepreneurship is natural for most people. Every one of us possesses the talents and abilities required to start and build a successful business, take control of our lives, and achieve financial freedom. What is often missing is simply knowing how to do it.

If you can drive a car, you can learn to be a successful entrepreneur. As Richard Branson once said, "Once you learn how to start and build a business, you can do it over and over again. The principles are the same." The wonderful news is that all business skills are learnable. Whether it's customer service, marketing, or administration, these skills can be acquired and refined.

In *The Book of Human Empowerment*, the focus is clear: purpose and mindset. Success doesn't just hinge on what we do but also how we think. Over my career, I've found that the wealthiest and most successful people think in specific ways that drive their decisions. To start a business or achieve financial independence, you need courage, optimism, and persistence—three qualities found in every successful entrepreneur I've encountered.

First, successful entrepreneurs have the courage to launch without guarantees of success. They face the prospect of failure but push forward in pursuit of opportunity, freedom, control, and financial independence. Second, they are optimists. With a positive mental attitude, they keep moving forward, even when the road is tough. Third, they are persistent. They don't give up, even when things seem insurmountable. Failure, in their minds, is simply not an option.

The purpose of any business, I always say, is not just to make money but to create and keep a customer. Profits are the result of skillful customer acquisition and customer service, not the primary goal. Every business boils down to three simple activities:

- Find or create a product that people want.

- Marketing and selling it.

- Managing the people, money, and operations.

These basic principles apply not just to business but to life itself.

In the same way, when thinking about *The Book of Human Empowerment*, the question becomes: What do we offer the world? What value do we bring? The chapters in this book are about helping individuals discover that value within themselves, tapping into their potential to become the best versions of themselves.

The three questions to ask before starting a business are the same questions you can ask about life. Is there a market for what you offer—your skills, your knowledge, your mindset? Are there enough opportunities for you to grow and succeed? And finally, how will you reach those opportunities?

Building a wealthy mindset, like building a business, comes down to a few simple principles. You must specialize—identify what you do best and focus on it. You must differentiate—stand out from others by providing unique value. You must segment—understand your ideal audience and serve them effectively. Finally, you must concentrate—focus your energy on the areas where you can make the most impact.

This same mindset can be applied to personal empowerment. To succeed, you must know who you are, what you value, and how to use your strengths to serve others. The stories, lessons, and insights shared in *The Book of Human Empowerment* are powerful reminders of how we can transform our thinking and, ultimately, our lives.

As you read through the pages of this book, I encourage you to reflect on the three qualities I mentioned earlier—courage, optimism, and persistence—and how they apply to your life. Whether you are building a business, pursuing a personal goal, or overcoming a significant challenge, these principles are universal.

Life will always present us with challenges, much like the biblical story of David and Goliath. But, like David, we can conquer the giants in our lives by sharpening our minds, focusing on our goals, and never giving up. The path to a wealthy mindset and a wealthy life is not paved with luck but with intentional actions and the right mindset.

Remember, the key to success is simple: add value. The more value you add, the more success you will create. This is true in business, in relationships, and in every area of life. Your purpose, your mindset, and your actions will ultimately determine your level of success.

I hope you enjoy the lessons and insights shared within this book. It has been my honor to contribute to this series, and I want to express my deep appreciation to Erik Swanson for inviting me to be a part of all of these important projects. May you find the inspiration you need to reach your fullest potential and make a lasting impact in your life and the lives of others.

~ Brian Tracy, Chairman and CEO, Brian Tracy International

Photo Credit: Cathcart Institute - CPE™ Awards, La Jolla 2024

BRIAN TRACY

Brian Tracy is Chairman and CEO of Brian Tracy International, a company specializing in the training and development of individuals and organizations. Brian's goal is to help you achieve your personal and business goals faster and easier than you ever imagined.

Brian Tracy has consulted for more than 1,000 companies and addressed more than 5,000,000 people in 5,000 talks and seminars throughout the US, Canada, and 70 other countries worldwide. As a keynote speaker and seminar leader, he addresses more than 250,000 people each year.

He has studied, researched, written, and spoken for 30 years in the fields of economics, history, business, philosophy, and psychology. He is the top-selling author of over 70 books that have been translated into dozens of languages.

He has written and produced more than 300 audio and video learning programs, including the worldwide bestselling Psychology of Achievement, which has been translated into more than 28 languages.

He speaks to corporate and public audiences on the subjects of Personal and Professional Development, including the executives and staff of many of America's largest corporations. His exciting talks and seminars on Leadership, Selling, Self-Esteem, Goals, Strategy, Creativity, and Success Psychology bring about immediate changes and long-term results. Brian Tracy is the recipient of many awards including The Habitude Warrior Lifetime Achievement Award.

He has traveled and worked in over 107 countries on six continents, and speaks four languages. Brian is happily married and has four children. He is active in community and national affairs, and is the President of three companies headquartered in Solana Beach, California.

www.BrianTracy.com

ERIK SWANSON

ALIGN YOUR MINDSET WITH YOUR TRUE PURPOSE

"I am here for a purpose and that purpose is to grow into a mountain, not to shrink to a grain of sand. Henceforth will I apply ALL my efforts to become the highest mountain of all and I will strain my potential until it cries for mercy."
~ **Og Mandino**

Practicing Purpose at an Early Age

What does it mean to have purpose in life? What does it mean to follow your purpose? Why is it so vitally important to keep your purpose in front of you at all times?

These were questions that were instilled in me at an early age. I started my self-development journey when I was in my teens and always knew I had a purpose in my life! I could feel it like a burning desire!

But, looking back at it now, I realize that I had purpose in my mindset even earlier in life. I remember when I was in kindergarten, I had a major crush on a girl named Kirsten. Wow! I was so in love with her. I'm not totally sure she knew it back then. I would follow her around like a little puppy dog every day. Today, I'm sure that would be called 'stalking.' But there I was, each and every day, following her around and trying to strike up conversations with her. You know, like, "What's a girl like you doing in a kindergarten like this?"

I was determined to at least get a kiss from her by the end of the school year. I did everything in my power to make sure I showered her with gifts throughout the year. You know, like swiping an extra milk box to gift to her at recess. I would bring her candy. I would bring her cookies. I would hold the class door open for her. I was always there, ready, and waiting for the one chance she may lean over and give me a kiss. Of course, I was always a gentleman. I learned the value of being a gentleman, which I carried into every year of my life.

So, there I was one day at recess and some other kids were picking on Kirsten and trying to bully her. Here was my chance to not only be the gentleman, but to be her protector. I sprang into action and marched right over to those kids and stood up to them for her. When I say stood up to them, well, they were much taller and bigger than me so I literally had to stand taller than I normally would. But I did it! I stopped them in their tracks because they had never been stood up to before. I guess they didn't really know what to do so they simply walked away and left her alone. Thank God!

I did it! I really, really did it! I saved her!

As I started to turn in her direction to make sure she was okay, I quickly realized this is the moment I had been waiting for all year long. It was going to happen. Am I ready? Can I handle this? Don't screw this up! She leaned over to thank me with a kiss on my cheek. WOW! She just kissed me! I was in heaven!

This was literally my sole purpose in life at the time and it really came true. I stayed the course. I held my ground. I followed my purpose and passion to accomplish what I set out to do and it came true. I kept my mindset on the goal.

I learned a lot of valuable lessons back then. I learned that if you set your goal and intention and keep your mindset focused on that specific goal, you can achieve it. I learned that focusing your mind is vital. Too many people these days have too many things going on in their minds that dilute their ultimate goal and purpose. They allow other things to occupy their minds that do not have a direct correlation to their purpose.

Success Leaves Clues

Sir Richard Branson only keeps three tasks on his plate any given day, and these task have a direct correlation to his ultimate goal. He doesn't think about anything else. Everything he does is either leading to that goal or he doesn't do it.

My Mentor, Brian Tracy, taught me a valuable technique that he calls 'single-handling.' This is when you have a goal and you keep on task to complete it in a certain time period. You are handling everything that comes at you during the day to make sure you are on target for that specific single task or goal. These could be smaller tasks or projects that lead to that goal which ultimately keeps you on your purpose.

What is Purpose?

So, what is purpose? I mean, really, what is the true definition of the word purpose? Here is my definition of purpose: Purpose is to have a life-long goal that is so clear and defined in your mindset and in all of your being that is based on your integrity, morals, and ultimate outcome to better the world!

In Viktor Frankl's book in 1946, *Man's Search for Meaning*, Viktor chronicles his experiences as a prisoner during World War II, and describes his method of staying alive, which involved identifying a purpose to each person's life through one of three ways: the completion of tasks, caring for another person, or finding meaning by facing suffering with dignity.

Defining Your Purpose

Defining your actual purpose in life is super vital. Without a well-defined purpose for your life, you may find yourself wandering aimlessly and hopping from one thing to another. People with a well-defined purpose find themselves more focused and determined and consistent in their goals.

How would you define your purpose? Here are a few suggestions to help you define your true purpose:

1. Ask yourself why you do the things you do each and every day.

2. What are the most important values in your life?

3. Who are the most important people in your life and why?

4. Why do you get up every morning and what makes you excited to jump out of bed and start your day?

5. If you are asked toward the end of your life what you are most proud of accomplishing, what would it be?

Creating a Mission Statement for Your Life

I would suggest that each of us should have a mission statement for our lives. I'm sure we have all heard of mission statements for companies and associations, but have you ever considered having a mission statement for YOU?

In business, a mission statement is a short statement of why an organization exists, what its overall goal is, the goal of its operations: What kind of product or service it provides, its primary customers or market and its geographical region of operation. It may include a short statement of such fundamental matters as the organization's values or philosophies, a business's main competitive advantages, a desired future state, or their vision.

So, what is your goal? Why do YOU operate? What is your actual vision? When you close your eyes and imagine yourself in the future, what do you see? Or, better yet, what would you like to see? How would you like others to describe you? What are the fundamentals that matter to you?

Much like Napoleon Hill taught us in his famous book, *Think and Grow Rich,* we must develop and have a definite purpose in life. Let's each develop a mission statement for our own lives and allow that to shape and define our actual purpose in life. This is your homework for today.

Mindset is Crucial

I shared many stages with the infamous Bob Proctor. One of the lessons he instilled in me and reminded me each and every time I met up with him, is the fact that thoughts are things. He is so right! Thoughts truly are things and they direct our focus and determine our future.

What you think about will ultimately determine how you feel. It's very difficult to have two or more thoughts simultaneously in your mind. Therefore, be careful about what you think on a daily basis. In fact, I would suggest being careful in what you are thinking even on a minute-by-minute basis.

So, one of the secrets to achieving any specific goal and to be aligned with your actual purpose in life is to keep what you want to achieve in your mindset on a consistent basis. It may sound strange to do this, but I would rather people think it strange and achieve my goals than for people to think I'm not strange and see me unsuccessfully wandering around the world.

My main goal and purpose in life is to help others and be kind to others. I call this "NDSO! No Drama - Serve Others!" It is the meaning of my life. You see, when you remove the drama in life, you allow space to serve the world.

ERIK SWANSON

As an Award-Winning International Keynote Speaker and Multi-Time #1 International Bestselling Author, Erik Swanson is in great demand around the world! He speaks to an average of more than one million people per year. Mr. Swanson has the honor to have been invited to speak to many schools around the world including the prestigious Harvard University. He is also a recurring Faculty Member of CEO Space International as well as an Alumni Keynoter at Vistage Executive Coaching. Mr. Swanson is also the recipient of 2024's International Book Impact Award and the United States Presidential Lifetime Achievement Award presented by the White House in 2024 for his ongoing community service and philanthropy work. Erik's speeches can be found on Amazon Prime TV as well as joining the Ted Talk Family with his speeches called, "A Dose of Awesome," and "NDSO ~ No Drama, Serve Others."

Erik got his start in the self-development world by mentoring directly under Brian Tracy. Quickly climbing to become the top trainer around the world from a group of over 250 handpicked coaches, Erik started to surround himself with the best of the best and very quickly started to be invited to speak on stages alongside such greats as Jim Rohn, Bob Proctor, Les Brown, Sharon Lechter, Jack Canfield, Lisa Nichols, and Joe Dispenza—just to name a few. Erik has created and developed the super-popular Habitude Warrior Conferences and Speaker Hearts Mastermind & Retreats, which have a two-year waiting list and include 33 top-named speakers from around the world. They are 'Ted Talk' style events which have quickly climbed to the top 10 events not to miss in the United States! He is the creator, founder, and CEO of the Habitude Warrior Mastermind, Global Speakers Mastermind, and Cafe Mastermind. He is also the creator and publisher of many book series such as *The 13 Steps To Riches* book series as well as *The Principles of David & Goliath* book series. His motto is clear: "NDSO!" No Drama – Serve Others!

www.SpeakerErikSwanson.com

BRIAN SMITH

BUILDING PURPOSE THROUGH THE BIRTH OF A BRAND

Starting UGG® Boots was one of the biggest challenges of my life but also one of the most rewarding. There were moments when I thought it wasn't going to work out, but each time I hit a roadblock, I found a way through by learning to serve my market better and finding solutions that aligned with the needs of my customers. My story is about finding that alignment, facing challenges head-on, and focusing on what truly matters to create a successful business.

I had a grand vision when I first brought five hundred pairs of boots from Australia to California. I was going to make a huge push, and I was confident it would take off. But when we went out to do our sales run through the surf shops, we were shut out by all the shoe stores. They couldn't understand why anyone in California would want sheepskin boots, especially in a warm climate. But I knew surfers who had been to Australia would understand. They were familiar with UGG® Boots.

My first-year sales? A disappointing twenty-eight pairs in December. That's it—just twenty-eight pairs. I had thought we would blow the market open, but it just didn't happen. I kept grinding, though, and took a summer job to stay afloat. The following year, I thought, "Let's do some advertising." I hired two models—a guy and a girl—and posed them at the beach in La Jolla. It was the perfect setting: perfect clothes, perfect hair, perfect sunset, and the boots were front and center in the ads.

The result? A modest $6,000 in sales. I was baffled. How could that be? The following year, I decided to hire better-looking models and more expensive photographers and do the same thing but at a higher level. The results? We only made about $10,000 in sales. Again, I couldn't figure out what was going wrong.

At that point, I thought I was done. I decided to quit, sell off my remaining stock, and move on. But then something interesting happened. The first winter storm hit the coast, and all my retailers started calling me. "Brian, everyone's in the store asking for UGG® Boots. Do you have any left? I've run out!"

Suddenly, I realized I couldn't quit. People were finally interested. I called up Australia and ordered a whole new batch of boots. But I knew one thing: my marketing wasn't working. So I went back to the drawing board and had a beer with my buddy at South Coast Surf Shop in San Diego. I explained my advertising dilemma, and he called over a group of kids hanging around the shop and asked, "What do you guys think of UGGs®?"

These 12- and 13-year-old grommets just laughed and said, "Oh man, those UGGs® are so fake! Have you seen those ads? Those models can't even surf." I realized at that moment that I was sending the wrong message. My ads were entirely out of alignment with my market. These kids didn't want models—they wanted authenticity. When I saw the ads through their eyes, I cringed. It was embarrassing.

So, like any entrepreneur who hits a wall, I called another buddy who was running a surf team in Orange County and asked, "Do you have any young kids about to go pro?" He gave me Mike Parsons and Ted Robinson—two talented young surfers. We went down to Blacks Beach in La Jolla and Trestles in San Onofre, took some shots of them surfing, and I ran those ads in October and December.

The result? Sales jumped to $220,000. That was when I realized what had been going wrong for so many years—I hadn't been in alignment with my market. These surfers wanted credibility, authenticity, and to feel like they were part of the cool, inner circle of surfing. Instead, I had been showing them glossy, commercialized ads that didn't speak to them at all. Once I aligned with what they really wanted, everything changed. And that lesson—understanding and aligning with the needs of your market—was crucial to building UGG®.

After that, the business never stopped growing. I applied the same lesson to snowboarding and ice hockey markets, where people didn't surf, and the results were similar. It was all about aligning with the target audience and serving their real desires.

But that wasn't the only time I learned the power of alignment. One of the most important marketing lessons I learned came from an experience with a girl shopping in one of my surf shops. She was touching the sheepskin boots, looking at different sizes and colors, and she asked the manager, "What are these like?"

He shrugged and said, "I don't really know." She responded, "Well, they look hot." He said, "Yeah, they sure look hot, and they're so delicate, you know. And expensive, too." She put the boots back and walked out of the store.

I stood there, stunned. I couldn't believe this was happening but quickly realized it was my fault. I should have someone in the store who was an advocate for the brand. So I came up with the "six-pair stocking plan." If a store put six pairs of UGG® Boots on its shelves, I'd give the store manager or owner a free pair to wear in the store. This way, they could speak from experience when customers asked about the boots.

The next time I was in the store, I saw it firsthand. Someone picked up a pair of UGG® Boots and asked, "What are these like?" The store manager, now wearing a pair, said, "Oh, they're fantastic! I'm wearing them now. They're perfectly foot-temperature and super durable. Yeah, they might seem expensive, but they're the best deal you'll ever get." The customer bought the boots right then and there.

That strategy transformed the way UGG® Boots were sold. I made it a policy that only my salespeople could sell a pair of UGG® Boots to a retailer if the retailer had tried them on first. That was a game-changer. It cost me one pair of boots per store, but the returns were incredible. Within a year, word of mouth had become so strong that I no longer needed to give away free pairs.

These two moments—aligning with my target market through authentic marketing and ensuring that store managers were true advocates of the brand—were absolutely critical to UGG®'s success. They both came from realizing that I wasn't serving my customers in the way they needed and then finding solutions to better meet their needs.

Of course, there were many more challenges along the way. After we started getting profitable, the knock-offs began showing up. Everyone was trying to copy us. One company even went as far as calling themselves "Thugs" instead of UGGs®, hoping to capitalize on our success. But they didn't understand that it wasn't just about making boots. There was so much infrastructure needed to make a business like this work—warehouses, distribution systems, customer service, and most importantly, credibility with the customer.

You can't patent colors or shoe designs, so our strategy was simple: "Get out front and run faster." We'd see all these knock-offs coming to the trade shows with last year's designs, but we'd already moved on. We spent our summers creating new designs and colors, so by the time they caught up, we were already ahead. That mantra—getting out front and running faster—became the foundation of how we dealt with competition.

Through it all, I learned that success comes from staying true to who you are and serving others. Whether it was listening to the feedback from the kids in the surf shop or creating a system that helped store managers sell more boots, it was all about understanding what people needed and then finding a way to give it to them.

There were times when I felt like giving up—in fact, I almost did. But I always knew deep down that the product wasn't the problem. The problem was me—I wasn't in alignment with the market, and I needed to figure out how to serve them better. Once I did, everything started to fall into place.

I also learned something important about mindset. Disappointments are inevitable, but they often turn into our greatest blessings. I talk about this in my book *The Birth of a Brand*. One of the key lessons is that "You can't give birth to adults." Businesses, like people, need time to grow and develop. And nearly always, your biggest disappointments will turn into your greatest blessings if you stick with it and find the right solution.

I often ask audiences when I'm speaking, "Raise your hand if something happened in the last six months that at the time seemed like the biggest disaster in the world, but now you look back and think, 'Thank God that happened.'" And most of the audience raises their hand. It's a universal principle—setbacks are part of the process but often lead to something much better if you keep moving forward.

I remember one particularly tough day when everything felt like it was falling apart. Sales were flat, I was broke, and I wasn't sure if I could keep going. I sat on the beach, watching the waves roll in, and it hit me: this wasn't just about me. UGG® wasn't just my business; it was something bigger. People loved these boots. They needed them. And I was responsible for finding a way forward—not just for me, but for the surfers who lived in them, the store owners who believed in them, and the customers who were waiting to discover them.

When I started UGG® Boots, I didn't just want to build a company—I wanted to create something that would have a lasting impact. There was a deeper sense of purpose behind the brand, even when I couldn't see it clearly in the early years. UGG® was more than just a pair of boots; it represented a lifestyle, a connection to a laid-back, authentic way of life that surfers and outdoor enthusiasts could relate to.

I realized that purpose wasn't just about making money or selling a product—it was about creating something people could love and rely on. It was about crafting something that served a real need in people's lives, and when I finally understood that, my mindset shifted. I wasn't just an entrepreneur trying to sell boots; I was someone on a mission to deliver a product that brought comfort, style, and authenticity to people who valued it.

That purpose kept me going through the most challenging times. Even when sales were low, and I felt like quitting, I knew deep down that UGG® Boots could be something special if I could align with what people needed. My purpose wasn't to build a company overnight but to create a brand that stood the test of time, built on trust and connection with the people who wore the boots.

But even with all those challenges, I don't regret the journey. After nineteen years of growing the company, I reached a point where I realized I couldn't finance the next level of growth. We had done $15 million the previous season, and the next season looked like it would be $25 million. I just couldn't do it alone. Luckily, I had a good friend, Doug Otto, who had started a company called Decker's Corporation. He took his company public and had the cash reserves to support the growth we needed. So, I sold UGG® to him, and it was the right decision. Today, UGG® is doing billions in sales, and I'm proud of the role I played in building it.

One of the biggest lessons I learned in building UGG® is that mindset is everything. The truth is that business is hard, and life throws challenges at you constantly. But what determines whether you succeed or fail isn't the circumstances—it's your mindset in the face of those circumstances.

Early on, I could have given up when things weren't working. There were moments when I seriously considered it. But what kept me going was my belief that I could figure it out—that there was a solution, even if I hadn't found it yet. It's easy to get bogged down in setbacks, but I've always believed that our most disappointing moments can become our greatest blessings. I've seen it time and time again, both in my business and in life.

This mindset of perseverance—of looking for the opportunity in every challenge—became the foundation of how I approached building UGG®. Every time something didn't work out, I didn't see it as a failure; I saw it as a chance to learn and grow. Whether it was the marketing missteps or the competition from knock-offs, I approached every obstacle with the belief that there was a way forward.

That mindset isn't just something you're born with—it's something you can develop. You must train yourself to look at challenges as steppingstones rather than roadblocks. Every entrepreneur faces difficulties, but those who succeed are the ones who keep their mindset focused on solutions, not problems. For me, aligning my mindset with my purpose—serving my customers and staying true to the vision of what UGG® could be—was the key to turning setbacks into success.

Looking back now, I realize that UGG®'s success was built not just on good marketing or business strategies but on the combination of purpose and mindset. My purpose—creating a product that genuinely served people's needs—motivated me to keep going, even when things were tough. My mindset—the belief that I could figure out a way forward, no matter what—allowed me to navigate the many challenges along the way.

It's easy to get lost in the day-to-day grind of running a business, but staying connected to your purpose gives you a sense of direction and fulfillment. And when you combine that with a mindset of resilience and adaptability, you become unstoppable. UGG® taught me that you can overcome any obstacle and build something that lasts with a strong sense of purpose and the right mindset.

Every challenge I faced, from aligning with my market to dealing with knock-offs, became an opportunity to grow. My purpose drove me, and my mindset kept me going. Together, they allowed me to build something far bigger than just a company. They helped me create a brand loved by millions of people worldwide, and that's something I'll always be proud of.

Looking back, I learned so much from the journey, but the most important lesson was this: alignment and service go hand in hand. When you align with your market, your customers, and your team and focus on serving others, success will follow. It's not always easy, but it's always worth it.

Cardiff-by-the-Sea, California

BRIAN SMITH

Brian is Australian-born and was raised with an enduring passion for surfing and the surf culture. In his youth, he enjoyed the epic waves on both coasts of his home country. He was educated at the Institute of Chartered Accountants Australia, where he received his first of many business credentials.

After ten years as a public accountant, Brian felt a burning desire to do something that would fit his passion for surfing while looking for a business idea that would allow him to support himself. He turned in his resignation notice, got on a plane to the States, and became a regular at the classic surfing destinations up and down the southern California coastline. He called Malibu, Cardiff-by-the-Sea, and Swami's Beach his "office."

One day, while pulling on his sheepskin boots after a cold surf session, he realized there were nothing like them available in California. He and a surfing buddy shipped six pairs from Australia to show them around, in search of interested takers. It was at this moment that the UGG®® brand was born.

Brian called on every surf shop up and down the California coast, enthusiastically showing prospective retailers the UGG®® prototype. Most of the shop owners would deliver the same disappointing reaction: "Brian, we sell flip flops, not boots." Not willing to give up his idea, he then embarked on a laser-focused effort to gain endorsements and support from the surf community, of which he was becoming a respected member. Finally, with two young Pro-surfers on "the UGG®® team," a new cult was born and "UGG®" became the cool word on California campuses and beaches alike.

Had he not diligently stuck to his vision, the idea of UGG®® Boots would never have come to fruition. Undaunted by the surf shop owners' initial rejections, Brian forged forward with his dream and we all now enjoy our much loved and favorite casual footwear—our UGG®® Boots.

After seventeen years, Brian sold his company and the brand to Decker's Outdoor Corporation. With their resources, the "casual comfort" segment of the footwear industry came to life and the UGG®® Brand now garners more than a billion dollars of sales per year, year after year.

Having developed the art of storytelling throughout the years, the stage became the perfect place for Brian to present to business owners the ups —and downs—of being an entrepreneur. He found that he not only enjoyed giving these talks, but his audiences were responding in wide embrace to his stories like he never could have imagined. The size and scope of the audiences grew and now he is one of the most sought after speakers in the world today. He brings a magical mix of real world street smarts, kindness, compassion and respect for the entrepreneurial drive— all of which fits business of any size. And, yes, he still continues to surf when he's not on tour.

www.BrianSmithSpeaker.com

DAME DORIA CORDOVA

FINDING YOUR PURPOSE: EVER-EVOLVING, DISCIPLINED MINDSET

Have you ever wondered how some people seem to have it all figured out? They're successful, prosperous, passionate about their work, they are making a difference in the world, and they seem to navigate life's challenges with grace and ease.

Happily, it's not magic or luck—it's about finding your purpose and cultivating the right mindset. And I should know, because I've been on quite a journey for the past forty-eight years (yeah, you heard right!). I have been working on myself since I was twenty-six years old.

Let me take you back to my twenties. I was like many young adults—full of energy and ambition—and very successful by the time I was twenty-four years old. I was an official court reporter in the Los Angeles Court System, and later in the Hawaii Judicial System. I was headed to being an attorney... and though I had tremendous success, health, beauty, and had many friends (and suitors), I was not a happy girl.

It may have been because I had experienced tremendous loss at eighteen years old when my fiancé was killed in a car accident, or the miscarriage of his baby on his birthday four months later; or the additional thirteen friends I lost in the next three years, and another miscarriage... plus, witnessing everyday horrific tragedies in my work environment in the legal system. When I look back, I wonder how I didn't lose my mind. Well, I came close to it.

I didn't have the time to deal with my feelings since I had full-time college studies, I was a college cheerleader, and writer for the college paper. I was paying for my court reporting education working as a Spanish and English interpreter; plus, I had a boyfriend and a very active social life. It was the '70s. Who had time to feel anything? I was too busy living the life that I had been conditioned to have.

In my heart of hearts, though, I was confused as to why I wasn't the happiest person on earth. I knew there was more to life, but I couldn't quite put my finger on it. That all changed after moving to Hawaii to pursue happiness. I became a "sailing bum" in a beautiful yacht, traveling around the most beautiful islands on the planet, simultaneously being the first official court reporter on Maui.

And then my mindset journey began… I had a profound enlightenment experience at twenty-six years old. This led me to start my "inner discovery" journey, which took me to attend *EST* (Erhard Seminars Training, Inc.), one of the most successful human potential programs, which led me to the incredible fortune of meeting a remarkable individual who would shape the course of my life: Dr. R. Buckminster Fuller ("Bucky", as he liked to be called).

Now, if you're not familiar with Bucky, let me tell you—he was a visionary like no other. An architect, systems theorist, thinker, inventor, futurist, and author, Bucky had this extraordinary ability to see the world as it could be, based on Generalized Principles (physics), research, science, and the study of nature.

When I first heard him speak, it was like a lightbulb went off in my head. Here was a man talking about how we could solve global problems through design and technology, and how we could create a world that works for everyone. His ideas about "comprehensive anticipatory design science" might sound complex, but at their core, they were about using our creativity and innovation to uplift all of humanity. And most importantly, something very close to my heart: we now had enough resources to eradicate hunger and poverty.

The floodgates of good fortune had opened for me at the young age of twenty-seven! Within a year, I attended the first Burklyn Business School for Entrepreneurs—the first of its kind. These programs were co-founded by the second genius who influenced by life, Marshall Thurber, along with Bobbi DePorter, the woman who put experiential trainings for teens on the planet.

Meeting incredible thinkers, masters, and experts in business, technology, systems, and human potential was like finding the missing pieces of a puzzle I didn't even know I was trying to solve. Their ideas resonated within something deep inside me, and, suddenly, I could see the outline of my purpose taking shape. I realized that I wanted to bridge the gap between business and personal development, resulting in positive global change. I wanted to help people unlock their potential not just for their benefit, but for the benefit of all.

That realization was the spark that ignited my journey. From that first business school, the *Money & You*® program was created. This became the answer to what had then become my driving question: *"What is my job? How am I going to express my gifts?"*

With all the knowledge that I had gathered in the legal system, the constant deep mindset work that I was doing (and still do), and bringing breakthrough entrepreneurial education to the world, my economic engine started forming, which not only sped up the actualization of my purpose, but it took me to live the wealthy life of my dreams.

On July 8, 1985, after the co-founders of the work went on to follow other endeavors, I inherited the intellectual property (IP) rights to the most magnificent curriculum of entrepreneurial trainings using experiential learning methods, which are 100% transformative and create extraordinary results to all who apply the principles and tools taught in their businesses or organizations.

This platform became my way of passing on the wisdom I'd gained through my own process of self-mastery and mindset work, while helping others find their purpose and develop the mindset needed to achieve the life of their dreams.

At the core of all of this success: Clarity of purpose and an ever-evolving, powerful, and disciplined mindset.

Finding your purpose isn't always a lightning bolt moment. For many people, it's more of a gradual unveiling. But there are definite steps you can take to speed up the process.

First, start paying attention to what truly excites you. What are the topics that make you lose track of time when you're reading about them? What are the problems in the world that make your heart ache, that make you think, *"Someone should do something about that"?* These are all clues pointing towards your purpose.

Next, reflect on your unique skills and experiences. What are you particularly good at? What life experiences have shaped you in significant ways? Your purpose often lies at the intersection of what you're passionate about—or what makes you angry—and what you're good at.

Don't be afraid to experiment. Try new things, volunteer for different causes, and take on diverse projects at work. Each new experience is an opportunity to learn more about yourself and what resonates with you.

Talk to people who inspire you. Ask them about their journeys, and how they found their purpose. You'd be surprised how many people are willing to share their stories if you just ask. And more than anything else, work on yourself!

And remember, your purpose doesn't have to be some grand, world-changing mission (although it certainly can be!). It could be as simple as being the best parent you can be or bringing joy to others through your art. The important thing is that it gives your life meaning and motivates you to be your best self.

One of the best stated purposes that I have ever heard is from my mentor: *To Love, Earn, and Learn!* Mine is a little longer: *To Uplift Humanity's Consciousness Through Socially Responsible Business.*

What say you? Can you just start "drive testing" some statements? Talk to yourself. You have nothing to lose.

Finding your purpose is just the first step. The real magic happens when you pair that purpose with the right mindset. And let me tell you, cultivating the right mindset is an art.

When I talk about mindset, I'm talking about the lens through which you view the world. It's the voice in your head that interprets your experiences and shapes your responses. And that voice can be your biggest cheerleader or your worst critic.

Speaker Erik Swanson & Dame Doria Cordova

In my early days of running *Money & You®,* we had the privilege of launching Tony Robbins as he was heading towards astronomical success a decade later. Even then, his ability to harness the power of mindset was evident. He understood how our internal narratives shape our reality, and how by changing those narratives, we can change our lives.

When I inherited the work in 1985, I took on a partner who, after nine years of working together, we supported him to go towards the work that made his heart sing by working on his mindset, and it resulted in the co-creation of one of the most successful financial literacy books, *Rich Dad Poor Dad.* That was Robert Kiyosaki. And that book was based on the *Money & You®* work.

Developing the right mindset is not positive thinking. It's about developing a deep awareness of your thought patterns and consciously choosing which ones to nurture. It's about building resilience, so you can bounce back from setbacks. It's about cultivating curiosity, so you're always learning and growing.

I've practiced Transcendental Meditation (TM) without missing a session twice a day for the past fifteen years. TM has opened me to new levels of clarity and peace in my life. It has allowed me to approach challenges with a sense of mastery and love, rather than fear or anxiety.

Another crucial aspect of mindset is moving from scarcity-thinking to sufficiency-thinking, which will lead you to abundance. This is something we focus on heavily in our programs. So many of us operate from a place of "there's not enough"—not enough money, not enough love, not enough time, not enough opportunities. But when you shift to a sufficiency mindset, you start to see possibilities everywhere, and the world opens up.

And that way of living ties to the realization that I had a couple of decades ago: True wealth is Access! Wealth isn't just about the money in your bank account. It's about having access to resources, wisdom, knowledge, and support. When you cultivate this kind of abundance mindset, you start to see that you're rich in ways you never realized before.

Developing this kind of mindset is a practice, something you need to work on every day. There will be days when it's easy, when everything seems to be going your way. And there will be days when it's a struggle. This is when you must consciously maintain that positive, sufficiency-focused mindset.

And then, as you continue to align your actions with your purpose and cultivate a supportive mindset, you'll find that you're not just changing your own life. You're changing the lives of those around you. You're contributing to that world that Bucky envisioned, a world that works for everyone.

I've seen this play out countless times over my forty-five years of leading a training company that has resulted in over 200,000 alumni from over eighty-five countries. I've watched people come into our programs feeling stuck or unfulfilled and leave with a clear sense of purpose and the mindset tools to achieve it. I've seen them go on to start businesses that solve real problems, positively transform their communities, and become leaders in their fields.

There's nothing more rewarding than watching someone step into their power like that. When you're living your purpose with the right mindset, you become a beacon. You inspire others to do the same. And that's how real, lasting change happens.

Finally, I want to leave you with some encouragement. Finding your purpose and developing the right mindset isn't always easy. There will be challenges along the way. There will be times when you doubt yourself and wonder if you're on the right path.

It's worth it. It's worth every moment of struggle, every setback, every doubt. Because on the other side of all that is a life of meaning, a fulfilled life, of joy. A life where you're not just surviving, but truly thriving. A life where you're making a real difference in the world.

We are all in the process of "continuous improvement"—it doesn't stop.

Keep exploring, keep learning, and keep growing. Your purpose is out there, waiting for you to discover it. And when you do, embrace it with all your heart. Pair it with a powerful, positive mindset, and of course, tools to create wealth. And then watch as you transform not just your own life, but the world around you.

You have unique gifts to offer the world. You have been given the power to create positive change. And the world needs what only you can give. So go out there, find your purpose, cultivate that empowering mindset, and shine your light brightly. I can't wait to see what you'll achieve.

Dame Doria (DC) Cordova
CEO/Owner of Excellerated Business Schools® / Money & You®
www.MoneyandYou.com

Dame Doria Cordova & Speaker Erik Swanson

DAME DORIA (DC) CORDOVA, PHD (HON.)

Dame Doria Cordova owns *Excellerated Business Schools® for Entrepreneurs* and *Money & You®,* a global organization with over 165,000 participants for the past forty-two years from over eighty-five countries, especially from Asia Pacific and the Americas. The programs are taught in English, Chinese, and Japanese—soon expanding to Tamil, Hindi, and other Indian languages—plus Spanish, Bahasa, and more… Many of today's wealth and business leaders have attended the Money & You program and transformed the way they teach and run their organizations.

Through these graduates, including her business partnership of nine years in the 80s and 90s with Robert T. Kiyosaki of *Rich Dad Poor Dad* fame, Dame Cordova's work has touched the lives of millions all over the world. The essence of her work is to not only focus on the bottom line and profits but also to offer products and services that add value to humanity.

She is the only Latin woman who was part of the group of pioneers, led by Marshall Thurber and Bobbi DePorter of *www.Supercamp.com*, who began the development of the transformational, experiential, entrepreneurial training industry. She inherited the work over thirty-six years ago, which has expanded to what it is today through countless partners, associates, teams, graduates, and the support of many.

Along with Robert Kiyosaki, of the *Rich Dad Poor Dad* series, in 1985 they opened that industry in Australia, New Zealand and later Singapore. Subsequently, along with new partners, the Malaysia, Taiwan, Hong Kong, China, Indonesia, India, Thailand, Philippines, Cambodia and other markets have been opened. Their larger market is in the Chinese language—having been in China for nineteen years. Dr. Willson Lin and his team have put the programs "on the map."

Her latest expansion of the work is the *English Global Excellerated Business School for Entrepreneurs*. This global gathering of global social entrepreneurs was held in Port Douglas, North Queensland, Australia on November 6 – 14, 2021.

www.DoriaCordova.com

LUCAS FOSTER

RIDING WITHOUT LIMITS: EMPOWERMENT THROUGH SNOWBOARDING

My definition of empowerment has evolved over time. As a kid, I wasn't really thinking about "empowerment," but that's precisely what was happening. My motivation came from a place of feeling like an outcast. I didn't fit in with the system in elementary and middle school. Public school and team sports just weren't for me. I found my escape in skateboarding and snowboarding. These weren't just sports to me; they were my way out, a means of creating a place for myself in a world where I felt like I didn't belong.

In those early days, I was driven by insecurity. I figured that if I could just be the best at something, people would finally notice me. I'd be the "super cool kid" if I mastered snowboarding. I saw one of the riders from my town, Telluride, go to the Olympics and win a medal, and I watched the attention and praise he got. I thought, "That's going to be me." It wasn't about fame at that point but about proving something to myself. I was super competitive, and I had this mentality that becoming a pro snowboarder was my only option. I never needed anyone to tell me I could do it. I'd already made up my mind.

Now, things are a little different. I've done much of what I set out to do as a kid. I've realized that empowerment isn't just about achieving personal goals; it's about the impact you can have on others. I started to see that accomplishing something doesn't just lift you up—it can lift your whole community. I've learned that I have a platform, and I can use that platform to create change and give back. That's what keeps me going through the tough parts—knowing that I can help the next generation of athletes in ways I wish I'd been helped.

But let me be real: it hasn't been easy. Empowerment often comes from pushing through obstacles; for me, those obstacles have been both physical and mental. Growing up in Telluride, I didn't have the resources kids from bigger ski towns had. There was no half-pipe to train in, and the snowboarding program in my town was pretty loose. We didn't have the structured coaching and training that other places had. It was me figuring things out on the mountain.

U.S. Ski & Snowboard

In addition, people—even some in my family—doubted me. They asked why I was wasting my time; some thought it was hopeless. And you know what? I thought it was hopeless at times, too. But I kept going. That's one of the biggest lessons I've learned—empowerment is about finding your own way through the obstacles. I didn't have access to everything I needed, but I figured out how to make the most of what I did have. For example, I didn't have a half-pipe, but I taught myself visualization and meditation so I could mentally practice my half-pipe runs. I realized empowerment is about seeing the gaps and figuring out how to bridge them. It's about taking what you have and doubling down on that.

There's a misconception that success in sports is all physical, but the truth is that the biggest obstacles are often mental. Snowboarding, like life, is full of challenges. When one obstacle is gone, another one comes up. That's just how it works. These days, my obstacles are more mental—learning how to handle the pressure of performing at the highest level, learning death-defying tricks, and managing the spotlight. But I've come to realize that overcoming these mental barriers is just as important as any physical achievement.

I've had proud moments in my career, and some of my accomplishments stand out. Recently, I pulled off the best result of my career—a trick that had never been done before. I was in a mental slump for most of the season, almost burnt out. I was staring at two roads: I could quit or embrace the struggle. I chose the latter, which led to one of my life's most surreal contest days.

But as proud as I am of that moment, I'm even more proud of how I've used my success. I love coming back to Telluride to teach kids at the skate camp. Giving back to the community, especially to kids, is a huge part of what drives me. I haven't let fame or glory change who I am. I've seen other athletes fall into that trap, thinking they're rock stars and letting their careers fall apart as a result. But that's not what I'm about. I'm proud of living a more humble life and focusing on helping others. There's no better feeling than knowing you've made a difference in someone's life.

Empowerment, to me, is about more than just my career. It's about giving back, sharing what I've learned, and being a positive influence. I've had the chance to do some amazing things, like speaking to military personnel at Fort Carson, Colorado, and sharing my knowledge with them. Those moments mean more to me than any contest result.

When I look to the future, I see it as a blend of personal achievement and giving back. Competing in the next Olympic cycle is definitely on my radar, and I'll be in my prime when the time comes. I want to go for a medal—I've been to the Olympics before, and now I feel like I'm ready to really go for it. But beyond that, my biggest goal is to use whatever I accomplish to give back. I want to be the kind of athlete who's accessible to everyone, especially kids who are just getting started. I want to create free events, programs, and camps open to anyone, regardless of their resources.

U.S. Ski & Snowboard

I've met some of my heroes, and they weren't as approachable as I hoped. That's something I never want to be. I want to be someone whose kids feel comfortable talking to, who inspires them and helps them see that no matter what obstacles they face, there's always a way forward.

I also want to find ways to support athletes who are financially compromised. I know how hard it can be because I benefited from grants when I was younger. One of my dreams is to create a foundation or program that provides financial help to young athletes who need it. I've seen firsthand how much of a difference that kind of support can make.

Growing up, my family situation wasn't easy. My parents split when I was eleven, and things got tight financially after that. But my mom was a tremendous support. She worked overtime, sacrificed so much, and made sure I had the basics, like a roof over my head and a ski pass. If I wanted to compete, though, it was a stretch. But she believed in me and helped in every way she could. Her one rule was that if I was going to do this, I had to give it my all. She didn't want me fooling around or wasting her hard-earned money. That drive, that hunger to give my best, has stuck with me ever since.

I was determined even when my parents weren't sure this path would lead anywhere. I took it upon myself to make things happen. When I was fifteen, I wanted to switch to online school so I could snowboard more, but my parents were against it at first. I researched every option, laid out a detailed plan, and convinced them. I didn't just rely on them to figure things out—I took charge. That's what empowerment is all about—taking ownership of your dreams and doing whatever it takes to make them happen.

Looking ahead, I know that empowerment means continuing to push myself in snowboarding and life. It means using my platform to help others and to inspire the next generation. I believe empowerment is about what you achieve and how you use your success to lift others.

LUCAS FOSTER

Lucas Foster, a Telluride, Colorado local, is a professional snowboarder who has emerged as a standout talent in the snowboarding world. A member of the U.S. Olympic Snowboard Team since 2019, Lucas competed in the 2022 Winter Olympics, where he placed 17th in the snowboard halfpipe competition. His rise to success is remarkable, considering that, growing up, Telluride didn't even have a halfpipe. Lucas could only practice on a halfpipe five to ten times a year in other areas. It wasn't until later in his career that he could truly focus on mastering the halfpipe, a dedication that has led to a series of impressive achievements.

Lucas's competitive record includes multiple podium finishes in major events. He has earned two podium spots in the NorAm Cup and placed second at the U.S. Championships in 2022. In 2024, he made history by landing the first-ever Alley Oop Double McTwist 1260 in competition, securing a podium finish at the Dew Tour with a score of 94.00. His performance placed him third behind Japan's Ayumu Hirano and Yuto Totsuka, marking a defining moment in his career.

In addition to his success in snowboarding, Lucas is passionate about health and wellness and credits skateboarding as the greatest influence on his snowboarding career. Known for his humble approach, Lucas has made it a priority to give back to his community, teaching kids at local skate camps and staying connected to his roots in Telluride.

Lucas's commitment to excellence extends beyond competition. He serves as an Executive Board Member of the United States of America Snowboard Association (USASA) and International Freeski Association, advocating for the next generation of athletes. Supported by high-profile sponsors such as Monster Energy and Salomon, Lucas continues to push the boundaries of the sport while remaining dedicated to fostering growth in the snowboarding community.

Lucas Foster's journey is a testament to perseverance, passion, and the power of self-belief. As he enters what many consider his "golden era," Lucas aims to continue competing at the highest level, all while using his platform to inspire and empower young athletes.

Notable Awesome Achievements:

- 17th place, Snowboard Halfpipe, 2022 Winter Olympics
- Podium Finisher, Dew Tour 2024 (first-ever Alley-Oop Double McTwist 1260)
- 2nd place, U.S. Championships, Copper Mountain, 2022
- Multiple podium finishes in the NorAm Cup

Lucas Foster is not only a snowboarding trailblazer but also a role model dedicated to inspiring the next generation of athletes through his passion for the sport and his commitment to giving back.

www.Instagram.com/LucasFoster

AARON GIBSON

THE FIRE WITHIN THE BELIEF

Dedicated to my Mother, Jo-Anne Gibson

Where do you go when the world's overwhelming weight appears to be crushing you into insignificance?

The "self-doubting thoughts" of failure rip away at your soul, leaving you raw to the core. The never-ending barrage of negative adversities shadowing you away from the warmth of light. The constricting demands of surviving feeling like they're tightly squeezing your will to press forward from your lungs. Crawling one step ahead one day only to fall three steps back the next.

How does one focus when there is nothing left in the tank? Shriveling away into the shadows requires less effort and appears so much more appealing than receiving another wound to your soul. Getting up again and again—metaphorically battered, broken, bloody, and bruised within your consciousness—to try and tackle the day can be daunting. Then, you "one-up" your scenario by adding a mental adversity to an already monstrous pile of obstacles in your walk of life.

I have always known war—from childhood to my days as Infantier in the Canadian Forces, and to where I stand now after more than two decades destroying my body in skilled trades. At times, I have been knocked right off my climb up the mountain and left for dead, dangling by the tinniest thread.

That thread is the strongest material known to humankind and the omnipotent.

That thread is made from one simple word: "Believe."

Believing in another's abilities because you can see their potential is so much easier than investing the time, effort, and commitment to honoring and repairing the belief in yourself. I feel there's many factors throughout our life hindering our advancement, contributing to belief's greatest adversary—fear.

However, what if we no longer have the good graces of fear as an option? When you feel you've lost everything within your capability and need to live to support others dependent on you, must overcome fear. It's that moment where you are forced to close the door on fear and commit to the door of "basic necessities" to live.

My walk has been one where I know the precarious paths of hell very well. Making that descent alone is overwhelming, with a healthy reflection that, even in my situation, I narrowly escaped. This is also why I have no reservation in going back to help walk with a fellow soul struggling from the corrupted and consuming climb out of the darkness.

I bore witness to and endured abusive situations in my childhood from my father's alcoholism, as a boy being charged at and thrown six feet into a wall, breaking through the drywall to slump on the ground in agony.... This molded me into a defender of others, not really understanding my place or purpose.

The desire to be stronger, wiser, more aware, led me to volunteer a three-year commitment to the Canadian Forces. A new perception of humankind emerged through my service and tour of duty. I watched children fight other children for food, the devastation that comes from war, how greasy and vile humans could be to other humans, and in the same token, have no regard to take another soul's life.

What was the big picture in all of this harsh exposure to the world and its broken parts? What could I do, being just one small drop in the pond?

I was released from the army with an honorable discharge. I committed to the only thing I'd seen value of this world, which is love. Seeing so much hate so far into life, I could only embrace the small, simple things that made this world worth living in. Regrettably, I'd forgotten that, after living as a cog in greater machine, that I was to assume the role as the new machine I had to serve if I was to help serve others.

An unknown sliver would start to fester, changing my perception. I got complacent and only focused on a small picture. I never really considered the unthinkable realities or truths which we quickly dismiss because we don't enjoy the awkward uncomfortable feelings or "crystal-balling"—a feasible reality that may happen when we don't want to evolve with unwanted change.

Fifteen years later, that's exactly what would happen for me. A healthy conversation between two souls who reflected on the truth that they were no longer in love or happy, my ex-wife and I reverted to being dear friends with an amazing son. However, the divorce would thrust me back to my beginnings with a very sharp blade.

Who was I? What do I like to do? What is my passion? My goals? What priorities do I need to focus on, being a single parent?

I was trying to comply with what's comfortable and start my own new little "box of world" that just makes me feel sheltered because it's what I've been patterned into. Looming thoughts and overwhelming feelings of failure that I couldn't make the last box work lingered on my mind.

In life, we are all thrown misfortune. I was driven to rock bottom. I lost my corporate job, had to sell what belongings I could, lost my rental home, rang up credit card debt to ensure child support payment, had to sit and watch my son eat with only the contentment of knowing he wasn't going hungry to feed myself.

My mindset didn't start to change until I took a moment to be genuinely vulnerable to my reflection in the mirror and reached out. I sought therapy, discovered I lived with PTSD, and learned to believe that I was worth fighting for. I learned to believe that every day is a day to start anew, that, if I embraced seeing the positive rather than focusing on the negative, I can change my current downward spiral destiny.

That belief allowed me to heal, to feel again, and to close up the raw, gaping wounds of my own bad patterns, and enlighten me to new vision and perception.

It was through these hardships that I had grown. I gained the ability to have honest reflection with myself. I could now see others silently struggling, visibly tired, feeling defeated and afraid that they were alone through similar adversities I had already traveled. This led me to reach out to them, giving them that one moment to be heard.

With commitment and integrity, I found my purpose. Two steps up, only to get knocked down one—yet, still, I found myself moving forward. Tiny, minute moments at a time led me to challenge my comfort zone and get rid of my box all together, no matter what came my way. Fighting, digging deep, reaching out for support, and holding that line because you believe in what you're working towards is imperative.

When you embrace yourself and stand true, genuine, and authentic, you begin to project an energy. Others that share that energy and have walked similar paths are drawn to each other with similar focus to help the next soul in need. That reminder that they are not alone, a perfect stranger who takes a moment to just be appreciative for the person you are, can change a person's course or frame of mind. Those people are the ones that can become family and change your charted course into new waters.

This was the greatest gift I was to receive in my journey. A family with no judgement, unconditional love and support, insights to share with new methods to apply, and see the gift that is you—helping to magnify your purpose and provide balance to your mindset.

Today, I stand here rebuilt from all that was lost, with the ability to help others reclaim their own happiness through my own Late Night Mental Health Talk Show, helping to guide others through adversity.

AARON GIBSON

About Aaron Gibson: Aaron Gibson is a dynamic and multifaceted professional best known as the host of Soul Man LIVE!!! As a remote livestream producer, Aaron brings stories to life with Voice Your Vibe and contributes to the highly regarded N.I.C. - Top Inspirational Connections on LinkedIn. He is a #1 International Bestselling Author and a respected National Technical Trainer. A proud veteran, Aaron's diverse background includes roles as a video producer, mental health advocate, and dedicated volunteer. His commitment to inspiring and empowering others extends to his personal life, where he is a devoted parent. Aaron's ability to connect and uplift individuals through his various platforms has made him a standout figure in both the Livestream and LinkedIn communities. His passion for mental health advocacy and storytelling continues to positively impact audiences worldwide.

Author's Website: *www.linkedin.com/in/aaron-g-801a2ba4/*

Book Series Website: *www.TheBookOfHumanEmpowerment.com*

ALANA CAHOON

SHIFTING GEARS TO FREEDOM

If you took charge of your life as you might a sports car, how long would you stay in first gear before you shifted into second? When would you dare to shift into fifth?

For me, purpose is about discovering what makes you feel alive, happy, excited, and needed. Mindset is about living that purpose fully!

First Gear

My dad used to take us to Watkins Glen racetrack on occasion. We would watch the cars go around and around and around. As a seven-year-old girl, I thought it was the most BORING family outing that existed. Why couldn't we go to an amusement park like other families?

Second Gear

Fast forward nine years, and I soon learned to appreciate those afternoons at the racetrack. I was now sixteen years old and ready to get my driver's license!

Who do you think my teacher was? None other than my father. As a car enthusiast, he only bought manual transmission vehicles and was determined to teach me how to drive one. He said that if I could master this, I could master any car. And he was right.

Shifting gears was tough to start, but with practice, it became a fluid movement toward gaining power—a power that increased not only speed but adrenaline.

"This is so cool! It's like flying."

What challenges prevent you from pursuing your purpose in life? Are you ready to master these and drive forward?

Third Gear

Freedom is what driving was—and I was craving freedom. We had moved out of my childhood home and into the countryside. It was beautiful and full of things I had only read about in books—like farms with pigs and chickens, friends with horses, and strawberry fields where you could spend the day picking and eating so many strawberries that when you closed your eyes at night, all you could see were strawberries.

We were out in the wilderness. We lived in the sticks. Driving a car would be my key to culture, people, pools, and fun!

Don't get me wrong. I love nature. Its beauty inspired my paintings and poetry then and still does. But I was lonely and yearning for adventure.

I was given a new sense of responsibility, and with that responsibility, I set my mind to be responsible! I set my mind to drive skillfully and to get myself out of the wilderness and into a place where I felt more alive with people, culture, and opportunities. A place where I could be myself, where I could live my true purpose.

What is your key to freedom? What makes you tick? What intention are you making today to live your life fully?

Fourth Gear

I started working at a job that filled my gas tank and gave me a sense of being needed. This, in turn, built my self-esteem.

When you're living with intention or purpose, you feel valued. You feel alive.

I also learned that life is filled with stages. We progress usually from the bottom up, whether that's grades in your school or positions at your workplace. As you climb the ladder, you take on more responsibility. With each step, you are rewarded with more lucrative benefits like financial compensation and elevated respect.

During this blossoming leadership role, your purpose may become even more clearly identified.

Have you shifted your mindset to take responsibility for the direction your life is heading?

Fifth Gear

I never became a race car driver, but I did kick it into fifth gear every now and then!

The stronger your desire to live life fully, the more likely it is that you will shift your life into fifth gear. Authoring books? Total fifth-gear living!

It's about trusting the Universe, seeking guidance, and getting the training and knowledge required to pursue your purpose. With a positive mindset and a can-do attitude, you will always move forward.

When was the last time you took a leap of faith and pursued your dreams?

Learning how to drive the car was a profound experience in independence. I felt a sense of freedom I had never felt before. It was my pathway toward self-exploration.

Driving is symbolic of leading your life. You're in charge. You're responsible, and you're free.

Use this as a metaphor to help you understand your purpose and to shift into a positive mindset as you move courageously forward, one gear at a time.

Does anyone really have a purpose? Or is that what we're here for, to discover our unique paths by living fully through trial and error until we come home to our authentic nature?

In the story above, I shared my journey into adolescence. This is a monumental time in our lives, one where we make choices about who we plan to be.

I stepped into my power at the age of sixteen. By seeking independence, I went out into the world and discovered, through trial and error, my purpose in life.

Was it truly to be a singer? To act on stages? Was it to express the creative nature I was born with? Or was it something else altogether?

I was interviewing a guest on my podcast, Creating Abundance, recently, when the topic of having a life purpose arose. During the discussion, we pondered whether we would land in this world with a predetermined purpose.

Could it be that living your life with all of its trials and tribulations is when your true life's purpose arises?

Throughout my life, I've discovered that my calling is to teach people how to access their inner wisdom so that they can live their lives in harmonious abundance. Some of these teachings include developing a meditation practice and learning mindfulness techniques. I also uncovered that I have been gifted with mystic intuition! I get to help others to heal from within naturally.

With this newfound knowledge of self-awareness, I was now able to be more selective with my choices. I studied and trained to become more skillful in my life purpose as a healer and coach. The music and creativity are simply aspects of my nature. They make my life fun and colorful! They help me to execute my calling joyfully.

It is in helping others that I feel truly connected to my purpose.

What do you think your purpose in life is? Who do you serve? What are your natural gifts?

Your talents may range from art to science to business to math—the list is endless. You might be the person who makes everyone laugh in the room. If so, write down humor! If you love to heal, write down medicine.

Let's shift the question from, "What is my life purpose?" to the following list of questions:

"What do I find myself doing most often during my spare time?"

"Where do I tend to go when the choice is completely my own?"

"Who do I like to spend time with?"

"What livelihood am I most drawn to applying myself at?"

Ask yourself each of the questions above and then ask the following question:

"How does this activity make me feel?"

It is how your activities make you feel that will determine if you are living your purpose or not.

If you wrote down that you like to spend time playing your guitar in your basement, follow it with how it makes you feel. Does it bring you closer to your emotions? Are you inspired to share your music with others?

Maybe your go-to place is out on the soccer field kicking a ball around. Does it encourage you to be more active in other areas of your life? Does it remind you of your childhood?

Finding your life purpose is not really a mystery. It's how you live your life.

Create a new list now of everything that makes you happy, including your favorite places to explore, like the beach, a ball game, or a restaurant. Then, take it to a deeper level.

What do you like to do when you're on the beach that brings you so much joy? Is it lying in the sun? Is it playing volleyball with friends? Is it swimming, kayaking, water skiing? The deeper you go, the more you'll know.

Whether you find yourself at the gym to support your physical health, in the yoga studio to connect with your spirituality, at an entrepreneurship conference to bolster your networking skills or at a reading club for social justice, pause and ask yourself, "Does this make me feel alive, happy, excited, and needed?"

Shift your mindset to those things that do and live your purpose fully!

ALANA CAHOON

About Alana Cahoon: Alana has helped entrepreneurs grow their ventures into 7-figure businesses while developing conscious leadership. Drawing on that depth of experience as a Coach and Energy Healer, Alana supports high-achieving women professionals and entrepreneurs who feel uncertain in a challenging world at work and home to gracefully step into higher leadership roles where they can gain recognition, respect, and financial independence while prioritizing their own self-care.

She founded Grow 2 B U, LLC, is the bestselling author of Mindfulness, Mantras & Meditations, and is the host of the Creating Abundance podcast.

Author's Website: *www.AlanaCahoon.com*

Book Series Website: *www.TheBookOfHumanEmpowerment.com*

ALEXANDER ZOLTAN SZINEGH

I PLAN TO LIVE FOR 120 YEARS

"Be miserable. Or motivate yourself. Whatever has to be done,
it's always your choice."
~ **Dr. Wayne Dyer**

Everyone has a different definition of success; however, there are certain steps you must take along the way. I, Alexander (Alex) Zoltan Szinegh, was no exception to that rule.

I was born September 9, 1949, in the little town of Keszthely, on the south end of Lake Balaton in Hungary, during very turbulent times. It was only a few years after the second world war, but the occupation by the former USSR was weighing heavily on the population. In 1956, the people had enough and rebelled against their oppressors. I watched as the Russian tanks drove over the fence at our farmhouse and took over our house and property. My father, Zoltan, fought in the uprising and was forced to flee the country when the revolution was over, leaving behind me, my mom, and two brothers.

It took seven years for us to reunite with our father in Canada on October 31st, 1963. I didn't speak any English at all. My first English words I ever learned were, "Trick or treat, give me something good to eat." There is no Halloween in Hungary. My brother and I put on our costumes, grabbed a bag, and went out to knock doors. People gave us free candy, we thought "What a cool country!"

We were out until 10 pm and went home with a huge haul. The next night at 5 pm, we got dressed in our costumes again and went out on the street.

We thought, "Wow, we got here before the competition—we will get more candy." We knocked on the first door and said our script, "Trick or Treat," but the lady opening the door was talking to us in English, which we didn't understand. We just kept repeating, "Trick or Treat." She finally gave up speaking to us, went to the kitchen and gave us some candy.

At the next door, there was an angry man, who yelled at us and slammed the door. I said to my brother, "It was easier yesterday; they were much nicer." After an hour of being rejected, yelled at and receiving a few meager pieces of candy, we headed home. The Hungarian friends we were staying with laughed and ridiculed us in Hungarian. Even though we felt silly and disappointed, I learned three valuable lessons that helped me in my life and career as a realtor.

1. As long as you are persistent, some people will respond positively.

2. If you don't listen to people's negativity, you can succeed. Sometimes people tell you "You can't do that or you are not good enough" (in our case, we didn't speak English).

3. The right script, even on the wrong day, WORKS (if you know what to say, you can communicate with people effectively).

We eventually moved to a small, cramped, rented house in Toronto, but I always had huge goals and aspirations by watching, "The Lifestyles of the Rich and Famous" on TV.

After only completing a 10th grade education in high school, I struggled to get a decent job and my vision of great success was only a fleeting dream. I was very bitter, frustrated, and angry at the world for not giving me the success and riches I so strongly craved. I felt "the world owed me a living" since I came from such a hard background. I moved from job to job, searching for the right opportunity to make me rich.

While searching around, I met a man named Jim Rohn, who told me about a book called, *Think and Grow Rich.* Jim also ended up coaching me for several years and gave me a lot of insights into myself and my potential. I devoured the book cover to cover in a few short weeks, taking copious notes and going back over and over some of the key principles. The information was simple to understand and gave me hope that I can control my own future instead of depending on anyone else to make me successful.

I realized that if I started to change my MINDSET on how I viewed the world and me in it, my life would improve. The book taught me about goal setting and discovering my true PURPOSE. I became an avid reader and started attending live seminars. I ended up reading several hundred books and attended hundreds of hours of seminars, which I figured gave me a college education about entrepreneurship and business. I got married and as my family expanded, I realized that I needed more space and more money. My motivation increased by having more and more financial and personal responsibility.

I started several businesses, began earning large sums of money and my personal satisfaction grew. However, there was a little void in my heart. I knew that there had to be more than business and money. A few years later, I met another great speaker and businessperson, Robert Kiyosaki. He introduced me to the DISC personality profile assessment system and worked with me to become more aware of who I was and my purpose in life. He and I spent many hours together, digging deep down into my personality to flesh out my true purpose and driving force.

This is when I discovered what really drives me—besides money and the feeling of business success. I realized that one of the main reasons I work so hard is to provide my family with a much better life than I had as a child growing up.

When my father had to flee Hungary to avoid persecution for his involvement in the 1956 uprising, we had no place to live. We lived on the street for a few weeks in Budapest until a caring person helped us get a roof over our head. It wasn't much, a 15-foot by 20-foot room with no windows, no bathroom, no heating—just four walls and a door. We lived there for almost seven years until we were able to escape the Communist Regime. We were very fortunate to make it to Canada and a free life.

With Robert Kiyosaki's help, I was able to dig deep to find and visualize my purpose, which I have been living for over forty years. I discovered that, not only am I committed to my own family's better future, but also that I'm committed to helping others also discover their true purpose in life. I love to train, coach, and mentor people and organizations to assist them in discovering their purpose in life. So, I need to live to at least 120 years old, as I have a lot to still accomplish.

I do a lot of visualization and write affirmations daily as my way of working on me and working toward my goals.

This is an important activity to continue pursuing my PURPOSE and shifting my MINDSET.

Anyone who is serious about empowering themselves and their business needs to continually refine their definition of PURPOSE. One of the most difficult things to change is a person's MINDSET. It is a constant work in progress. I coach individuals and businesses to advance to the next level. If you need assistance, please reach out to me at *AlexSzinegh@gmail.com.*

ALEXANDER ZOLTAN SZINEGH

About Alex Szinegh: Alexander Zoltan Szinegh has been a Realtor for the last thirty-six-years. He has sold over 3,600 properties. Alex is involved with several charities and raises funds for Heroes, the American Cancer Society, JDRF, Leukemia & Lymphoma Society, the Eye Institute, and many other local organizations. He also volunteers and speaks at local schools and colleges. His subjects include real estate, sales, effective communication, DISC personality profiles, conflict resolution, and motivation.

Alex is the Founder and CEO of Superstar Performance Inc., a training, teaching, and coaching company for sales professionals and business owners. The company's motto is, "We are committed to your Growth." Alex is a "rags to riches" success story. With only a grade 10 education, this Hungarian immigrant has overcome many obstacles. He is now a Bestselling Author, collaborating on *Speaking of Success* with Ken Blanchard, Jack Canfield, and Stephen R Covey; *Hey... Are you talkin' to me?* with Dr. Robert A. Rohm; and *Everything is Subject to Change* with Greg S. Reid.

Alex is a Trainer, International Real Estate Developer, Entrepreneur, and Performance Coach. During his long career in business, Alex has opened, owned, and operated many successful businesses, including several real estate brokerages and regional state franchises, and he was a high-level corporate executive. Alex is the creator of several online training systems. Alex has been instrumental in helping to build one Real Estate franchise, taking it from two offices to 1,250 with an agent count of over 36,000. He has the ability to inspire small and large audiences. Alex is funny, entertaining, informative, controversial, and, at times, "In Your Face."

Author's Website: *www.AlexSzinegh.com*

Book Series Website: *www.TheBookOfHumanEmpowerment.com*

ALLISON DOSS

SERVICE IN THE SUN

I nestled my shoulder underneath my Mama's armpit and wiggled my bottom to squeeze between her and the tiny space in the oversized, burgundy recliner. This was my space, my safe space. Every evening, as the sun set and the dinner dishes were cleaned and put away, the family would settle in to watch the usual family-friendly programming. Believe it or not, the Cosby Show was every household in the nation's 7 pm viewing pleasure back then.

On this particular night, we were missing one of the usual suspects who typically join us: my older brother, Bill. An invitation to the Rick Springfield concert, who my brother thought hung the moon and the clef notes in the sky, had him out for an evening with our uncle. My brother, nine, my sister, Kathryn, seven, and I, four, weren't allowed to do much that didn't involve a parent or two, so the fact that my brother was allowed to attend that concert was a really big deal!

As usual, by the time the credits began to roll on the Huxtables, I was fast asleep on my Mama's arm. I have no idea how much time had passed before I was jolted awake by a huge commotion. My brother had returned from his hero's gathering and, held high above his head, was his newest and dearest prized possession. "Look, everybody! An autographed poster of Rick Springfield! Look! Look!"

My family excitedly gathered around as my brother unrolled his treasure. He began to pass it around. As the poster made its way to my four-year-old fingers, my brother shouted, "Stop! No. Mama don't let her touch it! She'll just ruin it!"

And though history proved that I definitely never valued my siblings' things, by evidence of my sister's toy horses having two to three legs and not four, and my brother's action figures having disfigured faces with my teeth's imprints, Mama still confidently responded to my brother, "Bill, let her see it. She won't ruin it. Will you, little girl?"

She glared at me. I slowly shook my head from left to right as if to say no. The poster was carefully placed in my hands. I looked up at my brother. He looked down at me. We locked eyes. And without hesitation or even a blink, I ripped that 80s rockstar's iconic photo right down the middle! The slow, steady, deliberate motion shredded with such a sound that seemed to mimic the halt of rotation of the earth on a rusted, unhinged gear. Everything stopped. All was quiet, but not for long. At that moment, the crown of The Littlest and the Meanest was placed on my head, and a belt was placed on my backside!

At four years old, that was the beginning of the only nickname or narrative I heard, or can still recall, bellowing from my family members within the walls of our childhood home—little and mean. A few more labels were used to shape my view of myself during my childhood—bad and black sheep being on repeat. It's who I was. How could I not believe that? The people who brought me into this world and knew me better than anyone thought that of me, and they said it often. So that MUST be who I am—mean, born bad, the black sheep.

You're probably wondering why a story about me at four years old ripping an 80s rockstar poster down the center is here in a book about purpose and mindset. It's because, at four years old and repeatedly being told that I was mean shaped who I thought I was. And my mind was set!

Continually being told by the people that know you the best, birthed you, raised you, that you were born bad and that you were mean and that every consequence from your behavior that falls upon you is your fault because you are bad has a miraculous way of becoming the negative self-talk that plagues a child who turns into a reckless teen and an irresponsible adult. I spent a lifetime finding evidence to support that title because it was a part of my life, my self-talk, and a huge part of my story.

If I was a betting woman, I would bet that, in this moment, you are acutely aware of the labels that have been placed upon you as a child by a parent or teacher, or even a bully at school. And if you are like me, I can connect many of my actions and behaviors over a lifetime that have corroborated the identity that was given to me in my earliest years.

I wonder what my life and relationships would have looked like if my parents had spoken a different narrative toward me—perhaps curious, precarious, or investigative! I would've even settled for meddlesome! It's true that I was always getting into things and causing some type of trouble, but now, as a wise forty-eight-year-old woman looking back on my life, I know that I wasn't born bad or even mean.

But I believed to the deepest part of my core that I was inherently exactly what was told to me when I was a child. And when you're told something long enough, you rise to the occasion, convinced and you wear it like a name tag forever stitched to your soul. Because that's just who you are. Your mind is set and your purpose is to be exactly who you were told you are.

Let me ask you a very important question. Who were you told that you are? We don't have to think too long or too hard about this because it's a part of us. And if you are one of the few lucky ones whose parents and support system consistently and willingly bestowed nothing but positivity, love and acceptance onto and into you for a lifetime, I'm overjoyed for you! Please know you have a responsibility to continue that energy and flow into the world around you! And smile, knowing that you have been provided for in the most special of ways.

But for the rest of us, let's dive deeper and find out what we believe of ourselves and whose voice it is that creeps in that you've heard in whispers throughout your years. Whose voice is that? Have you ever wondered where that self-talk comes from? Where did you get that? How did it start? One thing I know with absolute certainty is that you weren't born with it. It was given to you. And it's not yours!

And today, we decide what we will bring with us into our future. Will you hold onto old narratives or bravely renounce them forevermore? Would you be willing to consider that every voice inside of your head that has been spoken over you and into you is from people who had voices spoken over them and into them—and the pattern goes on and on. This is some generational negative narration that we have the power to stop right here, right now.

I can go down a rabbit hole for a moment or two and think to myself, "If only there had been someone in my life early on to honor and see the light inside of me in a way that would've made me rethink all of the things that were told to me." Well today, you don't have to go down that hole because I am here for you! Let me be that voice that affirms you and sees the light inside of you and rejects every negative label that has been given to you in your lifetime.

As a woman who, for a lifetime, tried to hectically outrun her four-year-old self to prove to the world that I wasn't born bad, I now sit on a stage of certainty, knowing I was born of pure love. So were you. A spotlight shines upon you, as it does me, as a purposeful soul who is valuable and worthy simply because you are. Your existence is a miracle and, because you are here, the world is a better place.

When you say the words, "I am," are you immediately pressured to end the sentence with a descriptive word or noun? Do you feel like you must put something after the "I am?" I am a wife. I am a husband. I am a mother. I am a brother. I am a boss. I am a student. I understand why you may feel that way as we are told as a society from a very young age that we are the things that we do and that we must DO something to BE something.

Even without your credentials or honors or status or relationship with others, your energy and your spirit is vast. You are important. And you are purposeful. For today let me suggest that you emphatically proclaim, "I am." PERIOD.

"I am" is the most powerful statement there is. It will free you to be who you want to be because it's the power of God being spoken into you! I've always believed that I received divine messages from the people that God places in my life. And I give so much gratitude for those who have come into my path and breathed life into me so that I can stand today with confidence, knowing that "I am!" And that is enough.

My purpose today is to breathe that life into you. You have the power to create and offer a beautifully crafted tapestry of truth, authenticity, and acceptance of self and others, simply because you exist. You ARE, as I AM.

Life is different now than when I was a child, and through social media we are allowed to be a part of intimate moments between moms, dads and their children. I see courageous and willing moms and dads holding their toddlers steady on the bathroom counter while looking in the mirror and prompting them to say the most wonderful things about themselves: "I am kind. I am sweet. I am powerful. My voice matters. I have boundaries." And I think to myself, how wonderful for those children that their self-talk will support their every footstep in the path that they forge.

No matter where you are right now, reading this book, whether you're in your car listening to audio or cozy on the couch with a blanket, please allow me to affirm you now. The world is yours and you are deserving and valuable. And every narrative of negative thought that creepy crawlies into your brain is not your own.

These words and feelings were given to you at some point in time and I'm giving you permission to let them go. Being aware of this is the first step towards breathing life into your own existence. Once you are aware and you notice when it's happening, ask God to take away those thoughts as they do not serve you.

Who are you? You decide—not the parents that raised you. Not the teachers that taught you. Not the boyfriend or girlfriend that broke up with you. And not the boss that fired you. You decide.

I have decided for myself. I am creative and expressive and energetic and curious. I know I am loved, and with the most certainty I have in life, I know I am a child of God and here to serve others. Today, I serve you.

Close your eyes for a moment. Take a deep breath—breathe in exactly who you want to be and breathe out all of the things that you were told as a child that you know you are not. Sit still in beautiful silence for a moment and answer the question: Who are you?

ALLISON DOSS

About Allison Doss: Allison Doss is a woman who has defied the odds and transformed her life through resilience, self-love, and unwavering determination. Allison's journey is a testament to the power of personal growth and the strength found in choosing oneself.

Once trapped in the grip of addiction and homelessness, Allison made the courageous decision to break free from those chains, embracing a life of sobriety and self-discovery.

However, her journey took an unexpected turn when her husband came out as transgender. With immense strength and self-respect, Allison prioritized her own happiness and well-being, choosing to honor her own journey and forge a path that is true to herself. Allison's story is a powerful reminder that no matter the challenges we face, we have the power to reclaim our lives, trust ourselves, and create a future filled with authenticity, love, and personal fulfillment.

Author's Website: *www.AllisonDoss.com*

Book Series Website: *www.TheBookOfHumanEmpowerment.com*

AMY KEIDERLING

EMBRACING THE PRESENT MOMENT—LIFE IS NOW

LIFE IS NOW! LIFE IS NOW! LIFE IS NOW!

As I reflect on my journey and the experiences that have shaped me, I realize that the mentors who have come into my life have been more than just guides—they have been lifelines, anchors, and sources of inspiration in moments of triumph and despair. The power of mentorship is profound; it's not just about receiving advice or direction but about the transformation that occurs when someone truly sees you for who you are and believes in your potential, even when you cannot see it yourself.

My journey with cancer, starting with that first phone call on March 17th, 2020, has been filled with lessons, each one more powerful than the last. However, the most significant lesson I've learned is the importance of living fully in the present moment, and this lesson was solidified through the wisdom of my mentors.

One mentor in particular, Elaine, who urged me to take action with her powerful words, "Life is now," taught me that every moment is a choice —a choice to live, to love, and to embrace the life that is unfolding before us, regardless of the circumstances. She didn't just give me advice; she held up a mirror that reflected my inner strength and resilience. Through her, I learned that life does not wait for us to be ready; it happens in real time, and it's up to us to decide how we respond.

But Elaine wasn't the first mentor to guide me, and she certainly wasn't the last. As I navigated the turbulent waters of cancer, COVID-19, and the challenges that life threw my way, other mentors stepped into my life, each bringing their unique perspective and wisdom. They reminded me that I am not alone, that my struggles are not in vain, and that the power to create the life I desire lies within me.

Dr. Wayne Dyer, a mentor through his words and teachings, once said, "Change the way you look at things, and the things you look at change." This quote resonated with me deeply during my second round of cancer. It wasn't just about battling the disease—it was about transforming my mindset, changing how I viewed my situation, and recognizing that every challenge is an opportunity to grow, learn, and become more than I ever thought possible.

In its truest form, mentorship is about seeing beyond the surface, beyond the immediate obstacles, and into the possibilities that lie within us. My mentors saw potential in me that I couldn't see at the time. They believed in my ability to survive and thrive, pushing me to look at my life from a different perspective. They taught me that my life wasn't just happening to me—it was happening for me.

Through their guidance, I learned to embrace each moment with gratitude, to approach each day with a sense of wonder and curiosity, and to trust in the journey, no matter how uncertain it seemed. I realized that the present moment is all we truly have, and it is in this moment that we have the power to make choices that will shape our future.

As I continue to navigate my road of life, with its twists, turns, and unexpected detours, I carry the lessons my mentors have taught me. I've learned that the most important thing we can do is live fully, embrace the present, and trust that everything we experience is leading us to where we need to be.

My journey isn't over—there will be more phone calls, more challenges, and more moments when I'll need to dig deep and find the strength to keep going. But I know that, with the support of my mentors, the love of my family, and the belief in myself that I have cultivated, I will continue to rise, overcome, and live my life with purpose and passion.

In the end, life is now. It's not something that happens later, when things are perfect or when we feel ready. It's happening right here, right now, amid the chaos, the uncertainty, and the beauty of it all. And it's up to us to seize it, to live it fully, and to become the people we were meant to be.

So, as I move forward, I do so with the knowledge that I am not alone. I am supported by the wisdom of those who have come before me, the love of those who stand beside me, and the strength within me. Life is now, and I choose to live it with all I am. That is my mindset and purpose.

LIFE IS NOW! LIFE IS NOW! LIFE IS NOW!

AMY KEIDERLING

About Amy Keiderling: Amy Keiderling is a Rebel Soul Guide. She helps to navigate you to find your soul's purpose. Think of her as a co-pilot on the road of life. When the road gets bumpy, curvy, or just seems full of obstacles and detours, we will pull out our Rebel Roadmap and navigate it together.

Amy Keiderling is the owner of Rebel Roadmap, MOdville, as well as an adventure guide with MO Adventures. Amy has always been an avid collector of anything vintage; the instant connection a piece gives you to a memory or story is why she loves her fab finds and creating memories. Amy's passion grew stronger when she met Keith, as his passion for custom vintage cars, motorcycles, and random collectibles grew their collection. When Amy and Keith are not taking adventure lovers on chartered vacations/retreats, or riding around on their motorcycles, you will find them lounging in the middle of MOwhere on their 30-acre Mid-Century Modern Retreat Property. LIFE IS NOW! Amy's battle cry—as she's experienced life from everything from divorce, body image struggles, self-worth, bankruptcy, food stamps, single parenthood, starting four businesses, being a Rock Star Mom and Mimi to her Bigs and Littles, and a cancer warrior fighting Non-Hodgkin's Lymphoma! Amy's road may be "bumpy," but she's grateful for her "off road" adventure called LIFE. Amy encourages everyone to navigate their road of life and follow their inner GPS full of MO Adventures, MO Fun and MO Memories with the ones you love.

Author's Website: *www.ItsAMoAdventure.com* & *www.RebelRoadmap.com* *@RebelRoadmap*

Book Series Website: *www.TheBookOfHumanEmpowerment.com*

BOPI VILLARINO

FINDING PURPOSE THROUGH MINDSET & RESILIENCE

In life, we often find ourselves at a crossroads, wondering about our purpose and how to navigate the challenges that come our way. Some of us have found we are in this place at many various times in our lives. The journey to discovering our "why" is deeply intertwined with our mindset. As a firm believer that our mindset shapes our reality, I want to share some insights and reflections that can help you on this path. This chapter is dedicated to those who might feel lost or uncertain, offering a message of hope and guidance.

The Power of Mindset

Our mindset is the lens through which we view the world. It influences our thoughts, actions, and, ultimately, our outcomes. A positive mindset, grounded in gratitude, can transform our experiences and open doors to new possibilities. When we feed our minds with positive and empowering thoughts, we create a fertile ground for growth and resilience.

Gratitude: The Foundation of a Positive Mindset

Gratitude is more than just a feeling; it's a powerful practice that can shift our perspective and elevate our mindset. By focusing on what we have rather than what we lack, we cultivate a sense of abundance and appreciation. Start each day by acknowledging the things you are grateful for. This simple practice can set a positive tone for your day and help you navigate challenges with a lighter heart.

Discovering Your Purpose

Finding your purpose is a journey, not a destination. It's a process of self-discovery that unfolds over time. Sometimes, our purpose becomes clear through our experiences, while, at other times, it may feel elusive. Here are some key points to help you discover or rediscover your purpose:

1. **Reflect on Your Passions & Interests:** What activities or topics ignite your enthusiasm? Your passions often hold clues to your purpose. Spend time engaging in activities that bring you joy and fulfillment.

2. **Listen to Your Inner Voice:** Trust your intuition. Often, our inner voice guides us towards our true calling. Pay attention to the moments when you feel most aligned and at peace.

3. **Consider Your Strengths & Talents:** What are you naturally good at? Your strengths can provide valuable insights into your purpose. Leveraging your unique talents can lead to a fulfilling and meaningful path.

4. **Look for Patterns in Your Life:** Reflect on your past experiences. Are there recurring themes or lessons that stand out? These patterns can offer valuable clues about your purpose and direction.

5. **Seek Inspiration & Guidance:** Surround yourself with positive influences and mentors who inspire you. Their experiences and wisdom can provide valuable insights and encouragement on your journey.

The Servant & Warrior Heart

Navigating life's challenges requires a delicate balance between compassion and resilience. Having a servant's heart means approaching life with empathy, kindness, and a desire to help others. It's about making a positive impact on those around you. However, it's equally important to cultivate a warrior's mindset—one that is determined, resilient, and steadfast in the face of adversity.

Compassion & Empathy

A servant's heart is rooted in compassion and empathy. It means being there for others, offering support, and understanding their struggles. This compassionate approach not only enriches the lives of those around you but also brings a sense of fulfillment and purpose to your own life.

Resilience & Determination

A warrior's heart embodies resilience and determination. Life will inevitably throw challenges your way, but it's your response to these challenges that define you. Never give up, even when the path seems difficult. Embrace setbacks as opportunities for growth and learning. Each obstacle overcome strengthens your character and brings you closer to your purpose.

Finding Hope & Moving Forward

Life can be unpredictable, and setbacks or tragic losses can leave us feeling lost and uncertain. However, it's important to remember that hope is always within reach, even when that seems completely unrealistic! It isn't—it just may seem that way right now. Here are some strategies to help you find your way or regain your footing:

1. **Embrace the Journey:** Understand that finding your purpose is a journey. It's okay to feel uncertain or lost at times. Trust that, with patience and perseverance, clarity will come.

2. **Stay Open to New Experiences:** Be open to new opportunities and experiences. Sometimes, stepping out of your comfort zone can lead to unexpected discoveries about yourself and your purpose.

3. **Practice Self-Compassion:** Be kind to yourself, especially during difficult times. Acknowledge your feelings and give yourself permission to heal and grow at your own pace.

4. **Connect with a Supportive Community:** Surround yourself with a supportive network of friends, family, or like-minded individuals. Their encouragement and understanding can provide the strength you need to move forward.

5. **Set Small, Achievable Goals:** Break down your journey into smaller, manageable steps. Celebrate each achievement, no matter how small, as it brings you closer to your larger purpose.

6. **Keep a Journal:** Writing down your thoughts, feelings, and reflections can be a powerful tool for self-discovery. It allows you to track your progress and gain insights into your journey.

Embracing Grief with Compassion & Hope

For those suffering from grief, the path to discovering purpose and maintaining a positive mindset can feel particularly challenging. I know this seems cliche because everyone's grief and the way they process this is their own. Just know you are not alone. Grief is a natural and deeply personal response to loss, and it can sometimes cloud our sense of direction.

During these times, it is essential to allow yourself to grieve and to honor your feelings. Be patient with yourself. There is not a magic solution to make this go away, although we wish more than anything that there was and would do anything to make the feeling and reality disappear. Remember that, even in the depths of sorrow, hope and purpose can gradually emerge. Be gentle with yourself, seek support, and trust that healing and clarity will come in their own time.

Finding your purpose and cultivating the right mindset is a deeply personal and transformative journey. It's about aligning your actions with your inner values, embracing gratitude, and approaching life with a balance of compassion and resilience. Remember, your purpose may not always be clear, but with an open heart and a determined spirit, you can navigate through life's challenges and discover the path that is uniquely yours.

As you embark on this journey, carry with you the wisdom of a servant's heart and the strength of a warrior's heart. Embrace each day with gratitude, never give up, and trust that your purpose will reveal itself in time. Your mindset truly shapes your reality, and with the right mindset, you can create a life filled with meaning, joy, and fulfillment.

BOPI VILLARINO

About Bopi Villarino: Raised in the picturesque La Costa, Carlsbad, California, Bopi, has always been driven by a passion for education and real estate. She holds a Bachelor of Arts Degree in Liberal Studies/Elementary Education from Point Loma Nazarene University. As a dedicated mother to her beloved son Ross Villarino and cherished daughter-in-law Chelsea, Bopi takes pride in her role as a family-oriented individual. Bopi's remarkable journey into the world of real estate commenced at the young age of 18 when she served as a real estate assistant to a top-producing agent. She then ventured into the financial sector, establishing a mortgage company and expanding into the realms of real estate and escrow services.

After fifteen years, Bopi successfully sold their business to a prominent nationwide brand. Bopi continued to soar in her career, assuming pivotal roles such as Vice President of the Western Region for a division of Lending Tree and Managing Partner for a substantial team in the bustling city of Los Angeles. Her versatile skill set encompasses positions such as manager, director of sales, and team lead across various real estate companies, spanning Southern California, Vail, Colorado, and Park City, Utah. Bopi became a certified real estate coach, extending her expertise to business owners and agents throughout the nation. Bopi took the courageous step of resigning from her role as the Utah Principal State Broker, where she oversaw a thriving community of 600+ agents. She founded Distinctive Properties, a real estate company nestled in the scenic beauty of Heber City, Utah. She finds solace and fulfillment in being in nature, and in various activities, including waterskiing, skiing/snowboarding, hiking, SUPing, snowshoeing, and camping.

Author's Website: *www.DistinctivePropertiesUtah.com*

Book Series Website: *www.TheBookOfHumanEmpowerment.com*

BRIAN SCHULMAN

LIVE YOUR PURPOSE

"Your purpose in life is to find your purpose and give your whole heart and soul to it."
~ **Buddha**

In a world where the noise of daily life can easily drown out the whispers of our inner calling, living on purpose stands as a beacon of clarity and empowerment. It is the conscious and intentional pursuit of a meaningful and fulfilling life, aligned with our deepest values, passions, and goals. To live on purpose is to recognize that we are not mere passengers on the journey of life, but active architects of our destiny, capable of shaping our paths with deliberate choices and actions.

The Essence of Purpose

"The meaning of life is to find your gift.
The purpose of life is to give it away."
~ Pablo Picasso

At its core, purpose is about more than just setting goals or achieving success; it is about understanding who we are and why we are here. It involves a deep introspection and alignment with our authentic selves. Purpose is not a destination but a journey, an ongoing exploration of what brings us joy, fulfillment, and a sense of contribution to the greater good.

Living on purpose begins with a clear understanding of our values—those fundamental beliefs that guide our decisions and actions. Our values are the compass that directs us towards our true north, ensuring that we remain aligned with what is genuinely important to us. When our actions reflect our values, we experience a sense of harmony and integrity, fostering inner peace and contentment.

Discovering Your Purpose

"Don't ask what the world needs. Ask what makes you come alive, and go do it. Because what the world needs is people who have come alive."
~ Howard Thurman

The journey to discovering your purpose is deeply personal and unique. It involves asking profound questions and being open to the answers that arise. Reflect on what excites you, what you are naturally drawn to, and what activities make you lose track of time. Consider the challenges you have overcome and the lessons you have learned—these experiences often hold clues to your purpose.

It is also beneficial to seek feedback from those who know you well. Often, others can see strengths and passions in us that we may overlook. Take time to journal, meditate, or engage in activities that quiet the mind and allow your inner wisdom to surface. Remember, discovering your purpose is not about finding a single, static answer but about uncovering the themes and patterns that resonate with your true self.

The Power of Mindset

While discovering your purpose is crucial, cultivating the right mindset is equally important. Mindset is the lens through which we view the world and ourselves, influencing our thoughts, behaviors, and, ultimately, our outcomes. A purpose-driven life requires a growth mindset—a belief that our abilities and intelligence can be developed through dedication and hard work.

Embracing a Growth Mindset

"With the right mindset, we can't lose, we either practice what we've learned or we learn what we need to practice."
~ Nidhal Mahgroubi

A growth mindset fosters resilience and perseverance, enabling us to navigate setbacks and challenges with a positive and proactive attitude. It encourages us to see failures as opportunities for learning and growth rather than as insurmountable obstacles. With a growth mindset, we are more likely to take risks, embrace new experiences, and continuously strive to improve ourselves.

To cultivate a growth mindset, practice self-awareness and self-compassion. Recognize and challenge limiting beliefs that hold you back, and replace them with empowering thoughts that support your growth. Surround yourself with positive influences—people, books, and environments that inspire and uplift you. Celebrate your progress, no matter how small, and remain patient with yourself and give grace, as you navigate the ups and downs of your journey.

The Role of Presence & Mindfulness

Living on purpose also requires being present and mindful. In our fast-paced world, it is easy to become distracted and disconnected from the present moment. Mindfulness is the practice of bringing our full attention to the here and now, allowing us to fully experience and appreciate life as it unfolds.

Mindfulness enhances our ability to make intentional decisions that align with our purpose. It helps us to become more attuned to our inner state, recognizing when we are acting out of alignment with our values and purpose. By cultivating mindfulness, we develop greater clarity, focus, and emotional regulation, all of which are essential for living a purpose-driven life.

Decision-Making Strategies for Success

Purposeful living involves making choices and decisions that reflect our authentic selves and contribute to our personal growth and well-being. Effective decision-making strategies are essential for navigating the complexities of life and staying true to our purpose.

Clarity of Purpose

First and foremost, be crystal clear about your purpose. Having a clear sense of purpose acts as a filter through which all decisions are made. When faced with a choice, ask yourself whether the option aligns with your purpose and values. Does it bring you closer to your goals? Does it contribute to your overall well-being and fulfillment?

Prioritization & Focus

Prioritization is key to managing the many demands and opportunities that come our way. Not all tasks and activities are created equal; some will have a more significant impact on our purpose and goals than others. Learn to prioritize your time and energy on activities that truly matter, and be willing to say no to distractions and lesser priorities.

Focus is also crucial. In a world filled with constant stimuli, maintaining focus on what is important can be challenging. Develop habits and routines that support your focus, such as setting specific goals, creating to-do lists, and minimizing distractions. Regularly review your progress and adjust your plans as needed to stay on track.

Flexibility & Adaptability

While it is important to have a clear purpose and plan, it is equally important to remain flexible and adaptable. Life is unpredictable, and circumstances can change unexpectedly. Be open to adjusting your course when necessary, and view challenges as opportunities for growth and learning. Flexibility allows you to stay resilient and maintain your sense of purpose even in the face of adversity.

Decision-Making Tools

Several decision-making tools can aid in making purposeful choices. One such tool is the Eisenhower Matrix, which helps prioritize tasks based on their urgency and importance. Another useful technique is the "10-10-10" rule, which involves considering the potential impact of a decision in 10 minutes, 10 months, and 10 years. These tools can provide valuable perspectives and help ensure that your decisions are aligned with your long-term goals and values.

The Ripple Effect of Purposeful Living

Living on purpose not only transforms your own life but also creates a positive ripple effect that extends to others. When you are aligned with your purpose, you naturally inspire and uplift those around you. Your passion and enthusiasm become contagious, motivating others to pursue their own purpose and dreams.

Purposeful living also contributes to the well-being of society as a whole. When individuals act in alignment with their values and passions, they are more likely to engage in activities that benefit others and contribute to the common good. Your unique talents and gifts are meant to be shared, and by doing so, you make a meaningful impact on the world.

Empowering Future Generations

One of the most profound ways to extend the impact of purposeful living is by empowering future generations. As role models, our actions and choices serve as powerful examples for young people. By living authentically and purposefully, we demonstrate the importance of following one's passion and values.

Mentorship is another way to empower others. Share your experiences, knowledge, and insights with those who are seeking their own path. Provide encouragement and support, and help others navigate the challenges and uncertainties of their journey. Empowered individuals are more likely to empower others, creating a cycle of positive influence that spans generations.

To the Journey Ahead

Living on purpose is a journey of self-discovery, growth, and contribution. It requires a deep understanding of our values, a commitment to cultivating a growth mindset, and the practice of mindfulness and intentional decision-making. By embracing our purpose and living authentically, we not only transform our own lives but also create a positive ripple effect that empowers and inspires others.

Remember, your purpose is not a destination but a guiding light that illuminates your path. Embrace the journey with an open heart and mind, and trust that each step you take brings you closer to a life of meaning and fulfillment. Your unique talents and passions are gifts to be shared, and by living on purpose, you contribute to a brighter and more empowered world for all.

BRIAN SCHULMAN

About Brian Schulman: Named 'The King of Community on LinkedIn' by Forbes and known as 'The Godfather and Pioneer of LinkedIn Video' and one of the world's premiere live streaming & video marketing experts, Brian Schulman is a 17X #1 Bestselling Author (and 5X #1 International Bestselling Author) and internationally renowned Keynote Speaker, whose expertise, insights, and two Global Award-Winning LinkedIn LIVE Shows have been featured on NASDAQ, Forbes, Thrive Global, Bloomberg, Yahoo Finance, CBS, NBC, FOX, Viacom, Roku TV, Amazon Fire, PODTV, The CW, and hundreds of shows and podcasts, reaching millions worldwide.

Brian brings his twenty-plus years of experience, wealth of knowledge, and proven leadership expertise to C-Suite Executives and Entrepreneurs globally as an advisor and mentor through Voice Your Vibe's groundbreaking masterminds and heart-centered leadership programs.

Brian has been named a 6X LinkedIn Top Voice, LinkedIn Video Creator of the Year, 3X Top 50 Most Impactful People of LinkedIn, 4X Rising Star & Influencer to Watch on LinkedIn and 2X LinkedIn Global Leader of The Year, out of one billion business professionals on LinkedIn. Brian is also the Executive Producer, Creator and Cohost of VoiceYourVibe LIVE, which includes two global award-winning weekly LinkedIn LIVE shows broadcast in 120+ countries that have aired for over five years and 500+ consecutive episodes—and were named "Best LIVE Festive Show of The Year" at the IBM TV Awards.

Author's Website: *www.VoiceYourVibe.com*

Book Series Website: *www.TheBookOfHumanEmpowerment.com*

CHRISTOPHER HUNSICKER

TURN YOUR PURPOSE INTO A PRACTICE

I have so many friends who have yoga pants, a yoga mat, and even yoga blocks. What they don't have is a yoga practice—something they do every day, whether they feel like it or not!

In this book, many of my colleagues have shared amazing inspiration, tools, and frameworks to help you identify your purpose. This chapter is designed to help you live your purpose day by day and choice by choice for the rest of your life.

With each decision in our lives, we choose to step forward into growth or we step backward into comfort. Once you have identified your purpose, the most important thing you need to do is make and remake the decision to choose courage over comfort each and every day.

Far more people fail to live their purpose from a lack of courage than they do from a lack of clarity. The key to living your purpose is to turn your epiphany into execution; in short, your practice. You need a Purpose Practice!

Whether you have just begun to discover your purpose or are twenty years into living your purpose, here are three powerful tools to help you make your unique contribution to a world that desperately needs what you have to share. I call them behavioral mindsets:

1.   Get in the wheelbarrow!

2.   Your 3 things.

3.   Your Keystone 5-minute habit.

Mindset #1: Get in the Wheelbarrow!

It's almost 5:00 pm and Charles Blondin is about to cross Niagara Falls on a tightrope. There are hundreds, even thousands of people on both sides of the Falls in Canada and America. It's 1858, and this is high-end entertainment for the time. But, let's be clear, most of these people are not here to see Harry succeed. They are here to see him fail. They think it is impossible and that he is going to die trying to cross Niagara Falls on a tightrope.

Principle 1: Most People are Waiting for You to Fail. It's Your Purpose, Not Theirs!

The more you try to do something great, meaningful, or valuable, the more people will line up to see you fail. Most people really do not want success, especially success for other people.

For this crossing, Charles used a wheelbarrow full of bricks. After crossing from the Canadian side to the American side of the falls, a crowd of reporters were begging to talk to him. Most were sure he was going to die and now, to their complete surprise, he is here, and not only safe, but ready to cross back to the other side!

All the reporters are shouting questions. He asks them to quiet down, and states he will answer all their questions if they will answer one question for him when they are done.

When there were no more questions, Charles spoke up and asked each reporter if they believed he could make it back to the other side.

One reporter said emphatically, "No!" He was shocked Charles had made it once—there was no way he could do it again, and he strongly counseled Charles not to try.

Have you ever been told by authorities and experts or maybe loved ones that you can't do it and you should not try; that you should abandon your purpose?

Each of the next several reporters expressed some concern or fear that he would not make it back to the Canadian side.

Finally, one reporter shouted, "Yes, I think you can make it to the other side." Charles asked, "Are you sure, really sure?" Again, the reporter said, "Yes, I am; that is the most amazing feat of balance I have ever seen." Charles replied, "Thank you." Charles looked him straight in the eyes and asked again, "Are you really sure?" "Yes," came the emphatic answer, this time with more energy and certainty.

Charles smiled, walked over to his wheelbarrow, dumped out all the bricks, and said, "Get in!"

You see, it is one thing to believe—it is another to commit. It is one thing for the reporter to believe, even strongly believe in Charles' ability. It is another thing altogether to get in a wheelbarrow.

You have found your purpose—NOW commit to it with your whole soul. It is in the commitment to the purpose that the magic is found.

Mindset #2: Define Your Three Things

Your purpose will have a divine element to it, and with that comes access to universal wisdom. A practice is defined by our daily behavior. Ask yourself in a quiet moment, "What are three things (specific habits or practices) I need to do every day to live my purpose?"

1._____

2._____

3._____

Now, accessing that same inner wisdom, what are three behaviors, habits, or practices you need to stop doing, now, to live your purpose?

1._____

2._____

3._____

Mindset #3: Your Keystone Habit

In an ancient Roman arch, there is the keystone that sits at the top of the arch in the center and holds the whole arch together. The third mindset I want to share with you is the Keystone Habit, the one habit that you know will support all the other habits and behaviors you need to live your purpose. It may even be something you identified in Mindset #1. Get this one right and all the others fall into place.

My Keystone Habit

_____

Now, make the habit ridiculously simple. How?

Every year, I teach a master's class on executive coaching at CY Cergy Paris University. While I speak French, I do not have the chance very often to practice, so each year, going into my class, I am very rusty. The class is always the third week in May and I am the last guest lecturer before they finish the program.

Every March, I tell myself I am going to start my French practice so I can be ready for Paris. The Pimsler language app has lessons that are thirty minutes each. I have a busy and demanding schedule and so, inevitably, I do not have thirty minutes to practice my French.

So, I get from March 1 to March 30, and I have not listened to a single lesson! But, now, it is April and I only have seven weeks, so I recommit to starting my French practice. It's April 15 and I have listened to zero French lessons (because, again, I do not have thirty minutes).

Finally, I get to May and I am desperate to start listening to my French lessons. Around May 15th I break into a panic and cram a few lessons before I land in Paris, a few days before my class, and hope it all comes back. Sound familiar? I really want to practice French. It will really make a difference. But I don't. Why?

I am trying to do too much, too fast. It is so hard to get started, I never start. I have seen so many people come off the euphoria of finding their purpose only to get stuck on the shores of regret because they cannot find thirty minutes. What I needed to do, and eventually did, was make it ridiculously simple, and so easy I could not skip it.

I committed to five minutes of French while I showered. I shower every day in the morning. It takes about five minutes. When I turn on the water, I start the French lesson. The first year I did it, I started on March 1. By March 31st, I had thirty-one consecutive days! By the time I got to April, I was averaging thirty minutes a day. From mid-April to May 23rd, I was doing thirty-plus minutes a day. I had the best class ever that year.

So, how are you going to make your keystone habit so simple you cannot skip it?

Take the momentum, passion, and energy you gain from this book and turn your purpose into a practice.

1. Make a choice to get in the wheelbarrow of your own destiny!
2. Trust your heart and the divine spark in you to pick your three things to start and stop doing.
3. Find your Keystone Habit and make it so simple and so easy you cannot skip it.

Congratulations—unlike my yoga friends, you have a practice and, with it, the framework to live your purpose and give your unique gift to world. And we need it. We need you.

CHRISTOPHER HUNSICKER

About Christopher Hunsicker: Chris Hunsicker is a bestselling author and an internationally recognized authority on organizational leadership and change management. With a unique blend of warmth, humor, and dynamic presentation style, Chris is a highly sought-after speaker in both the corporate and public sectors. His keynotes and workshops are transformative experiences, known for their combination of education, entertainment, and energy (e3). Chris has a powerful gift for engaging both the heart and the mind, making him a trusted advisor to some of America's most successful companies.

As the founder of Hunsicker Coaching International, Chris specializes in helping organizations achieve two critical shifts: moving from insight to action and from data to dollars. His extensive experience includes working with diverse industries such as automotive retail and healthcare, and coaching teams from the C-suite to frontline managers. Chris's global impact is evident through his work in countries ranging from China to South Africa and from Europe to Brazil.

Chris holds a BA in Psychology from Utah State University and a Master's in Organizational Leadership from the University of Phoenix. He also lectures annually at CY Cergy Paris University. Chris and his wife, Sherrie, live in South Carolina, where they cherish their five children and six grandchildren.

Author's Website: *www.ChrisHunsicker.com*

Book Series Website: *www.TheBookOfHumanEmpowerment.com*

CHRISTOPHER MUSIC

A LIFE-CHANGING EXPERIENCE IN THE MARCHING MUSIC ARTS

Just imagine the setting: Saturday, August 15, 1987, Camp Randall Stadium at the University of Wisconsin in Madison, Wisconsin. The Drum Corps International (DCI) Finals, approximately 10:00 pm CST.

It was the culmination of an entire year of intense preparation, sixty days on tour though the central and eastern regions of The United States and Canada, and countless hours of drilling and rehearsal, bringing our production of Aaron Copeland's masterpiece, "Appalachian Spring," to its final legendary performance.

The activity is called drum and bugle corps. For those who are new to this term, it started generally after WWII as a summer activity for youth ages 13-21 through VFW organizations nationwide and developed into the marching music arts of present day. Similar to a corps-style high school or college marching band, these groups have only brass, percussion and color guard—no woodwinds—and one-hundred-twenty-eight on-field performers, plus instructors and support staff.

The corps compete throughout the summer with a scoring system based on technical precision and artistic quality for an 11.5-minute performance. The quality and difficulty of the repertoire increases each season as innovations in musical arrangements and drill designs push the activity to previously unimaginable productions.

The Finals are the last performance of the top twelve drum and bugle corps from around the world, showcasing the best and the brightest of the entire activity, which comprises what was hundreds of corps at the time, over a grueling but rewarding summer of commitment, dedication, persistence, physical and mental effort.

Personally, I began to study the trumpet in fifth grade and I became quite proficient at the instrument during my middle and high school years. Of course, I was in the marching band at my high school and had the good fortune of competing in band competitions in the Eastern Ohio and Western Pennsylvania circuits through my senior year. As I moved onto college, I took the summers of 1985, '86, '87 and '89 to participate in the drum corps activity, as it was a family tradition on my mother's side since the 1970s.

The Garfield Cadets of Garfield, New Jersey was the oldest and most revered drum and bugle corps in the country, founded as the Holy Name Cadets in 1934. In the early 80s, the corps found itself with a new Executive Director and a deep connection to Broadway, propelling the organization to ground-breaking and innovative musical and marching techniques that upended and re-defined the entire activity. Known for their musical difficulty and fast-moving drill, they had previously won the World Championships in 1983, '84 and '85.

1986 was my first season with the Cadets since I wanted to be with the BEST. At seventeen-years-old, I played the mellophone, which is a mellow sounding cross between a trumpet and French horn with a wide bell. The reason I chose this instrument was because we had the most melodic and interesting parts to play in the brass arrangements for the symphonic pieces we performed. The biggest lesson I learned in that first year with the Cadets was how to work—I mean, REALLY WORK.

1987 was, by all accounts, a dream season for the Cadets. We began in October 1986 with the monthly winter camps, which was one weekend a month where we all traveled to Teterboro, New Jersey to rehearse, eat, and sleep for forty-eight-hours and return home with the responsibility to memorize our parts. Once school ended in the Spring, people began to move to New Jersey for all day rehearsals beginning in mid-May. We had about one month to put a show together before the summer tour started in mid-June.

The show was beautifully designed and executed and we faired very well in competition during the whole summer, as we only had three early-season losses to the Spirit of Atlanta, an excellent drum corps headquartered in Atlanta, Georgia. The season comprised of roughly forty performances, all day rehearsals and sleeping on overnight bus rides to the next city. Sometimes, we were blessed with sleeping on high school gymnasium floors when we arrived or stayed more than a day in one place.

As we rolled into Madison, Wisconsin the second week of August, we had not seen the top two contending corps from the West Coast, namely the Blue Devils of Concord, CA and the Santa Clara Vanguard from Santa Clara, CA., so we had no idea how we compared to them in open competition with the same judging crew.

But it really didn't matter.

While the drum corps activity was based on a competition with other groups, one could never really determine who the ultimate winner would be because of the complexity of the performances and the judges' bias in the scoring. The competitive part of this activity certainly did provide us with motivation to do our best and win over the other corps, but that was not the reason we worked so hard.

No, we had the mindset of constantly and continually pursuing perfection from our position in the entire group. There was a perfect performance in mind for each person on that field. And when you are executing complex and fast-moving marching maneuvers while playing technically challenging instrumental parts, there is always a better way to place your foot or hit that note during a whole 11.5-minute show.

We had one instance where one of the baritone players was complaining about the baritone next to him, saying that she was not playing her part well. The instructor then immediately halted practice and made him stand in front of the entire horn line. He was asked if he could play his part perfectly and he responded by saying that he could play it better than the person next to him. He was then asked to play his part in front of everyone and he was stopped after two notes. The instructor merely asked if it was perfect, and we all could see that the attack on the note could have been sharper and cleaner.

The baritone player had to admit that his part was not perfect, and the instructor took the opportunity to remind us that we only need to worry about pursuing excellence in our own areas of control and not worry about the other person's performance. It was this relentless pursuit of perfection on an individual level and being the very best at our position that was the central lesson and philosophy we followed persistently the entire season.

This moment-by-moment mindset, along with our tireless physical and mental work, allowed us to achieve our purpose—to create an inspiring and emotionally-uplifting work of art. Our purpose was to do something that was never done before and to create magic, not to win a competition. We suffered through the toil and celebrated the successes together for a whole year to deliver a miracle in musical and visual pageantry.

Whether we won or not, every one of us knew that we did our very best, pushed our limits, and gained a new, expanded definition of personal excellence.

That night was our final show, and we were the twelfth corps to perform, due to our semi-final scores. After the performance, all twelve corps assembled on the football field in retreat, awaiting the scores and the final placements for the season. In the end, we won!

The Cadets edged out the Santa Clara Vanguard by one tenth of a point, as close a margin possible in the DCI scoring system of that era. As we celebrated, every one of us knew that winning the Finals was merely the validation of our mindset and our purpose. The true win was that we succeeded in bettering ourselves individually, and the group would make history as a result.

CHRISTOPHER MUSIC

About Christopher Music, MBA, RFC, CBEC: Christopher is a 31-year veteran of the personal financial planning profession. He has owned, built and sold two firms since 1992, improving the financial destinies of thousands of families in the US. He is a Wall Street Journal/USA Today bestselling author and international speaker on financial topics. As a Certified Business Consultant, Registered Financial Consultant®, and a Certified Business Exit Consultant®, he is committed to expanding his knowledge and expertise in the fields of personal finance and economics for the ultimate benefit of small business owners.

He has shared the stage and/or collaborated on projects with Grant Cardone, Forbes Riley, Steve Forbes, Brian Tracy, Erik Swanson, Robert Allen, Mel Robbins, and other leading coaches and consultants.

Christopher currently lives his life virtually as a digital nomad, traveling the world full-time as an investor and wealth coach.

He can be reached at *pchristophermusic@gmail.com.*

Author's Website: *www.ChristopherMusic.com*

Book Series Website: *www.TheBookOfHumanEmpowerment.com*

COREY POIRIER

MIND & PURPOSE MATTERS

In my latest book, *The Enlightened Passenger*, I shared that the most important word in the English language (based on my findings during over 7,000 interviews) is "Mindset."

A close second is "Purpose."

Having purpose may even be more important than having the right mindset, BUT, in my experience, it's much easier to start working on your mindset than it is to find one's purpose.

For help in finding your purpose, you can search my TEDx called, "How Schools Can Inspire Purpose," or check out one of my books (hint: one of them covers this, fully disguised as finding your why) as I think covering both in this one chapter may be a lot, even for me (someone who works with both mindset and purpose daily).

So, in terms of mindset, based on my extensive research during more than 7,000 interviews, one thing I have learned is that, like decision, mindset is one thing that is truly in our control.

We don't likely have control over much in our lives, but the decisions we make, and how we set our minds, are things we can control—as long as we don't give that control to others.

I read a comment by someone this week. They were commenting on someone's post saying we get to choose how we feel about things, how we act when good or bad things happen, and how we respond to what happens.

The comment the person made was something to the effect of, "Well, looky here, another hippy dippy manifestation; positive energy is always a rosy person."

My immediate thought was, even if we couldn't control how we react to things, or what we feed our mind, and even if we can't prove manifestation is happening, what is the upside to not believing it's possible?

I mean, the person saying, "Look at this hippy-dippy person," what are they gaining by thinking it's all a bunch of positive energy talk and affirmations?

I can tell you what I have gained by choosing how I respond to circumstances that happen to me, by believing it's possible to manifest, and by believing we attract stuff that is congruent with what we visualize.

My life has been, as described by someone just the other day, nothing short of magical.

I wonder if that person making the hippy-dippy comment is happy with their life.

I wonder, if they aren't, if their mindset may have something to do with it.

Because I believe the benefits to having the right mindset and believing manifestation is possible far outweigh the benefits of not believing, I want to share with you is three ways I believe you can use to interpret and respond to things in a way that serves your better good.

First: $E + R = O$

I learned this by attending a Jack Canfield (Chicken Soup) seminar years ago.

Jack said he learned it from his mentor, W. Clement Stone, and, I believe, he shares it in his *Success Principles* book.

The E in the equation stands for Event. The R stands for Response. The O stands for Outcome.

Every day, we are hit with events we can't control.

The only thing we can control is how we respond.

The response we choose will dictate the outcome we get (in most cases).

So, when an event happens, you can choose to respond positively or in a way that will get you the desired outcome, OR you can choose to react to the situation and perhaps make it worse, or you can end up with an outcome you wouldn't choose.

Ultimately, I always say the + sign is the pause in the equation—the moment you take to determine how you will respond.

So, basically, you get cut off in traffic and the person gives you the middle finger (aka. flips you the bird), you choose to yell and chase their car. You will have a different outcome almost ten times out of ten verses if you chose to simply say, it's likely not about me at all; maybe they are in a hurry for a legit reason, etc.

The second way you can improve the way you respond to situations is by feeding your mind the right stuff.

When you read the right books, attend the right events, listen to the right podcasts and so on, that becomes the mind food that you are feeding your mind.

The better the mind food, the better your mindset.

So, the question is, are you consciously feeding your mind the right things or are you leaving it to chance?

It truly is as simple as finding out what the right things are (perhaps talking to people you admire/respect to see what they are reading or listening to) and then feeding your mind those exact things.

The third way to improve your mindset and the way you interpret what happens to you is to surround yourself with the right people.

I do a relationship inventory once a year where I list the people I'm spending my time with and add a + to the ones who are bringing me positive energy, and a – to the ones who are bringing negative energy.

The more positive you have verses negative, the better your mindset. Again, very simple (see: not easy).

If you do this inventory and have more negative people in your life and fewer positive, you need to begin the work of removing some people, reducing time you spend with others, and adding some more positive ones.

For me, the result was almost unbelievable.

So, there you have it—in a short chapter, the three things I wish I knew when I started my journey about improving one's mindset, and the three things I had to do over 7,000 interviews to learn.

I hope it serves you as well as it did me.

Contact Corey Poirier:
Facebook: *www.facebook.com/corey.poirier.1*
LinkedIn: *www.linkedin.com/in/speakercoreypoirier*
Instagram: *www.instagram.com/thatspeakerguy*
Email: *blutalksbrand@gmail.com*
Website: *www.thatspeakerguy.com*

COREY POIRIER

About Corey Poirier: Corey Poirier is a multiple-time TEDx Speaker. He is also the host of the top-rated "Let's Do Influencing" Radio Show, founder of the growing bLU Talks brand, and has been featured in multiple television specials. He is also a Barnes and Noble, Amazon, Apple Books, and Kobo Bestselling Author, Award Winning Author, and the co-author of the Wall Street Journal/USA Today Bestseller, *Quitless.*

A columnist with Entrepreneur and Forbes magazine, he has been featured in/on various mediums. He is one of the few leaders featured twice on the popular Entrepreneur on Fire show. He has interviewed over 6,500 of the world's top leaders and has spoken on-site at Harvard, Columbia University, and more recently to Microsoft team leaders and at Kyle Wilson's Inner Circle retreat, which has featured everyone from Brian Tracy to Mark Victor Hansen to Phil Collen (Def Leppard).

He is a New Media Summit Icon of Influence, was recently listed as the #5 Influencer in Entrepreneurship by Thinkers 360, and was listed on the 2021 Brainz CREA Global Awards as an honoree. He is a Humanitarian Hero Award Nominee, Entrepreneur of the Year Nominee, Champion Award (Business from The Heart) nominee, and, to demonstrate his versatility, a Rock Recording of the Year Nominee who has performed stand-up comedy more than 700 times, including an appearance at the famed Second City.

Author's Website: *www.ThisIsTheBook.com*

Book Series Website: *www.TheBookOfHumanEmpowerment.com*

CRYSTAL LINDSEY

REJECTED

My empowerment story started when I was born. My mother never seemed to love me. She liked my older sister, but she never wanted to look me in the eyes or hug me. I knew I was treated differently. I got more beatings and less food. My sister got her share of beatings, too, but my treatment seemed to be different. I was scolded and mocked, while my sister was not.

I was constantly told that I would never be anything in this world. My mother's slogan for me was, "What do you think you are, special?" Or perhaps the lovely, "If I knew you were a girl, I would have aborted you." She already had two other girls by two men and wanted a son. Apparently, the ultrasound's misreading saved my life.

I was an outsider in my own family. My own mother rejected me. Little did I know this was the greatest gift someone could give me. My whole belief system about why I was treated this way was about to change in one afternoon when I was nine years old.

My mom arrived to pick me up after school crying. The tears must have blocked her vision because she was swerving all over the road. I could tell something was brewing. She seemed hysterical, and I was terrified. Finally, she pulled over and parked the car.

My heart raced as she spun her head around to look at me in the back seat. She yelled through her tearful eyes, "Your father is not your father, and your sister is not your sister. Your auntie is not your auntie. Your dad doesn't care about you. That's why he left you! He never wanted you." Then, she seemed to pull herself together and drive somewhat normally. The tears had ended after she had said what she needed to say.

I sat there stunned in the back seat of the car. Oddly, I don't remember any real emotions coming over me. I guess I didn't know what to think. I just stared out the window until we arrived home, where I could finally lay on my bunk bed. I began to sort it out. "Well," I thought, "I always knew I was different...." My mind trailed off into the million and one ways my sister and my mother rejected me. I could see now that I really was different.

I decided this was good news. My heart started to sing, and my feelings of confusion lifted. Finally, I had figured it all out! If my dad was why I was so different, then he must be really powerful! I just knew he was an alien from outer space with special powers that would rescue me. He would come back to get me. He had to, right? Wrong.

My dad never did decide to come to rescue me. He didn't have superpowers. Spoiler alert: he also wasn't an alien. But that didn't matter. I had already changed my expectation about my future, and thus I had altered my MINDSET and belief in myself. Suddenly I didn't spend my time wondering why my mother didn't seem to love me. I quit wondering why I was not enough. I stopped having feelings of despair. Now I had new thoughts of what my future would be like with my new family.

I thought of my new future with my dad so much that I even had a recurring dream about it. In the dream, my dad, an alien from outer space, would come bursting out of the attic on a motorcycle and swoop me up. He would take me away with our hair flapping in the wind. I was finally free. In this dream, I would laugh in joy and amazement. The moment had come; my dad was here to take me away from the suffering. Then I would wake up.

The problem is he never came. Instead, the abuse continued to escalate after my older sister had run away. At eleven years old, my mother attacked me, ripping my shirt off me and hitting me with an icepick handle. I ran away and was placed into the shelter for foster care children.

One day, the people who worked at the shelter sat me down. I remember they were clearly trying to say something difficult to me, but they couldn't get it out. "Come on," I told them. "You can tell me," I said with the most bravado I could muster at eleven. One finally blurted out, "Your mother left in the middle of the night, and we don't know where she went." I was shocked. I made them take me to the apartment I had lived in with my mom just last week.

The apartment was empty. She had taken every single item I owned.

Yet again, I went back to my bunk bed to lay down and sort it all out. See, I have always been committed to living a life of greatness. I remember telling my sister, "When I get older, I am going to make a lot of money. And the only thing I am going to buy you is an education!" This only got more intense after I learned about my dad not being the same as my sister's dad. I was different, and I knew it. That knowledge was power.

I decided I would be the victor, not the victim in the situation. And now, again, I lay on my bed and had to commit myself. I affirmed that "I was destined for greatness," and this was a gift. My MINDSET shifted. It was me and me now. That's it. With every ounce of my soul, I promised myself that I would take good care of myself. And that I did.

Now I am launching a whole new department for a digital marketing agency. I am also a proud accountability coach, artist, best-selling author, entrepreneur, and former college professor. I earned two master's degrees and continue to earn six figures with joy in my heart. Now, I have bigger dreams to do even more!

I have shifted my mindset from making six figures to making seven figures. Now I am becoming a multi-millionaire from foster care. My multi-millionaire empire will create a legacy I can pass down to help other foster youth when I am gone. Every day, I want to commit my life to helping people change the way they think to become who they are meant to be in this world.

How did I do it? That is for the next book. I will give you the exact strategy formula that I used to create the building blocks of my success. Right now, I want you to understand that I used what could have been the two biggest traumas of my childhood and turned them into my greatest turning points. The key to my future was my ability to shift my thinking about rejection.

Like how David had to shift his mindset to conquer Goliath, I had to change how I perceived myself without my mother's belief in me. David was rejected and dismissed as an unequal foe because of his diminished appearance. Likewise, I was rejected by my mother because my father left. However, like David, I believed in myself and committed to doing my best based on a belief I had from God.

I had to change my mindset. I knew that the rejection I felt was real, but I also knew I could decide what I believed. And I believed that I was going to be okay. I committed that I would always take great care of myself. I believed I had value in this world.

I was unprepared before birth to go up against a giant like Goliath. Then, as a child, I learned I was different. This knowledge allowed me to create a mindset that I was special and destined for greatness. I suddenly believed in myself even when all of the odds were stacked against me, and no one believed in me. I could not have created this mindset shift without the gift of rejection. God used rejection to allow me to take down the giant even while being woefully unprepared.

Let me clarify: you can only thrive out of trauma when you choose not to be a victim but the victor. You must see everything that has happened to you as a gift. So, if you are out there struggling with hardships, I want you to know you can change your life at any given moment by choosing to live intentionally and change what the trauma means.

I have news for you: your Goliath, your challenge, will always be there. Life will always throw you a curveball, even after you "make it." However, you can change other people's lives by changing what hardship means. In addition, this slight shift in your story will change your belief in yourself.

Remember, you change your beliefs and mindset by changing how you define your life circumstances. You can overcome poverty, rejection, fear, disappointment, or even loneliness by deciding you are worthy. You can change your mindset by speaking positive belief systems into your existence. You can change the meaning of your story. It is up to you. No one needs to give you permission.

Only you can do it, but first, you have to decide you can.

Please reach out to me at crystaljlindsey.com to let me know how you are changing the story of your lives. I would love to hear. Truly!

CRYSTAL LINDSEY

About Crystal Lindsey: Crystal overcame tremendous odds and became a bestselling author, public speaker, college professor, artist, and dynamic digital marketer. She is currently known as @GratefulMarketer! She teaches business owners the exact bio hacks and marketing hacks that she used to beat the odds. Crystal is currently the Digital Marketing Manager for Dallas for M. Roberts Digital.

Follow her on Facebook and Instagram, @GratefulMarketer, to learn how to achieve peak performance, grow your business, and leverage digital marketing.

Check out crystaljlindsey.com to learn more about her book, *Grit & Gratitude: The Former Foster Youth's Playbook for Adulting.*

Contact Crystal for Public Speaking, Emcee, Corporate Trainer, Inspirational Speaker, Panel Guest, Marketing Consultant, Corporate Sales & Marketing Training.

Author's Website: *www.CrystalJLindsey.com*

Book Series Website: *www.TheBookOfHumanEmpowerment.com*

DR. DEBORAH J. ANDERSON

LIVING WITH PURPOSE: DISCOVERING GOD'S PLAN

I have always known I am an Inspirer, and I get to live in that role every day. Having spent my life immersed in personal growth, I often emphasize finding your passion. Yet, I don't believe passion is something to be found. Instead, it's something to be expressed. It doesn't exist in a person, place, thing, or activity—it's within you, ready to be lived out in the world around you.

Sometimes, certain activities or circumstances may ignite that passion, allowing it to be expressed more fully, but the passion remains constant, regardless of external conditions. I believe in pouring my passion, especially my love for those who are less fortunate or dealing with injustice, into everything I do. Even mundane tasks can become fulfilling when they are driven by passion. I'm not searching for passion—I'm living it.

Reflecting on my life and those I have served, I realize that I have been expressing my passion all along. Whether through personal growth or acts of service, such as facilitating Fresh Start for All Nations groups, working with Open Door Mission, Heartland Kids Against Hunger, or my many opportunities to serve in the church, I see that I have lived in alignment with my passion without ever needing to find it. It was always there.

Purpose is a divine calling. In our culture, we are often told that we must find our purpose, as though it is hidden somewhere, waiting to be discovered. We attend workshops, read books, and take endless assessments, always feeling like something is missing if we haven't yet "found" our purpose. This search can leave us feeling inadequate, unworthy, or lost, as if we fail at life because we haven't stumbled upon that elusive purpose.

But I believe our purpose is not something to be unearthed; rather, it is something given to us by God. Our purpose is not just a personal mission to discover but is rooted in pleasing and serving Him. The Bible teaches that our ultimate purpose is to glorify God and enjoy Him forever. As Romans 12:1–2 reminds us, "…We are to offer ourselves as living sacrifices, holy and pleasing to God, and to be transformed by the renewing of our minds."

Our purpose in life, as God created it, involves five key aspects: to glorify God, to enjoy fellowship with Him, to build good relationships with others, to work diligently, and to have dominion over the earth. Yet, through man's fall into sin, much of this purpose became obscured. Fellowship with God was broken, relationships became strained, work became frustrating, and man's control over nature faltered. Only by restoring our relationship with God through faith in Jesus Christ can we rediscover and live out our true purpose.

Trusting God's Plan

Life is a proving ground. God sends us to earth to learn and grow through both pleasant and painful experiences, and He allows us the freedom to choose between good and evil. Our challenge is to have faith in His plan, even when we don't have all the answers.

One of the greatest questions we ask ourselves is not, "What is my purpose?" but rather, "What is God's purpose for my life?" Knowing and fulfilling God's purpose for our lives brings confidence in the midst of the confusion, fear, and distractions of this world. Scripture tells us that God's purpose is always at work, even when we may not fully understand how. As Isaiah 46:9-10 says, "I am God, and there is no other; I am God, and there is none like me, declaring the end from the beginning and from ancient times things not yet done, saying, 'My counsel shall stand, and I will accomplish all my purpose.'"

God's purpose is never random or haphazard. He is the supreme planner, with a strategy that stretches from eternity past to eternity future. His purposes for us extend beyond our individual lives—they are intricately connected to His larger, eternal plan for creation.

Purpose in the World to Come

From the very beginning, God had a plan. He created the heavens and the earth, setting the stage for His ultimate purpose to unfold. As Genesis 1:1 tells us, "In the beginning, God created the heavens and the earth," and later, in Genesis 1:27-28, we learn that He made mankind in His image, giving us dominion over the earth.

The Bible paints a picture of God's grand purpose, culminating in the new heaven and new earth. As Revelation 21:1-4 describes, "...in this renewed creation, there will be no more sin, suffering, or death (paraphrased)." God's ultimate purpose is to dwell among His people, redeem and glorify them, and share His glory with them.

As Jonathan Edwards so beautifully put it, divine love will be perfected in every heart, and every ransomed soul will burn brightly with that love for all eternity. This is God's ultimate purpose: to redeem this fallen world and to bring about a new creation where we live in perfect communion with Him.

Purpose in the Present World

But what about now? Between God's original good creation and the new creation to come, we live in a world devastated by sin, suffering, and death. Yet even here, God's purposes continue to unfold. His redemptive plan, carried out through Jesus Christ, transforms us in the present while preparing us for eternity.

Through Jesus' death and resurrection, God's kingdom is breaking into our lives. Jesus' followers, empowered by the Holy Spirit, were commissioned to spread the good news of God's kingdom across the earth. Today, more and more people are being brought into His family, as they are transformed by His grace.

As believers, our purpose is to be conformed to the image of Christ. This means that God's purpose for each one of us is to reflect His character more fully, living lives of love and good works. As Ephesians 2:10 reminds us, we are God's workmanship, created in Jesus Christ to do good works that He prepared in advance for us to do. These works are not the cause of our salvation but the fruit and evidence of it.

Living with Purpose Daily

This transformation happens in the ordinary affairs of daily life. God's purposes unfold in our families, work, and ministries. Every life is part of God's grand design, from the prophet Jeremiah to King David to each one of us. As Jeremiah 1:5 says, "Before I formed you in the womb, I knew you, and before you were born, I consecrated you."

Our task is to live out God's purpose in everyday life, seeking His guidance and direction through prayer, Scripture, and the wisdom of others. As Proverbs 3:5-6 tells us, "Trust in the Lord with all your heart and lean not on your own understanding; in all your ways acknowledge Him, and He will make your paths straight."

As we surrender to God's will, He leads us, even in the seemingly mundane decisions of life. As C.S. Lewis once noted, our choices shape us, "Every time you make a choice you are turning the central part of you into something a little different from what it was before."

Mindset: Surrendering to God's Wisdom

Purpose and mindset go hand in hand. Our mindset, attitudes, and beliefs shape how we approach our purpose. A godly mindset counts others as more significant than ourselves and focuses on things that are unseen rather than the visible circumstances around us. Philippians 4:13 reminds us, "I can do all things through Christ who strengthens me."

God calls us to replace toxic thoughts with His thoughts. His thoughts are higher than ours, and He gives us direction on how to think. By surrendering our minds to Him and seeking His wisdom, we can live out our purpose with joy and peace, regardless of the challenges we face.

Becoming Who God Created Us to Be

We are not defined by our circumstances, diagnoses, or mistakes. God has made each of us a treasured masterpiece created out of love and light. When life feels like it's falling apart, God reminds us that we are not breaking down—we are breaking through. We are becoming the people He created us to be people of light, love, hope, and courage.

As we journey through life, living out God's purpose and surrendering our mindset to His wisdom, we can trust that He is with us every step of the way. We are not falling apart—we are falling into place. And in the end, we will hear Him say, "Well done."

DR. DEBORAH J. ANDERSON

About Dr. Deborah J. Anderson: Dr. Deborah J. Anderson has worked as a special education teacher, administrator, and university professor. As a professional speaker, life coach, and author, Deborah inspires others to achieve a higher level of success through maximum productivity, action, and capitalizing on one's strengths. Deborah resides in her home state of Nebraska, where she has used her retirement as an opportunity to "refire:" serving others through various ministries.

In addition, she leads and facilitates Fresh Start groups for women who are experiencing the effects of offense, hurt, and loss through the transforming power of Jesus. Deborah is going ALL IN and saying "Yes" to whatever God is calling her to do.

Author's Website: *www.LinkedIn.com/in/Dr-Deborah-J-Anderson*

Book Series Website: *www.TheBookOfHumanEmpowerment.com*

EILEEN GALBRAITH

THE JOURNEY OF ELIZABETH

Transforming Your Mindset For A Better Life

Once upon a time, in the bustling city of Metropolis, lived a young woman named Elizabeth. Elizabeth was like many others—caught in the daily grind, dealing with life's ups and downs, and often feeling overwhelmed by the challenges thrown her way. But what set Elizabeth apart was her burning desire to change her life for the better. Little did she know the key to her transformation lay in her mindset.

Elizabeth's days began with a symphony of complaints. The alarm clock was too loud, the commute too long, and her job too monotonous. She felt stuck in a rut, believing that life was just a series of unfortunate events she had to endure. But one particularly dreary Monday morning, something changed. As she trudged to her local tea shop, she overheard a conversation that sparked a glimmer of hope.

Two distinguished women were sitting by the window, discussing the power of mindset. "Optimism is like a muscle," one said. "The more you use it, the stronger it gets." Elizabeth paused, intrigued. Could it be that simple? She decided to find out.

That evening, Elizabeth dove into researching mindsets. She discovered the concept of attitudes and how they shaped one's perception of the world. Attitudes, she learned, were like the lenses through which people view their lives. Optimism was the rose-colored lens that highlighted opportunities, while pessimism was the gray lens that emphasized obstacles.

Determined to test this theory, Elizabeth embarked on a little experiment. She called it the *Silver Lining Hunt*. Each day, she would find three positive aspects in her otherwise mundane or negative experiences. The next morning, when her bus was late, she seized the opportunity to savor her coffee, chat with a friendly stranger, and admire the blooming flowers in the park.

To her surprise, the more she hunted for silver linings, the more she found. Life began to seem less daunting and more like an adventure. Her optimism muscle was growing stronger.

Inspired by her small victories, Elizabeth decided to tackle her self-efficacy next. Self-efficacy, she learned, was like having an inner superhero who believed, "I can do this!" But her inner superhero was more like a reluctant sidekick. She needed to boost her confidence.

She read about the Superhero Pose—a simple yet powerful exercise. Every morning, she stood in front of her mirror, feet apart, hands on her hips, chest out, and declared, "I've got this!" At first, it felt silly. But over time, she noticed a change. The more she adopted her superhero stance, the more she felt like one.

With growing confidence, Elizabeth tackled new challenges at work and sought out opportunities for growth. She even volunteered for a project that required public speaking, something she had always dreaded. She stumbled at first, but each stumble was a steppingstone to improvement. Her belief in her abilities was transforming.

However, life wasn't without its setbacks. One day, Elizabeth received a rejection email for a job promotion she had been eyeing. Old habits threatened to resurface, but she remembered her training in resilience. Resilience was like being a rubber ball; the harder life threw you down, the higher you bounced back up.

Elizabeth created her Bounce-Back Plan. She allowed herself a day to feel the disappointment but then listed three actions to recover: seek feedback, identify areas for improvement, and apply for another opportunity. This plan was her lifeline, helping her navigate setbacks without losing momentum.

As Elizabeth continued her journey, she dove deeper into the beliefs that shaped her self-concept and self-worth. Her inner dialogue had always been harsh, filled with criticisms and doubts. But she learned that beliefs were powerful forces that could either lift her up or drag her down.

She embraced the practice of Positive Affirmations. Each day, she wrote down five things she appreciated about herself. These notes adorned her fridge, her bathroom mirror, and even her workstation. "I am creative," "I am resilient," "I am capable." These affirmations were her daily high-fives, gradually reshaping her self-concept into one of confidence and worthiness.

One of the most profound shifts came when Elizabeth explored the difference between a fixed and a growth mindset. A fixed mindset, she discovered, believed talents and abilities were set in stone. But a growth mindset? It believed in the power of effort and learning.

To cultivate her growth mindset, Elizabeth initiated the Growth Mindset Challenge. She picked a skill she wasn't good at—cooking. Each week, she set a small goal, like mastering a new recipe. Initially, there were burnt meals and kitchen disasters, but with each attempt, she improved. Celebrating these small victories with a happy dance became a ritual, reinforcing her belief that effort and persistence led to growth.

But Elizabeth's transformation wasn't just internal. She realized the importance of her relationships and the role of trust and empathy. Relationships, she learned, were like plants needing trust as water and empathy as sunlight.

She practiced the Empathy Exercise. The next time someone annoyed her, instead of reacting with frustration, she paused and thought, "What might they be going through?" This simple shift transformed her interactions, deepening her connections and fostering a more compassionate outlook.

Elizabeth's worldview also began to shift. She started seeing the world not as a series of traps but as an exciting adventure. She embraced the Adventure Mindset by trying something new every week—a new route to work, a new cuisine, or a new hobby. This kept her life vibrant and her mind open, adding a splash of color to her routine.

Adaptability became another key focus. Elizabeth learned to embrace change with a smile and a declaration, "Challenge accepted!" She saw each unexpected twist as an opportunity to grow. Flexibility, she discovered, was her secret weapon in navigating life's twists and turns.

To further reinforce her new mindset, Elizabeth started a Gratitude Journal. Every night, she wrote down three things she was grateful for, from a delicious meal to a kind gesture from a friend. This practice shifted her focus to the positive, enhancing her overall well-being.

She also embraced curiosity, setting aside time each week to learn something new—a language, a skill, or even random trivia. Curiosity, she realized, kept her mind sharp and her spirit youthful, feeding her brain a delicious, never-ending buffet of knowledge.

And then there was perseverance. Elizabeth adopted the Tenacity Test, choosing a long-term goal and breaking it into smaller, manageable tasks. She celebrated each small win along the way, understanding that perseverance was about staying on course, even when the going got tough. It was the turtle, not the hare, that won the race.

Elizabeth's journey wasn't without challenges, but her transformation was undeniable. She had unlocked the power of her mindset, reshaping her attitudes and beliefs to create a life filled with optimism, confidence, and resilience.

Changing your mindset, as Elizabeth discovered, is like upgrading your brain's operating system. It takes a little effort, but the results are so worth it. Remember, you have the power to shift your attitudes and beliefs. It's all about seeing the possibilities, trusting yourself, and bouncing back with style. So, grab your superhero cape (or just your favorite comfy sweater), and start transforming your mindset today. You've got this!

Crafting this narrative from my personal life experiences feels like an incredible achievement. Transitioning from a dark period marked by a suicide attempt in 1998 to working as a successful Women's Empowerment Strategist has been a journey shaped by a fundamental shift in my mindset. By reshaping my attitudes and beliefs, I've been able to extend support to numerous Women Entrepreneurs throughout my own entrepreneurial path.

Embracing an open mind and exploring boundless possibilities has been pivotal. In my work with clients, I prioritize mindset within our G.A.P Framework (Genius Aligned with Purpose). Developing your own mindset, rooted in your attitudes and beliefs, enables you to unearth your authentic purpose in life. I truly hope you will join me on this personal journey.

EILEEN GALBRAITH

About Eileen E. Galbraith: With an innate talent for connecting with others, Eileen champions a philosophy rooted in dialogue, believing fervently that communication is the linchpin of a better world.

Throughout her journey, mentors consistently hailed Eileen's joy in service, her intuitive grasp of people's desires, and her aversion to conventional sales tactics. For Eileen, sales were never about coercion; they were about understanding needs and offering solutions with sincerity and empathy.

However, it was adversity that propelled Eileen into the realm of entrepreneurship. Confronting personal crises, she discovered a reservoir of resilience and empathy within herself, prompting her to extend counsel to other women facing similar challenges. Thus, her accidental foray into entrepreneurship birthed two ventures in the early 2000s, now united under a single banner.

Today, Eileen is not just a sought-after speaker and multi-time Amazon bestselling author; she is the visionary behind "Implement to Impact," a coaching enterprise dedicated to empowering women entrepreneurs. With a focus on fostering time freedom, wealth creation, and a supportive community, Eileen's mission resonates deeply with those she serves, embodying the transformative power of empowerment. Learn more about Eileen at: *www.RenewedAbundance.com.*

Author's Website: *www.ImplementToImpact.com*

Book Series Website: *www.TheBookOfHumanEmpowerment.com*

ERIC D. JACKSON

HOW BAD DO YOU WANT IT?

Calls to Action: Keys to Expanding Human Empowerment

Raise Your Standard

In this book series on Human Empowerment, you get the incredible opportunity to learn from people who are dedicating their lives to becoming the fullest expression of themselves, and who want to encourage and equip you on your journey to living out your fullest potential.

My goal is the same, and in my chapters I will be weaving a continuous thread for you to focus on putting what you are learning into action so you can experience the expansion of who you want to become.

Maybe you have already accomplished a lot in your life, or maybe you are just starting out or starting over. We all have areas in our lives we want and even need to experience more expansion and fullness in.

Life is all about expansion, and just like the authors in the series have dedicated their lives to growth and development, this is your opportunity to continuously choose to dedicate your life to growth as well.

Life is going to demand all you have and more. The questions are, "How Bad Do You Want It?" and will you "Raise Your Standard" in order to meet the demands and overcome any obstacles along your journey? You must know your value and your why.

"The two most important days in your life are the day you were born, and the day you find out why."
~ Mark Twain

This quote addresses both Purpose and Mindset. If you haven't already considered—or accepted it—both days that Mark Twain references in that quote embody two truths: that you were both born from a unique purpose, as well as for a unique purpose—and considering those truths requires a shift in mindset to receive the fullness of them, as well as to take ownership, responsibility, and accountability to 'effectively affect' your best self in your life. Receiving the fullness of these truths will require each of us to 'raise our standard.'

This brings us back to dedicated growth. If we are to grow continuously, then our standards can never remain the same. This is also what makes milestone failures okay and even beneficial. (I say milestone failures because they illustrate lessons learned along the journey, not repeated failures from being stuck in unlearned patterns.)

If we choose not to remain the same, and to continuously grow, then we will continuously value the growth, learning, and failures of learning new things in all areas of our lives. You must raise your standard if you are going to experience the expansion of who you want to become.

"What you perceive is what you will receive."
~ Eric D. Jackson

A mindset of growth and learning will help us see more of the world and the people around us. It will help us to look at things from new and different perspectives, and to gain new understandings and become aware of new possibilities.

In my own personal journey, I am regularly reminded of how uncomfortable the growth process can be, and though I have come a long way, I am ever more conscious of how far I have yet to go. Both of these are sobering and humbling realities, but also encouraging—even in the face of fear.

When you are on your personal Human Empowerment journey, you will 100% encounter normal feelings of doubt, fear, fatigue, and more! This is when you have to ask yourself again, "How Bad Do You Want It?" and, "Am I willing to Raise My Standard, again? Am I willing to go a little further, a little while longer to that next breakthrough or level up?"

Here are two tips from what we have already covered, so you can remind yourself—and motivate yourself—of who you truly are and why it is worth fighting the good fight to move forward and upward in any circumstance:

* Go back to Mark Twain's quote and remind yourself that you were indeed born with a purpose and of all the reasons why you are here to make a difference.
* Refocus your mindset on growth and accountability, and remember that you are empowered to take agency of your life right now, wherever you are, in any moment—and choose to affect the future outcomes you want to realize in your life.

"You can re-calibrate your caliber in any moment."
~ Eric D. Jackson

Now, maybe you are asking what else is there to better understand my purpose and improve my mindset. Here are some of the steps I regularly teach that will help you focus your energy and keep you fueled toward living out your fullest potential:

Your Core: The ABCs of What Makes You, You!

Of all the things that you will uncover and discover about yourself and the world/others around you, there are three traits that will always serve the core of who you are, and the potential of who you are becoming: your personal Attitudes towards everything, a set of positive Belief systems, and a dependable Character of choices made over time.

I also will add to the ABCs a willingness to dedicate your whole self to your Decisions, and to always protect the boundaries of each of the Environments you want to thrive in. Remember, "At any moment, you

141

can re-calibrate your caliber." So, it doesn't matter what circumstances you are coming out of, or the ABCs you have lived out before, because you can, in every moment, change the ingredients to affect the outcomes of your life and influence the world around you for the better.

In nearly every way, you get to choose your ingredients, as mentioned above. There are also assessments that may show where your natural or dominant traits or strengths resonate from and toward. You may or may not appreciate assessments, but I recommend taking a variety of them to gain some data on what makes you uniquely wired to be who you are authentically and to do meaningful work that positively impacts others. Each assessment is just another sliver adding to a 3D picture of you.

Your Ikigai: The Famous Japanese Venn Diagram of Purpose

If you do a browser search for Ikigai images, you will see plenty of versions, and all will show the main diagram as four overlapping circles of categories: What We Love, What The World Needs, What We Can Be Paid For, and What We Are Good At. You will see on the diagram that where two of these circles overlap are categories of what would be your Passion, Mission, Profession, and Vocation. At the very center of it all would be your Purpose.

The Ikigai framework or model is very helpful in aligning and allocating your time and energy and resources toward the different areas and ways that are meaningful to you. I hope you do, too!

Your Focus: Values, Vision, & Victories!

Tony Robbins is known for saying, "Where your focus goes, energy flows." Recently, I heard this idea attributed to Abraham Lincoln, "Vision is like your North Star, and mission is like your map—you need to know where you are headed, but a map will show you the way through the swamp."

I always include your personal—or, in business, an organization's—Values, Vision, and Victories (missions) as the key components to your navigation system. These together have a gravitational pull that will keep you moving forward and upward, especially during the times you are discouraged or don't feel like taking another step forward.

All the ABCs and Ikigai will get you so far, but it is these last three that will get you the rest of the way. They will harness the rest and bring out the best in you. Your Values will help to govern you, guide you and guard you. Your Victories are those achievable moments of accomplishment that keep you on mission, doing the work of highest value and impact that you can contribute to the world.

Your Vision is that future-forward version of the world you are inviting others to see and to contribute toward alongside you, so that one day you might have a movement large enough to have 'made a dent in the universe.'

> *"Choosing growth in your aptitudes and attitudes is choosing your altitude."*
> ~ Eric D. Jackson

Attitudes alone will not get you to the altitudes you want to soar to. You must grow your aptitudes (skillsets) in all vital areas required for your overall achievement of success.

Think of your forward and upward trajectory that you desire in your life, starting with Your Core, working through Your Ikigai, and being pulled in the direction of Your Focus. Always remember who you are born to be (want to be, meant to be) at Your Core, and the reason why you are here making a difference through and toward Your Focus.

These will help align your time, energy and resources to fuel you, and keep you on your Human Empowerment journey. Pro Tip: Teach and share what you are learning, and help others as you go, teaching them to do the same so that there is a multiplying ripple effect in everything you do.

Calls to Action: Keys to Expanding Human Empowerment

- **Value People:** Are you modeling respect, honor, and dignity for all people?

- **Remove Self:** Will they be better when you are no longer beside them?

- Empowering Cultures: Are you engineering environments for people to thrive?

- **R2A2D2:** Raise the Standards of Reward, Recognition, Attitude, Accountability, Development, Discipline

- **Dedicated:** Be purposeful, intentional, even consecrated, toward your Purpose and Mindset so that you are continuously growing and becoming the fullest expression of your potential and who you are meant to BE!

ERIC D. JACKSON

About Eric D. Jackson: Eric Jackson has led high-performance teams for leading organizations in marketing and financial sectors and helped clients from family-owned to Fortune 100 companies achieve their desired results. He founded Transformational Leadership & Culture International, as well as Jackson Insurance and Financial Services.

As a Champion of people, leadership, and culture, Eric loves helping people create transformation in what matters most to them, and for their people so they can grow their influence, team, and impact. He helps leaders to GAIN, RETAIN, and TRAIN for high performance results for themselves and for their teams to create breakthrough and take practical action steps toward growth and improvement.

Eric is a Certified Leadership Coach, Trainer, and Speaker with the Maxwell Leadership Team and with SCALE Architects and the Predictable Success model. As a speaker, trainer, and coach, he is also a practitioner in his own life and businesses. He has studied people and leadership since he was in grade school, always driven to find a better way and to share what he has learned with people so they, too, can create their own desired life transformations.

In his free time, Eric enjoys playing golf and volunteering with youth leadership programs. Eric is passionate about helping others to make a difference in their lives and the world we live in.

Author's Website: *ItsYourLif.com/Books*

Book Series Website: *www.BookOfHumanEmpowerment.com*

EVELYN CUI
LIVING ON PURPOSE

It was a warm and peaceful afternoon in my piano studio. My student, not yet ten, was unusually quiet and thinking intensely. "What's on your mind?" I asked.

"I've been wondering about this for a long time, and I can't find the answer," he said as he paced between two pianos. "What's the point of all this? Life is so hard. We have so much to do every day, but why? We are born. We live, and then... we die."

I looked into his clear, bright eyes. He may have looked perplexed, but I knew he was no longer asleep in his walk of life. I wondered what he had suffered through that brought him to this quest, but I was more excited and grateful that he felt safe to ask me these questions knowing that I would answer him.

"Thank you for asking me these great questions," I smiled and took a deep breath. "I'd love to tell you what I think, but for now, I encourage you to hold onto these questions and keep searching. I'll share my thoughts when we get a chance later."

"Okay. Just don't forget it. Cuz I really want to know. I *need* to know," he emphasized. I reassured him as I took his questions to heart.

Many nights later, I received a phone call from a dear friend seemingly out of the blue. "Hey, how's it going?" I asked. "I'm okay. Everything's fine, but I don't feel fine. I don't find my job meaningful. I'm grateful that it pays the bills. I'm relatively healthy, and I have friends and loving parents. I have a pretty good life that others dream of having. So I feel wrong to feel not okay. Sorry for rambling. I just feel empty and lost... I don't know what my purpose is."

I was amazed at how quickly and powerfully God answered my prayer. I'd asked Him who this chapter is for and what He wants me to say. My friend's call made it clear to me that there are weary modern-day souls searching for clarity and hope, many of which are lost in the pursuit of what they thought they needed and wanted, just to realize the emptiness in those achievements alone.

We are made to want more from life than a mere sum of what we accumulate physically. We desire to know our purpose and live it so that we have the most joy from being in alignment with the truth of who we are. It's my honor to humbly carry this message to my beautiful friend, my young inquisitive student, and you.

Purpose: The reason for being, doing, or creating. It's the answer to the question of "why" when we choose to do something, create something, or simply exist.

Activate your imagination now. Envision a large whiteboard and a simple drawing of a person's head, neck, and torso. First, I'm going to describe the head. The head is labeled Purpose and has three parts from top to bottom as follows:

- Crown — Conscious

- Middle — Subconscious

- Base — Unconscious

(To see a sketch of this drawing as you follow along, check out my link in bio.) Let's now dive a little deeper into each type of purpose.

Art by Wesley Lin

The **Conscious Purpose**, or "CP," is what most people seek when searching for meaning. It often appears larger than life and transcends the need for purely personal gains. It points toward wholeness and love. It's the most powerful state to make decisions from because it's internally, and in my case, also spiritually driven. The conditions of this world do not define what Conscious Purpose can be achieved. If you are like me in believing that you are a spirit living in a body, then you can say that CP is the purpose of your spirit's existence. The empowering truth here is knowing that you and I can find our Conscious Purpose when we earnestly seek it. Take a moment to pause and examine the "why" and "who" you are when considering CP, and finish this sentence: "I am here to _____."

Remember: Your CP is not dependent on things in this world to be true. Dig deep into your identity to arrive at an answer that resonates with your whole being.

The **Subconscious Purpose**, or "SP," is shaped by external influences—education, family, religion, culture, or societal values. After all, what more could we want from life than being happy, healthy, and wealthy? A common answer I hear is, "I want to be a good person". While not inherently bad, these subconscious motivations should not be confused as one's primary purpose. If that were to be the case, what would happen if we fell short of our expectations? The caution here is not to dream smaller to avoid disappointment, but rather to ensure you don't miss out on fulfilling your Conscious Purpose by *only* operating from the subconscious. Reflect on what you have been pursuing in life, whether it's a career, status, or even a moral value, and finish these sentences with your SP:

"I live to be _____."

"I live to have _____."

"I live to do _____."

Now, check your answer against your CP. Is your SP in alignment with your CP? If so, congratulations! You've been living a consciously purposeful life. And if you find that they are out of alignment with each other, you may need to unlearn old beliefs, heal, and realign your life to reflect your true self.

Unlike CP or SP, **Unconscious Purpose**, or "UP," is not something we actively think about, yet it is always there. It's like the way our brain regulates breathing or our heartbeats without conscious effort. From the moment we come into existence, we are woven into a cosmic story filled with wonder, mystery, and beauty. My inquisitive young student may never fully grasp the joy and inspiration he brings to me simply by being himself. But it's not his or anyone else's responsibility to know the full extent of their life purpose if we can agree that there will always be things beyond our own understanding.

In this space of all possibilities of what we don't know we don't know, I hope some will find freedom and relief that we don't need to know all the wonderful impacts we make. As Unconscious Purpose is relational— whether that relationship is with others, with the environment, or with our Creator, God—it bears repeating that knowing our true identity helps us to better understand our purpose.

If Purpose is the head, then Mindset is the neck. It's a mode of operation —a way of thinking and deciding how to approach things. I coach and teach on mindset in my work because it leads to forming habits that either bring people to their goals or derail them from their pursuits. Think about the importance of the neck in connecting the head to the body. The body is Identity, represented by the torso in our drawing. Whether we can fully express our purpose in alignment with our identity lies in the mindset that we choose.

I will expand on this in the next volume of this series, but for now, I want to give you the tools to decide for yourself what kind of mindset serves you best. When examining a mindset from a high level, consider flexibility, direction, and strength, as one has with the neck of a human body. Take any mindset you find in this book or elsewhere, and check for yourself:

For flexibility: What kind of choices does this mindset offer me?

For direction and strength: Does it support or hinder my Conscious Purpose? Is it in alignment with who I am?

Here's to your courageous and full life! You are loved, and you are always enough. We're in this together. I am here for you.

— Love,
Evelyn Cui

P.S.: Let's connect.

EVELYN CUI

About Y. Evelyn Cui: Y. Evelyn Cui is a multilingual, award-winning music educator, certified NLP life coach (Neuro-Linguistic Programming), and the visionary founder and CEO of Elevation Language and Music School, as well as Evelyn's Musical Garden. Her specialty is in teaching emotional development through language and music lessons.

She is also a bestselling author and an international speaker on topics of Education, Music, and a Heart-centered Approach to Life and Leadership. She has spoken and conducted trainings at educational institutions, corporations, forums, and private events.

A passionate leader, Evelyn advocates for holistic education for her students, their families, and teachers. She believes that loving relationships form the foundation of all learning and transformations. Evelyn's unique methodology blends education with inspiration, leaving her global audience with applicable knowledge and an uplifted spirit.

To reach out regarding her latest works, lessons, speaking, or coaching, visit her websites and leave a message. She would love to hear from you. Visit *www.ElevationMusicSchool.com*.

Author's Website: *www.EvelynCui.com*

Book Series Website: *www.TheBookOfHumanEmpowerment.com*

FELISHA BUSTOS

INNER PURPOSE & CULTIVATING OUTWARD MINDSET

Purpose and mindset are two profound concepts that have the power to shape our lives in extraordinary ways. For me, understanding and integrating these elements has been a lifelong journey filled with discovery, challenges, and profound growth. I invite you to join me as I share my experiences and insights on embracing purpose and cultivating a mindset that aligns with your true self.

Understanding Purpose

When I think of purpose, words like "target," "reason," and "direction" come to mind. Purpose is that driving force that gets me out of bed in the morning; it's my "why." It's something bigger than myself that ignites a fire in my belly and compels me to take meaningful action because it truly matters to me.

Purpose encompasses my values and connects my past, present, and future into a cohesive journey from point A to point B. It's a deeply personal and unique experience for everyone, almost as if it's been divinely placed within us, waiting to be discovered and nurtured. When I'm not living in alignment with my purpose, life can feel stagnant, unfulfilling, and as though something critical is missing. On the other hand, living on purpose brings a sense of charge, energy, motivation, and excitement. I feel aligned, significant, and connected to others, knowing that my actions have meaningful impacts.

Purpose is, in essence, fuel for our souls.

The Power of Mindset

Mindset is the compass that directs that fuel. Our brains are incredible machines capable of handling numerous tasks simultaneously, often operating on autopilot. But our minds are so much more—they intertwine with our souls and spirits, representing the core of who we are. Mindset is like the wizard behind the curtain, consciously guiding and directing the automated processes of our brains.

When we actively engage our mindset, we become the captains of our ships, setting the rudder, consulting the compass, and navigating through life's vast ocean. A focused and intentional mindset aligns our thoughts and actions with our desired destination, ensuring that we're not just drifting aimlessly but moving purposefully towards our goals.

Mindset and purpose together create an unstoppable force. With a clear purpose fueling me and a focused mindset steering me, I can overcome obstacles and achieve profound fulfillment. Even in simple, everyday tasks—like going to the grocery store—I can find alignment when these two elements work harmoniously, transforming mundane activities into purposeful actions that contribute to my broader mission and values.

Discovering My Purpose

My personal journey of discovering purpose began in the 10th grade, during a time when my life felt particularly unsettled. My parents had separated when I was in the 6th grade, uprooting the stability I had known and leaving me yearning for security and direction. High school brought me into contact with a Christian church and a supportive youth group led by mentors who genuinely invested in me. For the first time, I delved into reading and memorizing scripture, which provided an anchor amidst the turbulence of my adolescence.

One verse, in particular, resonated deeply with me: the commandment to love God and love others as yourself. This simple yet profound directive struck a chord, leading me to ponder its true meaning and implications for my life. I found myself praying earnestly for God to grant me His eyes—to see people as He sees them and to love them with a radical, unconditional love that defies logic and expectation.

This prayer marked the beginning of a transformative journey. I started to notice changes within myself, a growing capacity to love and empathize with others deeply and authentically. People began to recognize and affirm this love in me, telling me that I embodied love in ways that touched and inspired them. These affirmations confirmed that I was living in alignment with my purpose, fueling my commitment to continue growing in love and service to others.

Reaffirming & Realigning with Purpose

Discovering purpose isn't a one-time event; it's an ongoing process of reaffirmation and realignment. Countless times throughout my life, I've revisited and reassessed my purpose, using it as a compass to guide me through decisions and challenges.

Whenever I find myself veering off course, I return to fundamental questions: Am I truly loving others, myself, and God at this moment? Am I acting in alignment with my deepest values and beliefs? These reflections aren't about self-judgment but about awareness and intentionality. They help me recognize when I'm straying from my path and gently steer myself back toward alignment.

Living on purpose requires conscious choice and commitment, especially when faced with difficult decisions or tempting distractions. It's about recognizing the long-term fulfillment that comes from aligning with my true self over the fleeting satisfaction of immediate gratification. This ongoing practice of realignment ensures that my actions consistently reflect the love and purpose that define who I am at my core.

Making Hard Decisions Aligned with Purpose

One of the most profound tests of aligning with purpose and mindset came through the journey of my marriage and eventual divorce. Marrying Luke was a decision rooted in love and hope, but over time, it became clear that our paths were diverging in ways that caused pain and discord.

Choosing to release our marriage was one of the hardest decisions I've ever made. It required putting aside my fears, ego, and the comfort of familiarity to act in genuine love—for myself, for Luke, and for our children. Letting go meant acknowledging that we both deserved the opportunity to find happiness and fulfillment, even if it meant walking separate paths.

This decision demanded immense courage and a steadfast commitment to my purpose. It involved facing the unknown, embracing vulnerability, and trusting that acting in love would ultimately lead to healing and growth for all involved. Through this process, I learned that living on purpose isn't always easy or comfortable but can be profoundly rewarding and transformative.

Releasing the marriage also meant creating a more peaceful and nurturing environment for our children and, with time, demonstrating the importance of authenticity, self-love, and courageous decision-making. It reinforced my belief that aligning actions with purpose and mindset can lead to positive outcomes, even in the face of significant challenges and heartache.

Guiding Others to Discover Their Purpose & Mindset

Helping others discover and embrace their purpose and mindset is a passion close to my heart. I believe that each person's answers lie within themselves, waiting to be uncovered through introspection and courage.

My approach involves asking thought-provoking questions and encouraging solitary, distraction-free time for deep self-connection. By creating space for individuals to explore their inner landscapes, they can uncover their true desires, values, and motivations, leading to authentic and fulfilling lives.

I don't believe in prescribing a one-size-fits-all purpose or mindset. Instead, I aim to facilitate a journey of self-discovery where each person identifies what resonates deeply within them. This personalized approach respects the uniqueness of each individual's path and empowers them to live in alignment with their true selves.

A Call to Action: Questions for Deep Self-Discovery

Embarking on the journey to discover your purpose and cultivate a supportive mindset begins with courageous self-inquiry. I invite you to explore the following questions thoughtfully and honestly, allowing your authentic self to surface and guide you:

1. What am I hiding from, if anything?

2. What am I avoiding?

3. What am I pretending not to know?

4. What becomes available to me when I carve out time and space to be alone with myself?

5. What are the costs of not living on purpose—for myself and for others?

6. How can I be gentle and kind with myself as I delve into deep self-exploration?

7. What does it look like for me to be my own best friend and support system during this journey?

8. Who was I as a child? What did I love, and what excited my heart when I was at the age of my earliest memory?

9. Who am I truly beneath societal expectations and external influences?

10. How can I honor and integrate my authentic self into my adult life, enriched by maturity, wisdom, and experience?

11. When was the last time I felt completely in sync with myself, joyful, and at peace? What did that feel like, and how can I take steps towards experiencing that regularly?

Take your time with these questions. Sit with them, journal your responses, and allow whatever arises to do so without judgment. This process may uncover discomfort or fear, but remember to approach yourself with compassion and understanding. Embracing your authentic self is a journey, not a destination, and every step you take brings you closer to living a life of purpose and fulfillment.

Embracing purpose and cultivating a supportive mindset have been transformative in my life, guiding me through joys, challenges, and profound growth. These concepts are not static; they evolve and deepen as we continue to learn and experience life.

I encourage you to embark on your own journey of discovery, embracing the unique purpose and mindset that resonate within you. Trust that the answers lie inside you, waiting to be uncovered through intentional reflection and courageous self-love.

Remember, living on purpose with a focused mindset isn't about perfection; it's about alignment, authenticity, and continual growth. As you navigate your path, be patient and kind with yourself, celebrating each insight and progress along the way.

May your journey be filled with discovery, empowerment, and the profound joy that comes from living authentically aligned with your true purpose.

FELISHA BUSTOS

About Felisha Bustos: Felisha Bustos is an accomplished visual artist, educator, and community leader with over twenty-seven years of professional experience. Born in Burbank, California, and currently residing in Northern Colorado, Felisha has created a legacy of powerful, meaningful art that reflects her values of personal growth, authenticity, and connection. Her work is characterized by vibrant colors, intricate details, and a deep sense of purpose, specializing in commissioned murals, fine art, and creative experiences tailored to clients' visions.

Felisha is renowned for her community-centered projects, including murals for schools in District 6 and her notable 270-square-foot mural, "You Belong," at Aims Community College. Her ability to bring people together through creativity is exemplified by her signature projects like "HerStory," which celebrates women's lives through art, and "Uncorked," a unique paint-and-sip gathering that encourages personal reflection and creative expression.

In addition to her artistic endeavors, Felisha is the founder of Be-ART-ifull, a platform that emphasizes the importance of being and creating authentically. Her work, both as an artist and mentor, continues to inspire and uplift individuals and communities across the United States.

Author's Website: *www.Instagram.com/Be_Art_Ifull*

Book Series Website: *www.TheBookOfHumanEmpowerment.com*

FRED MOSKOWITZ

LIVING YOUR PURPOSE

Have you ever spent significant time thinking about learning and defining your purpose?

The traditional definition of purpose is the reason why something exists or is done. When it comes to exploring our own purpose, I like to put it in terms of that thing or activity that you are passionate about doing. This also becomes the thing that keeps us going whenever we are facing adversity, despite all of the hardships and obstacles that stand in our way. Our purpose is meaningful to ourselves and, at the same time, is impactful to the world at large.

It has been said that there are two extremely important days in each of our lives: the day that we are born, and then the day that we discover why.

The Concept of Purpose

Your purpose can be defined by something that is an underlying intention that is highly meaningful to you. Having a clear definition of your purpose significantly helps to provide constant direction and motivation in your life. Think of it just like your personal internal compass or GPS that guides you throughout your life.

Knowing and being able to articulate our purpose provides a strong alignment, and this creates a congruency with our personal values, strengths, and passions. Some of us know our purpose all along. Others are still learning and determining their purpose, and it is important to understand that is completely okay. And, sometimes, we might think that we know our purpose, but then a life-changing event happens which results in making a significant shift. It is all part of the exciting journey of life!

Strategies for Finding Our Purpose

I'd like to share with you some of my favorite actionable strategies for finding your purpose.

- **Self-Reflection (Core Values, Strengths, & Interests):** I really like the idea about looking at our purpose through this lens: If you were extremely wealthy and no longer needed to work for the money, then would you continue to do the work or the job that you do? If not, then what could you see yourself doing? This is a great question to sit with and think about.

- **Partaking in Activities that Bring Joy & Fulfillment:** Get involved in your favorite hobbies and in supporting meaningful causes. Do you ever feel stuck and not sure what you can do? Any time this happens, place yourself somewhere that you can volunteer or be of service and add value to others. Actively taking part in the service of others really helps in discovering purpose and puts things into perspective for us.

- **Taking on Challenges & Growth:** Have you ever heard about author John Maxwell's lesson on the Law of the Rubber Band? In that law, he states that growth stops as soon as you lose the tension between where you are and where you have the potential to be. The theme here is to get into a heightened awareness, becoming aware of your comfort level where you are, and seeking to always push yourself to higher levels. Spend time going beyond the edge of your comfort zone.

- **Seek Out Mentors & Guidance:** Turn to mentors, coaches, trusted friends, and advisors for support and feedback on discovering our purpose. A couple of great questions to ask are, "What is it about me that makes me special?" or "What is it about me that makes you want to show up to support me?"

Living in Our Purpose

As someone who had a long career working in the engineering and tech industry, in the workplace I have sometimes encountered people who would go to work every day, uninspired and unmotivated, for months or even years. Any time I would see someone that was emotionally checked out, it was usually a sign that they might soon be seeking to move on.

And, in the majority of cases, if we were to deeply unpack why this happens, most of the time the answer is simple—that the work is not in alignment with the person's purpose. It could have been in alignment at one point in the past, but now the work is no longer meaningful or no longer fulfilling to the person.

If we seek out goals, opportunities, projects, and work that are aligned with our purpose, it can result in a major shift. Consider this idea, that every decision we make moves us towards our goals or away from our goals. When you are faced with a decision, you might find it helpful to stop and evaluate the alignment and congruency with your purpose. This can result in being able to make decisions quickly and with confidence.

As I mentioned previously, a great way to get started is to seek out opportunities to be of service to others through creativity or innovation. We can volunteer our time to help others or support a cause we care about. We can bring new ideas and products to the marketplace, adding value in that way. What better way to live in our purpose could there be than to bring value to the marketplace, in a way that is personally fulfilling and makes a profit at the same time? To me, that is truly living in alignment and congruency.

Think about some of the successful people that you know, those who are living a fulfilling and extraordinary life. A common trait that you will find is that their actions are in alignment with their goals and their purpose.

Mindset

If we want to up-level our mindset, a great way to start is to get into the energy of gratitude on a daily basis. Spending a couple of moments of quiet daily time thinking about our gratitude and appreciation, writing about it, and acknowledging the gifts we have received.

Our mindset is shaped by our beliefs, habits, and environment (content and influences). Our beliefs have been formed throughout our upbringing, education, and family environment. Even though beliefs have been formed over the course of a lifetime, they still can change gradually over time when we focus intentionally on controlling the other two variables.

When it comes to habits, we can start by setting the intention and starting out with very small steps. As it was mentioned earlier in this chapter, every decision we make will bring us closer to our goals or further away from our goals. Starting out with very small steps and new habits and doing them successfully with consistency helps us to build momentum and grow. And then, over time, we can stack more small steps and exponentially increase the momentum we are experiencing.

And if we focus some effort on changing our environment, this will amplify all of the other activities and progress we are experiencing. Changing up the content we consume, the places where we frequent, and the people that we spend time with will result in dramatic changes.

Consider this: If we put ourselves around a group of people that are playing the game of life at a higher level, then what do you think might happen over time? Simply, as a result of the proximity, we will start being exposed to reading what they read, listening to what they listen to, setting goals the way they set goals, and attending great events that they attend.

In this chapter, we learned about the value and importance of knowing and getting clear on our purpose, along with some of my favorite actionable strategies for exploring purpose and then making sure that we are living in alignment with our purpose.

Additionally, we covered and explored what I feel are the basic building blocks of mindset—our beliefs, our habits, and our environment. If you want to develop an unshakeable mindset, you can start out by working on these basic building blocks. And in no time at all, you will be well on your way to shaping your mindset in a way that best aligns with your purpose.

If you spend any time studying successful people, you will likely find that they are living in alignment and in congruency with their purpose and their goals.

FRED MOSKOWITZ

About Fred Moskowitz: Fred Moskowitz is a Bestselling Author, investment fund manager, and speaker who is on a personal mission to teach people about the power of investing in alternative asset classes, such as real estate and mortgage notes, showing them the way to diversify their capital into investments that are uncorrelated from Wall Street and the stock markets.

Through his body of work, he is teaching investors the strategies to build passive income and cash flow streams designed to flow into their bank accounts. He's a frequent event speaker and contributor to investment podcasts.

Fred is the author of *The Little Green Book of Note Investing: A Practical Guide for Getting Started with Investing in Mortgage Notes* and contributing author in *The 13 Steps to Riches* and *The Principles of David & Goliath*.

Author's Website: *www.FredMoskowitz.com*

Book Series Website: *www.TheBookOfHumanEmpowerment.com*

GWEN MITCHELL

THE RESILIENCE TO MANAGE LIFE'S ROLLER COASTERS

As a child, I loved riding roller coasters. I remember seeing their tall peaks and seemingly endless drops, repeating in a thrilling pattern. Every summer, my family would visit different amusement parks to try out the latest attractions and revisit our old favorites. Upon arrival, I'd dash straight to the newest ride, holding my breath and hoping my height wouldn't be a barrier to my ticket to ride.

Once I passed the height check, I'd join the long line, each step bringing me closer to the screams and cheers of those ahead. Finally, it would be my turn, and I'd jump into the seat, rush through safety check, and feel an electrifying tingle fill my body. As the ride began its slow crawl to the top of the first peak, following my daredevil brother, I'd ignore the guide's instructions and throw my hands in the air for the ultimate thrill.

After what felt like hours, the ride would end in just two minutes, leaving me with the choice to ride again.

As I grew older, trips to amusement parks were replaced by grown-up obligations. In hindsight, this childhood passion has taught me valuable lessons that drive my growth mindset.

Hello. My name is Gwen, and I approach life as a practitioner. I seek to understand, integrate, and inspire practical ways to meet challenges. As you read this chapter, I invite you to imagine we're having a one-on-one conversation in your favorite space.

By the end of this chapter, I hope to spark your curiosity or inspire your creativity to enhance your growth mindset.

A Moment of Acknowledgement

First, I'd like to acknowledge Habitude Warriors for the opportunity to participate in this project. Secondly, thank you for seeking different perspectives on human empowerment, specifically mindset. Give yourself a round of applause for taking action!

Minimize Life Fluctuations

In our short time together, I'll share three strategies from a model I created to help people struck in high or low moments in their lives. The Minimize Life Fluctuations (MLF) Model is rooted in neuroscience and integrates experiences from my consulting career and personal amusement park visits.

The purpose of the MLF Model is to help people understand how their internal saboteurs impact them and to build the mental resilience needed to handle life's changes with an ebb and flow approach. It provides practical 15-minute daily practices to build mental muscles for sustainable resilience.

The MLF Model helps me focus on goals, reduce stress, and tame my inner monster named Fear. Are you curious to explore how these three strategies can help you?

Why Me?

You might wonder what qualifies me to share these strategies. Here's a bit about my story. People often ask how I keep bouncing back from life's challenges—rebuilding after disasters, losing major contracts during economic downturns, dealing with partner betrayals, and more. How do I continually reinvent myself? I've felt uneasy, out of control, or full of self-doubt. Discovering how neuroscience impacts our mental resilience and communication with ourselves and others, combined with my years as a process improvement specialist, showed me how my early roller coaster experiences set the foundation for a growth mindset.

Visualize & Surrender

Let's dive into the first lesson I learned from my roller coaster days: I never lost focus on reaching the top of the first peak and feeling that energizing tingle. Setting goals with emotional attachment makes them more believable and achievable.

The biggest challenge is surrendering expectations of how and when your goals should happen. Just act in the direction of the goal and trust it will happen.

Are you ready to try the first strategy? Visualize what you desire and the feeling you'll have once it is accomplished, then surrender expectations of how it should happen.

Overcoming Barriers

The second lesson is about handling the inevitable obstacles that distract you from your goals. I view obstacles as tests of my determination.

A common mistake is to see obstacles as negative. I choose to label them as neutral—neither good nor bad, just to be determined. This perspective allows me to stay curious and ask: Why it is here? What is it trying to tell me? What are the short and long-term impacts on me, the community, and the world?

For instance, I couldn't control how fast I'd grow to meet the height requirements for roller coasters. Instead, I used the time to learn about the rides, their origins, and analyze every twist and turn. I prepared myself for the opportunity when it arrived.

I challenge you to try this for one day: When you have a negative thought about a perceived obstacle, shift your perspective. Say to yourself, "This is not negative. I choose to be emotionally neutral and curious about why it has shown up now." Remember, barriers are not about adversity; it's your response that matters.

Facing Fear with Your Hands Up

The final lesson involves stepping boldly outside your comfort zone. This doesn't mean ignoring the safety instructions on a roller coaster; facing fear is about challenging the beliefs that hold you back from your goals, not putting yourself in danger.

Metaphorically, focusing on your inner game means throwing up your hands and digging deep to examine your current belief and assumptions that misalign with your goals. The inner work requires modifying the outdated programs you've been running that no longer serve you.

This emotional roller coaster will have many peaks and valleys, but, in the end, you have a choice: continue with the status quo or tame your inner monster. This may require purging things and people to establish new boundaries by learning to say "No" or "Not now."

Three Strategies to Minimize Real-Life Roller Coasters

These strategies can help minimize the fluctuations as you navigate life's real-life roller coaster:

1. **Visualize & Surrender:** Visualize what you desire and the feeling you'll have once it's accomplished. Then, surrender expectations of how it should happen.

2. **Shift Your Perspective on Negative Thoughts:** When you encounter a negative thought about a perceived obstacle, shift your perspective. Tell yourself, "This is not negative. I choose to be emotionally neutral and curious about why it has shown up now."

3. **Face Fear & Challenge Beliefs:** Work on your inner game by stepping outside your comfort zone. Challenge beliefs and assumptions that misalign with your goals. Be open to modifying

outdated programs by releasing things and people that no longer serve you.

What's Your Next Step?

Consuming information is valuable, but the real power comes from acting based on what you've learned. Take time to reflect on what has sparked your curiosity and identify the next steps to enhance your mindset, preparing you to handle whatever life throws your way.

GWEN MITCHELL

About Gwen Mitchell: Gwen Mitchell is the visionary founder and managing partner of 3rd I Business Solutions. Additionally, she is a certified Global Team Coach Practitioner, motivational speaker, and author. Her mission is to provide businesses with the structure needed to empower performance excellence, bringing clarity to the chaos. In other words, she is a Change Coach: Promoting changes in the way you think, listen, speak, problem solve, and do business… changes that not only affect the corporate bottom line but also how you conduct yourself in life. The goal is to evolve into the best version of "you." The cornerstone of her process is communication —creating safe environments for all voices, an inclusive feeling, and critical listening skills. By implementing her proven techniques, people who work for the same entity become team players with a united goal, working in unison for the company's overall success.

Everyone has a job to perform, and everyone's job is essential to the business' accomplishments. With a commitment to inclusion and mentorship, Gwen develops and assists organizations in implementing processes that maximize the talents of their workforce. Her techniques and style are innovative, inspirational, time-efficient, and measurable, with strategies that bring people together and make them want to achieve because they feel they are integral to the organization's success.

During Ms. Mitchell's corporate career, she has developed a reputation for her ability to utilize resources judiciously streamline roles and responsibilities in multi-million-dollar projects. For over 20 years, her work and experience have directly benefited customers, vendors, contractors, and employees of client organizations.

Author's Website: *www.GwenKMitchell.com*

Book Series Website: *www.TheBookOfHumanEmpowerment.com*

JEFF KIST

IF I ONLY KNEW THEN WHAT I KNOW NOW

What do you want? What do you really, really want?

It's a question that seems simple, but as I've learned, it holds the key to living a life of true purpose and fulfillment. Everyone craves a sense of meaning, to know that what they're doing in this life has significance. We want to feel that our actions matter, that we're contributing to something larger than ourselves. But how do we arrive at that place? How do we discover what indeed drives us?

I've spent years working with people who are lost in the maze of life, searching for their true purpose. They come to me with a common frustration: "I don't know what I'm meant to do." The truth is, your purpose is not some elusive, predestined role waiting for you to discover it. Your purpose is what you decide it to be. It's what brings you joy, energizes you, and makes you feel alive. It's what makes you smile when you wake up in the morning—it's that first thought that comes to mind before your feet even hit the floor.

But let me tell you this—it's not a one-size-fits-all concept. Your purpose can encompass every aspect of your life: your time, your finances, your career, your relationships, and even something as seemingly trivial as finding the best cup of coffee today. Whether creating a multimillion-dollar corporation or simply living in the moment, your purpose is what you choose it to be, and the absolute joy comes from the journey of becoming, not from the destination itself.

Purpose is Fluid & Evolving

As we grow and evolve, so too does our purpose. What drives us today might be different from what inspired us five years ago, and it will likely change again in the future. Our purpose expands and adapts as we learn more about ourselves and our world. It's about being the best version of who we are in every role—whether as a parent, a business leader, or a community advocate.

I've seen people find profound purpose in the most straightforward roles. A housewife who finds joy in nurturing her family, a first responder who is driven by the call to protect others, a politician who genuinely works for the greater good—each of these individuals has found their own unique purpose. And I believe that's why we're all here on this planet: to connect with our higher power, to follow the natural gifts we've been given, and to make an impact on the world, no matter how big or small.

The Power of Imagination

There are six higher mental faculties that we are gifted with at birth, as eloquently quoted in Wallace Wattles' *The Science of Getting Rich*: "You are to become a creator, not a competitor. You will become a creator by employing the higher faculties with which you have been endowed: Perception, Reason, Will, Memory, Imagination, and Intuition. No other form of life was given these creative faculties."

Although we don't have time to delve into each of these faculties in detail, I want to focus on one particularly crucial to creating our purpose: imagination.

Think back to your childhood when your imagination knew no bounds. You could be a firefighter, a doctor, a race car driver, or an astronaut— whatever your heart desired. But as we grow older, societal expectations start to weigh on us. We're told to stop daydreaming, focus on practical goals, and conform to what others think is best for us. School teaches us to memorize and regurgitate information but rarely encourages us to dream big.

Yet, imagination is critical to creating the life we desire. It's through our imagination that we can envision the life of our dreams, whatever that may be. Imagination fuels our creativity, our energy, and our passion. It allows us to see beyond our current circumstances and to create a vision for our future that excites and inspires us. From there, the journey begins.

Purpose & Planning: A Powerful Combination

Purpose, as defined in the dictionary, is "the reason for which something is done or created or for which something exists." It's a sense of resolve, of determination. It's the act of purposing—having an intention or objective and committing to it wholeheartedly. And yet, most people spend more time planning their next vacation than planning the life they want. Why is that?

The answer lies in our mindset. When we start thinking about what we truly desire, our minds often wander to the obstacles and reasons why we can't have those things. We imagine the difficulties, the setbacks, the failures, and we use our imagination to create a life we don't want.

But what if we flipped the script? What if we used our imagination to create a vivid picture of the life we do want?

That's where the power of imagination meets the discipline of planning. When you can clearly see your vision in your mind and become emotionally involved with that image, you're more likely to fall in love with it. And when you're in love with your vision, nothing can stand in your way. You'll find a way to overcome any obstacle because your commitment to your vision is unwavering. As Bob Proctor famously said, "If you can see it in your mind, you can hold it in your hand."

Mindset: The Key to Success

All that being said, your mindset is the most critical factor in achieving your vision. Every person has to find their own path, and no two paths are exactly the same. Your mindset will determine your success. Life has a way of testing your resolve, throwing obstacles in your path to see if you're truly dedicated to pursuing your chosen path.

You must be comfortable with being uncomfortable because true growth comes with adversity. Find someone already doing what you want to do at the level you want to do it and learn from them. Surround yourself with like-minded individuals and seek out mentors who can guide you along the way. This journey of life is a continuous process of learning and growing. If you're not growing, you're disintegrating.

Bob Proctor and Earl Nightingale have both defined success as, "Success is the progressive realization of a worthy ideal."

So, pick a worthy ideal for yourself, and don't quit until you get there. Your journey will be filled with lessons, challenges, and growth, but the pursuit of that ideal will give your life meaning and purpose.

The Journey of Becoming

Reflecting on the lessons I've learned over the years, one truth stands out: The joy is in the journey of becoming, not the destination. If I only knew then what I know now, I would have embraced every challenge, every setback, and every victory with the understanding that they were all part of my growth. I would have spent less time worrying about the "right" path and more time creating a life that aligned with my true desires.

I encourage you to ask yourself, "What do I really, really want?" and then use your imagination to create that vision. Commit to it with everything you have, and trust that the journey will bring you the growth and fulfillment you seek. Your purpose is yours to define, and the pursuit of that purpose will make your life truly meaningful.

JEFF KIST

About Jeff Kist: Jeff Kist is a dedicated life coach and mentor whose journey to personal transformation began with a profound wake-up call that changed his life forever. After spending 25 years in the automotive industry, working long hours to chase a version of success that left him unfulfilled, Jeff experienced a pivotal moment that led him to reevaluate his life's purpose. This turning point sparked a deep dive into self-discovery, where Jeff realized that his thoughts were shaping his reality—a revelation that he now considers the secret to a fulfilling life.

Three years ago, Jeff's path intersected with that of renowned mentor Bob Proctor, whose guidance and teachings provided the framework for Jeff's own transformation. With Bob Proctor's mentorship, Jeff learned the powerful tools and principles that helped him reshape his mindset and, ultimately, his life. These are the same tools and insights Jeff now shares with others, guiding them on their own journeys toward meaningful change.

As a coach, Jeff is passionate about helping individuals unlock their potential by changing their thoughts and embracing the possibilities that lie beyond their current circumstances. He believes wholeheartedly that anyone can transform their life by mastering their mindset, and he is committed to empowering others to do just that.

Author's Website: *www.BigWheelConsultingInternational.com*

Book Series Website: *www.TheBookOfHumanEmpowerment.com*

JEFFREY LEVINE

EMPOWERMENT THROUGH CONNECTION & ACTION

Every day above ground is a bonus, and I wake up with that mindset, grateful for the opportunity to make a difference. My journey hasn't been linear, but the constant thread has been empowerment—both empowering myself and others. It's not about holding power over people but helping them unlock their potential to be the best version of themselves. Empowerment is about connection, trust, and taking action, and throughout my life, I've seen how these principles can change not only individual lives but the world at large.

I've had the fortune of connecting with extraordinary people, mentors like Bob Proctor, who truly changed my life. Bob taught me something that I carry with me every day: The key to empowerment is not about seeking external validation but rather finding the strength within. That message hit me hard and set the stage for much of the work I do now. My mission is clear—I help others discover their potential and live empowered lives.

Connection is the Foundation

When I think about empowerment, the first thing that comes to mind is connection. Throughout my career, whether it's writing, speaking, or coaching, I've learned that we are only as powerful as the people we surround ourselves with. As much as empowerment starts from within, it also thrives through the relationships we build and the communities we engage with.

Take the time I spent working on films like *Mastermind Secrets* or *Beyond Physical Matter*. In both cases, I found myself surrounded by people from all over the world, each with a unique perspective on life. There was a time when I interviewed two individuals from Hungary for a film. They didn't speak English, and I didn't have a translator. I felt like I was in uncharted territory, unsure of how to bridge the gap. But here's where connection transcends language. I asked for divine guidance, and before I knew it, I was asking questions that felt perfect for the moment, even without fully understanding their responses. That's empowerment through connection. When you trust that the right people and the right energy are around you, things fall into place.

This lesson of connection goes beyond film and interviews; it's at the core of what we do every day. Whether I'm working on books, like *The Book of Mentors*, or standing on stage in front of hundreds of people, the goal is always to connect with others on a deep, human level. You never know how many lives you'll touch or how your words will resonate. But when you show up authentically, that's when real empowerment happens.

Trust the Process

Another essential aspect of empowerment is trust—trusting the process, trusting yourself, and trusting the people around you. There was a time when I was intimidated by the enormity of certain projects, whether it was starting a new TV show, stepping onto a stage, or even contributing to a book. But I've learned that empowerment often comes from simply stepping forward, even when you're unsure of the outcome.

This reminds me of something I experienced during my work on *Beyond Physical Matter*. It's a project people have compared to *The Secret*, and its scope is massive. As we worked through it, I realized that I didn't need to control every element. Sometimes, you just need to trust that everything will come together as it should. It's funny—when I started, I thought I had to carry the entire weight of the project on my own shoulders, but once I let go and trusted the process, the entire experience transformed. The same applies to empowerment; sometimes, you just have to let go of your fear and trust that you have everything you need to succeed.

In my work, I've often said that empowerment comes from trusting that things will work out as they should. When I was awarded the Presidential Award for my contributions, it wasn't because I meticulously planned every moment of my career—it was because I trusted that the work I was doing mattered. That trust fueled me to keep pushing, to keep connecting, and to keep empowering others.

Take Action: Empowerment is a Verb

Empowerment isn't just a feeling or an idea; it's action. Every day, we have the opportunity to empower ourselves and others, but it requires action. I see this play out in every project I'm involved in—whether it's writing chapters for *The 13 Steps To Riches* and *The Book of Mentors* book series or speaking at events like Secret Knock. The difference between feeling empowered and being empowered is action.

When I work on books or shows, it's easy to get caught up in perfectionism or fear that what we're creating isn't enough. But the truth is, empowerment doesn't come from sitting around and thinking about what you could do—it comes from actually doing it. You have to step into your role, whether that's as a mentor, a creator, or a leader, and take action. The more you take action, the more empowered you become and the more you empower others around you.

For example, when I was preparing for a speaking engagement, I could have spent endless hours worrying about every detail. Instead, I focused on what I could control—my preparation, my delivery, and my connection with the audience. That's where empowerment lies—in taking intentional action and knowing that, with each step, you're growing stronger and helping others do the same.

Empower Others to Empower Themselves

One of the most fulfilling aspects of my work has been seeing how the people I've empowered have gone on to empower others. There's a ripple effect that happens when we share our knowledge, experiences, and energy with others. This is especially true in the realm of mentorship. I've had the incredible honor of contributing to *The Book of Mentors*, where I've been able to share my journey and the lessons I've learned from extraordinary people like Bob Proctor. The stories and strategies we share are not just meant for personal reflection—they're tools for others to use, adapt, and pass on.

Empowerment, at its core, is about legacy. It's about ensuring that our work today will continue to inspire and uplift others long after we're gone. When I think about the books, films, and TV shows I've been involved in, I don't just see them as accomplishments. I see them as opportunities to leave behind something that will continue to empower people for years to come.

Recently, I've been involved in projects that are larger than life, like *Beyond Physical Matter*. This film, which many are calling the next big thing after *The Secret*, is designed to challenge people's perceptions and expand their minds. It's the kind of work that has the potential to create massive shifts in people's lives, and that's why I'm so passionate about it. But the real power of this project isn't just in its message—it's in how that message will empower those who watch it to take action in their own lives.

Live Empowered Every Day

The path to empowerment isn't a one-time decision or event; it's a daily commitment. Every day that I wake up, I remind myself that I have the power to make a difference, and so do you. It's about showing up for yourself and for others, trusting the process, and taking action. Whether you're writing a chapter in a book, filming a documentary, or simply having a conversation with someone, remember that your words and actions have the power to change lives.

We are all here to grow, to connect, and to empower one another. As Bob Proctor once told me, "The only limits we have are the ones we set for ourselves." I've taken that to heart, and it's become the foundation of everything I do. My job now is to help others see that truth within themselves, to empower them to break through their self-imposed limitations, and to create a world where we all live empowered lives.

JEFFREY LEVINE

About Jeffrey Levine: Jeffrey is a highly skilled tax planner and business strategist, as well as a published author and sought-after speaker. He's been featured in national magazines, on the cover of *Influential People Magazine*, and is a frequent featured expert on radio, talk shows, and documentaries. Jeffrey attended the prestigious Albany Academy for high school and then went on to the University of Hartford at Connecticut, the University of Mississippi Law School, and Boston University School of Law, and earned an L.L.M. in taxation. His accolades include features in Kiplinger and Family Circle Magazine, as well as a dedicated commentator for Channel 6 and 13 news shows, a contributor for the *Albany Business Review*, and a talk show host for WGY Radio.

Jeffrey has accumulated more than 30 years of experience as a tax attorney and certified financial planner and has given in excess of 500 speeches nationally. Levine is the executive producer and cast member in the documentary *Beyond the Secret: The Awakening*.

Levine's most current work, Consistent Profitable Growth Map, is a step-by-step workbook outlining easy-to-follow steps to convert consistent revenue growth to any business platform.

Author's Website: *www.Strategies.org*

Book Series Website: *www.TheBookOfHumanEmpowerment.com*

JON KOVACH JR.

YOUR STRENGTHS EMPOWER THE WORLD

As a young boy, I was raised to be the mule. Yes, that's right—the mule. Like a pack horse, an animal that can bear lots of weight over long distances.

My family has a 75-year-old tradition of hiking and camping in the Wind River Mountains. We like to backpack, carry our outdoor essentials with us, spend days fishing from our favorite lakes, build memories, and have a great outdoor experience.

My dad loved to share the wilderness with our church group and scout troops. We would take groups of people on these high-adventure excursions. These guests varied greatly in their athleticism and strength. Some were in great shape, played sports, and had no trouble throwing on a backpack and hiking eight-plus miles a day. Others lived more sedentary lifestyles, did not exercise much, and were new to outdoor excursions.

These individuals would often slow down our excursions by taking two to three times as long to hike the distances. Expectedly, they would complain about the pain and the weight of the backpacks, much like I did as a young boy hiking in these mountains, primarily due to their lack of experience and the inability to endure pain for an extended period.

As the "mule," I was trained as a kid to run up the mountain with my own backpack, drop off my pack at our campsite, then run back down the trail and pick up my father's backpack to help him finish the trail. For a young, athletic kid like me, it was quite the workout and challenge, but it was very fulfilling to carry on a tradition that my dad started with his father, my grandpa. It's just one of those things the Kovach family always does, and I am happy to carry on the tradition.

However, there was a year when several people were struggling on the trail. It wasn't ever asked of me, but given our tradition and the opportunity to empower others and finish their journey, I could help them reduce the weight on their shoulders and continue with their heads held high. Motivated to serve, I ran up the mountain, dropped off my heavy backpack, turned around, and ran back down to help the next person struggling.

Some of our determined guests would say, "I'm good for another mile or two. Go help the next guy or gal." They would pay it forward, and I'd continue to run down the trail to the next struggling hiker. But usually, it came down to me running to the last and farthest person on the trail. I would grab their backpack and do the same thing—run back up to the camp, drop their pack off, and start back down the mountain again.

After doing this several times, I had accumulated more miles than I had ever done in a single day. On this trip, I hiked, backpacked, and carried heavy backpacks for almost eighteen miles, an extra ten miles I hadn't planned on or anticipated. But I was happy to do it.

Reflecting on these experiences, I wonder why I was so glad to do it. Did it hurt? Yes. Did I complain at all? Sure, I'm human, but only when I was alone. But why was I happy to do it? What motivated me to endure this voluntary pain?

After so many years of enjoying my time and experiencing the nostalgia, tradition, love, and camaraderie among family and friends, I wanted others to experience that as well. If I could carry a little of their struggle and weight, I knew they could have the same experience. It wasn't just about giving or some charitable act—it was about helping others overcome the physical challenges so that they could also simultaneously win the internal mindset challenges, much like I had to as a young mule-boy.

Empowerment, for me, is all about creation—creating moments, opportunities, and room for action. I wanted to create the opportunity for others to have the same positive, loving, and unforgettable experiences I had—whether it was catching that first fish, photographing a beautiful sunset over the mountains, or sharing conversations around the campfire. I wanted so deeply for others to experience it. Selfishly, I wanted to experience it with them. Carrying their weight up the mountain was a no-brainer for me.

I care so deeply about what others think. You could call it one of my love languages—my perpetual driver of vitality and belonging. How could an emotion like that empower someone like me to carry mine and other people's backpacks for eighteen-plus miles to enjoy time with others in the outdoors? I guess my purpose was to help others succeed, and my mindset overcame the pain I endured to achieve that.

Long ago, in college, I took the Gallup Strengths Finder test. My top strengths were Woo, Positivity, Communication, Leadership, and Inclusivity. I always laughed that backpacking, hiking, and running weren't on the list—nothing that described a mule.

I have always wondered what inclusiveness or including means. However, I realized I would go out of my way to involve people in everything I was doing because I empathically wanted to connect them with my surrounding joys and happiness. Through my positive, charismatic energy, enthusiastic leadership, and outspoken communication, I found I could curate environments and relationships. I also recognize that you can be a leader and strengthen those around you, no matter your strengths or assessment results.

Regardless of how many times I took the Strengths Finder Assessment—three different times throughout my life, to be exact—my number one strength was the "Woo" quality. My peers and those who took the assessment with me used to make fun of me for the "Woo" quality—to them, it was silly to be a 'wooer.' But over time, I've embraced being a "wooer."

In fact, under further research and understanding of the Strengths Finder tools, I've found that 'Woo' is one of the most marketable traits in the world and could help me achieve outrageous goals and aspirations such as sales, relationships, leadership, mentorship, creating communities—heck, even world domination if that was my desire.

Empowerment is more than just physical energy; it's a strength anyone can develop. It's emotional, spiritual, mental, intuitive, and conscious. Empowerment comes from within. It's a desire, a connection, a magnetism. The essence of human connectivity unites us all to the same frequency and desire for significance and meaning.

I once met a mentor who taught me about the six perpetual human drivers—the deep reasons why we exist and do what keeps humanity progressing. Although primitive in nature, they are deeply connected to our relationships and personal empowerment. The 6 Perpetual Drivers, taught by Levi McPherson at his Prosperity Gym workshops, were:

1. Meaning
2. Progress
3. Vitality
4. Survival
5. Belonging
6. Lifestyle

The one driver that resonated most with me was 'Belonging,' as it reminded me of my search for purpose and meaning. These drivers are crucial to understanding human behavior, especially when understanding why people say "yes" to offers and commitments. Which of these Perpetual Drivers resonates with you? Can you identify any of these strengths in your daily decision-making processes?

Looking back on our backpacking excursions, I realize that helping others on the trail wasn't just empowering myself—I was seeking to uplift others and help them find meaning and belonging while overcoming the challenges that the trail sometimes offered. By planting seeds of positivity and helping them overcome their physical and mindset struggles, I was contributing to their growth and achievements.

I'm well aware of the negative thoughts and physical pain that creep into our minds during tough times. But when you experience victories like relief from carrying weight, an increased sense of purpose and mindful energy, and an I-can-do-this attitude can develop—it improves your mindset, driving your attitude and leading to more significant progress and meaning.

Selfishly, I must admit, having company with you in the great outdoors who also have great attitudes makes the experience much better for everyone. A positive attitude transforms and empowers the journey for all of us, rather than dealing with someone complaining in pain the entire time.

Human empowerment is a powerful force of action. It starts with the soul and our desire to connect, find meaning, and live purposefully. The many elements of empowerment are essential. Using the example of the 'Woo' strength, although the rest of the world would dub my attributes as people-pleasing, sucking up, and showing off—once again tying me back down to the idea that 'Woo' is one of those strengths and traits others do not understand.

Instead of accepting their teasing, I have found that the 'Woo' mentality is one of the greatest strengths in creating relationships and serving people, causing experiences as a speaker, mentor, coach, and bestselling author in my professional life.

Early on, I learned that some of the keys to success in accountability and achieving personal goals were more than just developing discipline and strategic planning and following through. Add to the keys the continuous effort of repeating and reporting your daily efforts to others. The more I repeated my goals aloud, the more I held myself accountable.

However, when not held responsible by others, I could easily change and work towards new, shiny, exciting goals, forgetting the purpose and mindset I had set for myself. The more I told people my goals, the faster and more motivated I was to achieve them.

I saw this also play out to fruition in other people, as they told me their goals, and they, too, would have significant results. We should ask questions like, "How are you progressing and how close are you to achieving your goals?" This significant element was super crucial for me to share with others because, even though I am not responsible for the accomplishment and achievement and following up of their goals and achievements, it gave me great power knowing that if I asked how they were doing, it would add an element of responsibility to finish and achieve their goals in their minds. Some people would quickly draw conclusions, like, "Oh, I gave up on that," or "Why do you keep asking? Why do you care?"

And the truth is, I don't care. But I do know that if I continue to ask the questions, it's going to push them in the direction of actually achieving their goals. And I guess I lied a little because I do care. If somebody tells me something hard that they want to accomplish, and then, upon further follow-up and discovery, that they achieve it, it'll deepen our connection and relationship when I can celebrate with them the wins and the exciting accomplishments they are achieving.

It takes being human to be empowered and empower others. Empowerment is physically moving—it can lift and carry people up the mountain, emotionally climbing the mountains of depression, seeking happiness and fulfillment, or mentally empowering them by solving problems, cracking the code, finishing a puzzle, or finding the answers to life's great mysteries.

No matter what it is, empowerment starts with the soul and our magnetic, connected beads of seeking meaning and fulfillment and realizing the power of these human drivers, which ultimately give us a purpose in life.

Two of the most significant questions I've ever asked are, "What is the purpose of life?" and, "What is the meaning of our existence?"

Whether it be belief or through the evidence of scientific solutions, there is a magnetic unity, attraction, and connectivity that webs us all together. I implore that you discover your greatest strengths and learn to use them to help empower yourself and those around you.

JON KOVACH JR.

About Jon Kovach Jr.: Jon is an award-winning international motivational speaker and global mastermind leader. Jon has helped multi-billion-dollar corporations exceed their annual sales goals, including Coldwell Banker Commercial, Outdoor Retailer Cotopaxi, and the Public Relations Student Society of America. In addition, in his work as an accountability coach and mastermind facilitator, Jon has helped thousands of professionals overcome their challenges and achieve their goals by implementing his accountability strategies and Irrefutable Laws of High Performance. Jon is the Founder and Chairman of Champion Circle, a networking association that combines high-performance-based networking activities and recreational fun to create connection capital and increase prosperity for professionals. Jon is the Mastermind Facilitator and Team Lead of the Habitude Warrior Mastermind and the Global Speakers Mastermind & Masterclass founded by Speaker Erik "Mr. Awesome" Swanson.

Jon speaks on accountability, The Irrefutable Laws of High Performance, and The Power of Mastermind Methodologies. He is a #1 Bestselling Author and a featured keynote on SpeakUp TV, an Amazon Prime TV series, with his keynote speech titled, *Getting Unstuck*. In addition, he stars in over 100 speaking stages, podcasts, and live international summits each year. Jon's motivational messages have been viewed by over 300,000 people online. His voice has been used by global brands and creators on TikTok and Instagram Reels, such as: Red Bull USA, Michael Bublé, The NHL, Powell Books, GoDaddy Studio, Canada's Wonderland Amusement Park, and the LSU Cheer Team.

Author's website: *www.SpeakerJonKovachJr.com*

Book Series Website: *www.TheBookOfHumanEmpowerment.com*

JON NASH

FINDING YOUR OWN PURPOSE

To have the most meaningful life, you need to be able to discover your purpose independently of what others might say you should do. When we make decisions based on what others might believe is best for us, we risk being dissatisfied with those choices.

I struggled for a while because I was pursuing many things that were not part of my purpose. Others had told me that, since I was good at math, I should pursue a career in the engineering field. I started into degrees in electrical and mechanical engineering, and later pre-med and pre-pharmacy, all the while discovering that these career paths would not be right for me.

I turned to my own intellect to figure out what my purpose was, racking my brain to find what my life's purpose was outside of having a family of my own. All the avenues I was coming up with on my own left me frustrated and unsatisfied. This left me taking a break from educational pursuits and trying to figure this out for myself.

This became a period of intense self-reflection, and it allowed me to step back from my mindset of always needing to take a step forward. It was then that I was able to find a direction that I had never considered before. I had to stop and turn to God before I could clearly see my purpose in helping others. It was through divine inspiration that the seed of pursuing a career in therapy became planted.

Therapy and lifting others are things I couldn't imagine doing before because I could only see my weaknesses. A combination of being introverted and feeling fairly broken myself led me to feel unqualified to talk with people all day. Little did I know that these would play right into what makes me an effective therapist today. I am able to listen intently because I have never felt a need to talk over other people. My lived experience helps me to understand and connect with others in a way that I couldn't if my life had always been easy.

Lifting others through therapy and other means is now the only thing that feels right, and this helps me have the right mindset going into every day. I am keenly aware of the impact that deep, meaningful conversations can have for people. Seeing the progress that people make throughout their healing journeys invigorates me and keeps me moving through long days. I'm profoundly grateful for the journey that has led me to this point in my life where I feel I am really making a difference in people's lives.

I share this experience to illustrate four important realizations to help you on your journey:

1. Determine your purpose.
2. Realign yourself.
3. Weaknesses as strengths in disguise.
4. Life purpose.

You should get to determine your own purpose.

Feeling connected to your own purpose increases the traction toward fulfilling that purpose. Being told by others what your purpose is can create roadblocks to true ownership of that purpose. Other people may be able to provide valuable insight into your strengths and areas where you might excel, but this does not necessitate acceptance of what they tell you. You must agree with what is being shared to have it truly resonate with you.

If you get inspiration from a higher power in the same way that I did, there should still be personal confirmation. The quick nature of sharing the story in this format fails to capture the process that it took to be able to align myself with the idea that helping others was my purpose. This was a months-long process, and for others it can take even more time. Taking the time at the beginning to figure this out will pay off over the long-term, as most people tend to have fewer questions about whether or not they have made the right decision.

Bottom-line is that feedback from others is only valuable as long as it helps to propel the process of really understanding yourself and what will help you to move forward in a meaningful way.

Periodically, take a step back to realign yourself.

Our purpose in life is a dynamic part of ourselves, and not a static one. What may be true about our purpose when we are twenty-years-old may not be applicable when we turn forty. That is not only okay, but it can also be expected and embraced. As we make progress in life, our understanding of ourselves changes, and our abilities change. We will likely be able to take greater steps than we were able to at earlier stages in our lives.

The growth that we experience could alter the course that we take to fulfill our purpose—or could change what our purpose is. Ensure that you regularly have time to reflect on your actions, abilities, and progress. Doing so will help you make course corrections when it is easier, rather than waiting until when you are feeling a large amount of dissatisfaction with your direction in life.

Large shifts in our purpose are also possible, even when we are continuously doing course corrections. I have seen many individuals who have felt that they have completed what they needed to with a previously defined purpose and determined that they were ready to make a significant shift into something very different. You can only know this if you take the time to self-reflect.

Your perceived weaknesses could actually be strengths in disguise.

Wherever you are living, there are cultural factors that influence our perception of what is valuable. It's no secret that, in the United States, extroversion, an analytical mindset, ambition, and a competitive nature are valued for leadership and seen as ideal traits. This is true for many positions, but focusing solely on these characteristics reduces our ability to see how other characteristics can really be strengths in other types of pursuits. Not everyone wants to be in leadership. Not all leaders need to be extroverted or possess the other previously identified characteristics. There is space for other types of leaders.

Allow yourself space to recognize where your perceived weaknesses could actually be strengths. ADHD tendencies can lead to higher creativity. Anxiety can help one to prepare effectively for upcoming challenges and create higher success rates. Our society is opening up to more possibilities for careers that meet human needs in different ways. Take this further for yourself and find things that come naturally to you and that you enjoy, regardless of what the perception of others is. It may take some effort, but there is likely a way to turn those into a purpose inside or outside of a career. Believe in yourself and be willing to be vulnerable.

Life Purpose

This discussion has focused a lot on career purpose, but the principles apply more broadly to all of the different areas of life. Putting in the work to identify what matters to you is fundamental in propelling your life forward. You have worth and value. You can accomplish greatness in your own sphere of influence.

Once you figure out what you are aiming for, it becomes a lot easier to accomplish your goals and achieve your dreams, even the ones that you are not aware of right now and will discover on the journey. Keep pressing forward.

JON NASH, CMHC

About Jon Nash, CMHC: Jon Nash, CMHC, is a clinical mental health counselor who grew up in Fort Collins, Colorado. Jon is passionate about helping others to achieve their potential and overcome their own personal obstacles. He has a bachelor's in psychology from Brigham Young University and a master's degree in marriage and family therapy from Touro University Worldwide.

He has been practicing as a therapist since 2016. He has worked in a variety of mental health settings including residential treatment for youth, behavioral health unit at a hospital, substance abuse intensive outpatient program, and private practice. He is currently trained as a clinical supervisor, faith-based counseling, EMDR, DBT, couples counseling, and neurofeedback. Jon resides in Utah County, Utah, where he and his wife are raising their three children. *Inviting Christ on the Mental Health Journey* is his first publication.

Author's Website: *www.JonNashCMHC.com*

Book Series Website: *www.TheBookOfHumanEmpowerment.com*

JULIE DELGADILLO

SELF-LEADERSHIP, MENTORSHIP, & RECIPROCAL EMPOWERMENT

Leadership has always been an anchor of mine. More than just guidance, Leadership is an experience that transforms both mentor and mentee in equal measure.

Leadership as a Mutual Relationship

I have realized that leadership is not a linear path—instead, it is more cyclical; giving and receiving are interwoven in their existence. Mentors have played an instrumental role in shaping my path while learning something valuable from me. Leadership's powerful legacy lies within this reciprocity: its essence rests within its ability to recognize that, although people seek guidance, they also bring something of their own to offer in return.

Unknowingly, I found myself serving as an unwitting leader. It happened unexpectedly during one of those everyday interactions you might take for granted: A young woman in my community approached me asking for advice on balancing work and personal life. She admired my work while telling me she admired me as someone who had it all together despite her struggles. This realization was full circle for me when I realized that those challenges I had overcome could serve as roadmaps to others needing advice and guidance.

Mentorship isn't about having all the answers; instead, it is about sharing our journey, lessons, and vulnerabilities—walking alongside someone while they navigate their path with support when necessary, offering assistance when they stumble, or celebrating their victories as though they were your own! I was lucky to become friends with this young lady as she and I became mentor-mentee relationships—her unique perspective inspired me to keep pushing through even when the going got tough!

Self leadership is an evolving concept. My consideration of my mentors has allowed me to witness an evolution in how I view and approach mentorship. At first, mentors provided resources, and knowledge gaps were filled by providing tools like Miss Hazel (described in previous chapter contributions). She helped me navigate academic challenges while instilling confidence and resilience, which served me through an extremely transformative period by showing my potential and aligning me with my purpose.

Now, I find myself at another stage of leadership, one where the boundaries between leader and follower blur more fluidly than ever. Leadership doesn't just involve learning from more experienced people; rather, it should include taking advantage of all possible sources of wisdom if we allow it. Everyone you come into contact with has something valuable to impart if only we listen.

Self leadership is a collaborative experience. I no longer view it as something for which I need an external instructor as much as something I seek internally through peers and colleagues, including friends, mentees, or anyone who may seem unrelated. Some of my most influential leaders may even remain unaware that they're mentoring me; friends, colleagues or even my mentees provide challenges, push my comfort zone away and illuminate parts of myself that I may have otherwise failed to recognize fully.

Self-Leadership as an Agent of Change

Empowerment has always been at the core of my work, and leadership plays a central role. Leadership doesn't provide new power but reveals their existing power for greater independence. I strive to foster strengths by nurturing them to help discover potential within them while offering the support necessary to navigate any potential roadblocks they might come up against in life.

One of the greatest joys of leading others is witnessing their transformations. I have had the honor of mentoring many women and young people over time, and the greatest moments have come when they begin seeing themselves as I see them: capable, strong, and full of potential. Self leadership and reciprocal empowerment should not involve forcing someone into being someone they aren't; rather, it should assist individuals in becoming their very best selves.

Maria came to me feeling uncertain about herself and her career path yet lacking the confidence to step into them powerfully. Through our conversations and the challenges I offered her, over time, Maria began seeing herself differently, taking risks more frequently, speaking up more, and taking up opportunities she previously avoided. Watching Maria transform into an empowered leader is truly one of my life's most satisfying experiences!

Maria's journey taught me an invaluable lesson about patience in mentorship. Personal and professional growth does not occur overnight; it requires hard work, dedication, encouragement, and persistence from everyone involved. Mentors must remain patient while giving our mentees the space they need to develop, remembering that our role as supporters should not include pushing.

Self-Leadership is Essential

As much as I appreciate having mentors and leaders, one of the greatest sources of guidance and strength can come from within yourself. Self-leadership involves applying lessons you've learned from others into your everyday life while becoming your biggest cheerleader, guide, and source of strength.

As I matured, I became less dependent on external leaders and mentors to guide me. Now that I trust myself more and listen to myself more closely, I seek guidance within myself more frequently rather than externally. That doesn't mean I no longer seek guidance from leaders and mentorship—quite the opposite, in fact—but rather that I know how to balance external guidance with internal wisdom.

Reflection has become one of my primary forms of self-leadership, helping to keep me grounded and focused even when the road ahead may not always seem clear. I take time every week to reflect upon past experiences, examine lessons learned, and decide how they might apply in my everyday life moving forward. This practice has proven essential in staying grounded and focused no matter the obstacles.

Self-compassion is another critical aspect of self-mentorship that I found indispensable. Recognizing your humanity and realizing you will make mistakes is essential to treating yourself with the kindness and understanding you would show a mentee. Self-compassion has proven invaluable in helping me face life's obstacles with grace and resilience.

Mentorship isn't something to graduate from—it evolves with your life stages. My focus as a mentor lies in supporting others to become mentors while continuing my growth by finding opportunities to learn from others, challenge assumptions, and expand my understanding of what it means to mentor someone else. Successful leaders remain open-minded to new experiences while continually expanding on what they have discovered as empowered leaders.

Accepting Leadership as a Compass of Success

Technology has unleashed unimagined possibilities for connection and learning, making it simpler than ever to locate mentors worldwide. Virtual mentorship programs, online communities, and digital resources have revolutionized how mentors are approached, opening up endless doors of potential growth.

So, while we embrace new tools, resources, and modalities for empowerment through leadership, it's still vitally important to remember its core essence—relationships, connection, and a shared journey of growth and empowerment. Trust, respect, and mutual learning still hold true whether mentoring someone offline or online.

Digital empowerment through leadership can be just as impactful in my work. Throughout my mentoring experiences with women and young people from diverse cultures spanning multiple countries through video calls, emails, and online platforms, my engagement has expanded my perspective while deepening my appreciation of global challenges and opportunities.

As time progresses, I remain committed to exploring innovative methods of mentoring and being mentored in today's digital environment. By harnessing technology as we do so, mentorship can reach further—creating a more connected and empowered society in its wake.

Steps for Becoming an Empowering Leader & Mentor

Are you starting your leadership and mentorship journey? Below, I offer some practical steps I took to become an effective leader and mentor. These may change with time as you gain experience, but they provide a solid framework for empowering mentoring relationships.

1. **Active Listening:** One essential skill any mentor must master is active listening. Active listening goes beyond simply hearing what your mentee says—it involves understanding their needs, concerns, and aspirations without passing judgment. It gives each member of your mentee's community the space and respect they deserve to voice their opinions freely and independently. Take the time to actively listen without judgment so your mentee knows their voice has been heard!

2. **Ask Thought-Provoking Questions:** A mentor's primary job is not to supply all the answers for their mentee but instead help them discover them themselves. Asking thoughtful questions that encourage introspection and critical thought processes among your

mentees helps your mentor delve more deeply into their thoughts and emotions while stimulating critical thought for future decisions made by their mentees.

3. **Share Your Experiences:** Be bold and open up about your journey's successes and failures with your mentee; being vulnerable with them can build trust and rapport between both of you.

4. **Provide Constructive Feedback:** Feedback is critical for growth but must be delivered properly to be most beneficial. Focus on providing constructive comments that highlight areas for improvement while acknowledging and celebrating strengths within the mentee's life.

5. **Encourage Self-Reflection:** Encourage your mentee to use reflection as an effective method for personal growth and increasing self-awareness. When used properly, reflection can provide immense potential benefits and deepen self-knowledge.

6. **Celebrate Their Achievements:** Acknowledging and celebrating your mentee's victories is crucial in building their confidence and reinforcing positive behaviors. Acknowledging achievements helps reinforce positive behaviors while building self-confidence.

7. **Be Patient & Supportive:** Growth takes time, so when setbacks arise, mentors and mentees should remain supportive and remind themselves that setbacks are an inevitable part of the learning process.

8. **Foster Independence:** Mentorship should provide your mentees with the confidence and tools they need to become independent, self-sufficient individuals. Please encourage them to make decisions based on themselves alone while having faith in themselves and trusting in themselves and their capabilities.

Leadership and mentorship creates an ever-widening circle. When you mentor someone, you not only directly impact their life, but your influence also grows throughout their circle of influence. This effect creates lasting change while building communities of empowered individuals working toward a positive impact in our world.

One of the greatest joys of mentoring lies in seeing your mentees carry forward the lessons and values you've imparted. You see them mentor others with passion and dedication similar to what was shown to them. You know that your impactful mentorship will last beyond you, leaving an everlasting legacy of empowerment spanning generations.

As part of my work with Corazon and my personal life, I have witnessed firsthand the ripple effect mentorship has on the lives around me. One act can spark another and transform multiple lives through mentoring alone —this is truly amazing and represents its true power: making an impactful impression across communities that you may never fully comprehend!

Leadership and mentorship is one of the greatest gifts anyone can give; all it requires to be effective as a mentor is listening, sharing knowledge, and assisting on others' journey.

Leadership and mentorship can be an incredible catalyst for change—for mentors and mentees alike. Please take full advantage of its potential, share your light, and continue the journey, knowing its legacy will linger long into the future.

JULIE DELGADILLO

About Julie Delgadillo: Julie Delgadillo is a confident, enthusiastic, witty, and sought-after passionate servant leader and mentor with over 20 years of experience in non-profit management, leadership development, and confidence coaching. Julie is the Executive Director of Corazón U.S. & Mexico. Julie is a firm believer in leading by example and actively engages in developing community leaders. It's not uncommon to catch her rolling up her sleeves and wearing a tool belt to personally contribute to building homes in Mexico for deserving low-income families.

Julie's strengths and passions are rooted in empowering women to be confidence in every area of their lives. Julie has personally coached and developed teens and women from across the globe and serves as an International Ambassador for the economic development of women. Julie is also a former International Beauty Queen and a long-time Hunger Relief Advocate.

An alumna of the prestigious University of Notre Dame's Mendoza School of Business Non-Profit Business Management Executive Leadership Program, Julie's educational journey is a testament to her commitment to growth and learning. Her undergraduate studies at Mount Saint Mary College and her certification in transformational life coaching from the Life Purpose Institute further enrich her holistic approach to empowerment. When she is not out conquering the world, you can find her discovering new brunch spots, listening to audiobooks, or in the aisles of TJ Maxx, Marshall's, or HomeGoods. Let's Connect: *www.Linkedin.com/in/JulieDelgadillo*

Author's Website: *www.linktr.ee/SheConquersTheWorld*

Book Series Website: *www.TheBookOfHumanEmpowerment.com*

LAUREN FIELDS

FROM COMA TO CLARITY

When we think about purpose, we often think about joyful, upbeat, motivational goals. We think about our calling, dreams, and what we enjoy doing. But we usually overlook the fact that our most challenging moments also play a role in shaping our purpose. Struggles not only build character, but they also help us define our calling. They enable us to develop the mindset and skills needed to scale the mountains of life as we journey toward actualizing our potential.

Finding Our Purpose

Many of us are waiting for external forces to reveal our life's purpose. What I've come to find is that there is no shortcut to finding our purpose, and no one else can tell us what it is. After all, who knows us better than we know ourselves? We must look within to find the unique gifts developed throughout our life experiences.

A Spark of Purpose

Several years ago, I was in a horse-riding accident. The last thing I remember was galloping toward the jump in a show-jumping competition. Then everything went black.

Three days later, I awoke from a coma to discover I'd experienced a traumatic brain injury. Dazed and disoriented, I overheard the doctors telling my parents, "Keep Lauren out of school. She may have to relearn how to speak, she may have difficulty walking, and she may struggle with memory retention."

I was shocked. The next day, I walked slowly beside my father to the cafeteria down a hallway that seemed miles long, trying to piece together where I was and what had happened. At that moment, little did I know that this life-altering event would come to define my purpose. Upon leaving the hospital, I set out on a mission to defy expectations and show everyone I could rise gracefully from any setback.

Over the next few weeks, I defied all odds. I was out of the hospital and back on a horse in record time. Then, the first spark of my purpose began to form: I realized I was an overcomer who could go on to one day help other people overcome their unique challenges.

My Purpose Develops

I went on to study business and enter the corporate arena in NYC. After college, I became a lifestyle manager, helping clients maintain a sparkling external image. I booked their five-star hotels, elite galas, and dinners at the poshest restaurants and ensured their lives appeared beautiful on the outside. However, I realized something was missing in this work—the inner being. I dove into health and wellness coaching, life coaching, and eventually a Master's in Psychology to understand the science behind human cognition. This was another step toward finding my purpose, but my true calling would not be fully refined until I faced profound limitations and vulnerability.

Pain into Purpose

As time progressed, I developed nerve damage due to a blood spot on my brain from the equestrian accident, leading to an eight-hour tendon transfer surgery. Recovering from the surgery was one of the most challenging experiences I had ever had. For the first time, I felt helpless as I waited for a healing that I could not control the speed of.

Finally, I realized my purpose was not to prove to everyone I was okay. Instead, it was to do profound inner work to stabilize myself during this time so that I could help others who were also suffering in silence. I dove into wellness and self-empowerment books to stabilize myself during this challenging period of isolation.

This shift changed my life forever and ultimately led me to start my coaching method to help others in areas where they feel stuck. Many of us get knocked down and struggle to get back up. My mission is to help others reignite their spark for life and live fully, making every moment count toward a more prosperous, authentic life.

Purpose happens at the intersection of what you're good at and what you enjoy doing, and it often includes a deep-seated desire to help others overcome the same challenges you have gone through. Rather than waiting for purpose to find you, actively create it by discovering the unique treasures within yourself and taking bold action toward your desires.

Developing a Mindset of Resilience as We Pursue Our Purpose

Not only does our pain help us discover our purpose, but it also helps us develop the mindset of perseverance that we need to reach our goals. Several years ago, I went on an eight-day hike in the Himalaya. To complete the expedition, I needed to ensure my mind was focused and resilient.

This hiking trek was one of the most physically challenging things I'd ever accomplished. It pushed me out of my comfort zone in ways I was not prepared for. Every day, we hiked for up to eight hours. While I tried my best to prepare, some factors surprised me: extreme altitude, temperatures below freezing, unexpected terrain, overall discomfort, and exhaustion. Not to mention having to use nature as my bathroom!

I would tell myself, "Just one more step, just one more day. You're Lauren Fields; you got this." Ultimately, I learned that the reward is much greater when struggle is involved in working towards the destination. This trek became a metaphor for life. A resilient mindset is essential to overcoming the challenges on our path to purpose. Here are a few critical mindset shifts we need as we pursue our purpose:

- **Avoid Labeling:** Instead of labeling situations as good or bad, look for the ways the painful moments can contribute to your ultimate calling.

Take it as information that can guide your growth and deepen your understanding of your purpose.

- **Faith:** You can choose to have either faith or fear. Both emotions take the same energy. Choose to believe you're on the path and that you can do what you set your mind to.

- **Perseverance:** Keep going, and never give up. Ensure your "why" is strong enough to help you stay committed. After all, you have the rest of the time to figure out the how.

- **Embrace Failure:** As a perfectionist, I used to fear challenges or failures. Now, I welcome them with open arms. I have learned that this is where the growth happens. Failure isn't failing. It's just deciding not to get back up and into the arena.

- **Practical Action:** Write a plan for your life and break that plan down into actionable steps. Dream the dream, develop the systems, and take action! Action is one of the most critical steps toward purpose.

These mindsets not only enabled me to climb a literal mountain but also empowered me to help others by first helping myself. For nearly a decade after my injury, I envisioned myself as a coach, speaker, and podcaster. But I didn't dare to actually coach, actually speak, or even try to start a podcast. One pivotal day, that all shifted when I got up on the TEDx stage and told the story I had kept hidden for far too long. It was time to use all my certifications, degrees, and credentials, take action, and share my purpose. Once I did, my world changed forever.

Time and again, I've learned that my most challenging moments have come to shape who I am. They've given me purpose. Trials are a way to shape our purpose rather than a way to destroy it. As we pay attention to those lessons and build those mindsets, we'll experience the joy that makes us leap out of bed every day. We'll experience true and lasting purpose.

LAUREN FIELDS

About Lauren Fields: Lauren Fields is a Life Design Strategist, Podcast Host, and TEDx speaker passionate about helping individuals design and live extraordinary lives. With a diverse background in hospitality, health & wellness, and life coaching, she founded the Fieldswell Method to empower clients to overcome challenges with resilience and grace to tap into their full potential.

Currently pursuing a Master's in Psychology, Lauren draws from her recovery from a traumatic brain injury (TBI) to provide high-level insights and strategies tailored to personal growth. Her coaching is focused on transforming dreams into reality, ensuring that her clients' lives are fulfilling, both inside and out.

Author's Website: *www.Fieldswell.com*

Book Series Website: *www.TheBookOfHumanEmpowerment.com*

LORNA SHERLAND
LIFE IS A GAME

Life is a game.

Yes, you heard me—it's a game! It's a game of chance!

The sooner you realize this, the sooner you can start playing it to your advantage. But here's the catch: you need to figure out which game you're playing at any given moment. And then, you need to understand who made the rules and what those rules are.

Understanding the Game

Life throws different games at us. Sometimes, it's a game of survival, other times it's a game of success, love, or happiness. Each game comes with its own set of rules, often dictated by external sources—society, culture, media, and sometimes our own families. But who made these rules, and why do we follow them so unquestioningly?

Who Made the Rules We Grew Up With?

As I entered into the realm of transformation, I realized that I had been operating under someone else's rules. It was actually only recently that I had one of my mentors ask me the question, "Whose rule am I not willing to break?" This was when I realized that I had been, for the longest time, operating my life and making decisions under the guise of my mother's rules. It was a huge eye opener for me. And it was a moment of profound empowerment because, now that I am aware, I make my decisions with the question in my mind as a filter. It is a powerful position.

From a young age, we are handed a set of rules about how life should be lived. These rules come from our parents, teachers, religious institutions, and society at large. They tell us what is right and wrong, what is acceptable and what is not. These rules shape our beliefs, behaviors, and even our dreams.

For instance, we are taught to value education, work hard, and strive for success as defined by societal standards—money, status, and possessions. But who decided these were the measures of success? These rules were made by people before us, influenced by their own circumstances, cultures, and times. They are not absolute truths but rather constructs that have been handed down through generations. Isn't it time to create individual constructs? It would solve a lot of problems in the world and in relationships—even relationships with self.

For me, operating under those rules, while I am grateful, if you asked me before transformation, I would have wanted to do some things differently, make different decisions. For instance, I was gung-ho on going to medical school, not because I love medicine, but because I wanted to become a big-shot doctor so that my mother could tell her friends and everyone she knew that her daughter is a doctor.

Luckily, the universe had my back and shifted my path when I got to organic chemistry 2. The college I had been attending required that to attend organic chemistry 2, I had to go to school full time, and that wasn't going to happen because I had to work. Thank God the universe always has our back!

So, Why Do We Continue with the Same Rules?

Despite the changing world, many of us continue to live by these inherited rules. We follow them because they provide a sense of security and belonging. They give us a framework within which to operate, reducing the chaos and uncertainty of life. This is where I get to disrupt your thinking, and to invite you into challenging that safety and security idea.

These rules can also limit us. They can prevent us from exploring new possibilities and living authentically. We fear stepping outside these boundaries because of the potential consequences—judgment, failure, or isolation. But what if these fears are unfounded? What if breaking these rules could lead to a more fulfilling life?

What Are You Afraid Of?

Fear is a powerful force that keeps us playing by the old rules. We're afraid of the unknown, of making mistakes, of being judged or rejected. But these fears often stem from our own limiting beliefs and past experiences rather than reality.

Facing Your Fears

To break free from these fears, we need to confront them head-on. Ask yourself: What am I really afraid of? Is it failure? Rejection? Disappointment? Once you identify your fears, challenge them. Are they based on facts or assumptions? Have you ever tested them?

For example, if you're afraid of changing careers because you fear failure, ask yourself if this fear is truly justified. Have you tried and failed before? Or is it just a hypothetical fear? Often, we find that our fears are not as insurmountable as we thought once we shine a light on them. Then the bigger question is, is the fear REAL?

I remember when I walked out of the office of the last advertising agency I worked for after being a controller for five years. I had no idea what I was walking into from there. I recall the fear that gripped me as I made that decision, walked into HR and told them to approve my unemployment. When I left the building without a plan in place, if felt like I was walking into nowhere, an empty void of nothingness. There was no turning back! That fear had me lightheaded.

Yet, within two months, I got my real estate license and went on to serve people and closed twenty five deals in my first year when the average agent in the US still, even today, closes four deals per year. That's the game, using the fear to give yourself momentum.

Reclaiming Your Power

We are innately wired to be our own rudder, to steer our own course. However, over time, we allow external influences to decide our direction. People, education, media, arts, entertainment, and culture all play significant roles in shaping our beliefs and behaviors.

Education is responsible for a large part of our cultural conditioning. It teaches us what to think rather than how to think. It promotes conformity and discourages questioning the status quo. While education is important, it should not stifle our individuality and creativity.

The media is a powerful tool in the game of life. I am a parent who is guilty of raising my son in front of a television, because, while I was not raised on that, I came into a culture and learned. That is how powerful the media is. Arts and entertainment are powerful tools that shape our perceptions of reality. They influence our values, aspirations, and even our self-worth.

While they can be sources of inspiration and knowledge, they can also perpetuate stereotypes and unrealistic expectations. The things we see on the screens, in theatrical plays, and hear from music shape us in subconscious way that are so subtle yet powerful. It's a hard one to shift, yet we must.

Under it all, our parents and cultural backgrounds play a very crucial role in shaping our beliefs and behaviors. They pass down traditions, values, and expectations that can either support or hinder our personal growth. It is essential to honor these influences while also questioning and redefining them to align with our true selves. Now this is the work! This part is not a game!

Belief: Do You Believe the Universe/God Has Your Back?

A crucial aspect of navigating the game of life is belief—believing in yourself and in a higher power, whether it's the universe, God, or something else. This belief can provide a sense of purpose and direction, giving you the confidence to play the game on your own terms.

Believing that the universe or God has your back means trusting that there is a greater plan at work, that you are supported, and that everything happens for a reason. This belief can be a source of immense strength and resilience, helping you to overcome challenges and stay focused on your goals.

Cultivating belief takes work. It involves regular self-reflection, mindfulness, and gratitude. These are powerful weapons to slay fear and unbelief and bust open the past experiences that hold us back. Taking time to connect with yourself and your higher power is paramount. Practicing gratitude for everything, both good and bad, in your life and trusting that you are on the right path, even when the way forward is unclear is the way to play the game. It would help if you created your outcome by creating your own rules.

Conclusion

Life is indeed a game, but it's a game you can learn to play well. By understanding which game you're playing, recognizing who made the rules, and confronting your fears, you can start to play by your own rules. Reclaim your rudder and steer your own course, trusting that the universe or God has your back. When you do this, you'll find that life is not just a game—it's a game you can win.

LORNA SHERLAND

About Lorna Sherland: Lorna Sherland is a distinguished Mindset Leadership Transformation Coach at Freedom LifeStyle, where she specializes in helping driven female entrepreneurs overcome limiting beliefs to achieve six- and seven-figure milestones in their businesses to create time and money freedom. Lorna combines her extensive experience in real estate with her passion for empowering others, focusing on educating buyers and sellers to enhance their real estate experiences while empowering female entrepreneurs to go to the net level of growth and impact.

As the founder of Success Power Brokers Real Estate and Consulting Services, with over twenty years of industry experience, Lorna has established herself as a Real Estate Mega Agent, successfully closing over 1,000 deals. Her philosophy is centered around the belief that a well-informed buyer or seller is the best consumer of her services. This dedication to client education has set a high standard in her field.

Since August 2018, Lorna has dedicated herself to mindset empowerment and transformation coaching.

Lorna's impact extends beyond her professional achievements. She is a thought leader in the industry, frequently speaking on topics such as buyer and seller dynamics, real estate trends, mindset resets, and homeownership. Her insights and guidance continue to inspire and transform the lives of many, particularly female entrepreneurs aspiring to reach new heights in their business endeavors.

Author's Website: *www.LornaSherland.com*

Book Series Website: *www.TheBookOfHumanEmpowerment.com*

MARIS SEGAL & KEN ASHBY

EMPOWERING LEADERSHIP = THRIVING RELATIONSHIPS

From the time we wake up in the morning until our nightly sleep, we are in relationship with someone or something. Even through our dream state we are in relationship with ourselves. Every relationship, personal or professional, begins with a connection. Think of your day today, did you wake up to an alarm or your partner saying, "good morning," kids and pets jumping on your bed, then checked your messages, emails, news, took a shower, dressed, exercised, meditated, made breakfast and all before you headed to work or your first appointment. In our leadership coaching and consulting work, we call this relationship immersion, the RFactor. Relationships, like air and water, good or bad, may be avoided but overall, we would not survive without them.

Purpose

Part of our relationship journey is connecting with our purpose and charting a path to realize it in the future. Together, we inhabit a planet with over 7.5 billion humans. As a couple in love and business for over twenty years, we believe that we are all connected as humans and the bottom line begins with relationships, one connection at a time. Our purpose is a passionate drive to impact lives by uniting humanity and evolving human relationships across the globe. Everything we do and how we live supports our purpose. Finding your purpose begins with some key questions—have fun with it, "What do I want? What do I feel passionate about? What are my unique gifts? What problem can I solve?"

Each of us, unique and perfectly imperfect individuals, come into this world connected to each other by a number of universal birth rights; It is our birthright to be valued, happy, healthy, safe, loved, and feel a sense of belonging and accomplishment. If it were only that simple! How often does something occur or we get in our own way and sabotage one or more of the above? We are the leaders of our lives and as we lead daily, at home, work, or school, the choices we make determine our future.

Empowerment is a fundamental choice and commitment to elevating humanity. Imagine a world where all relationships are elevated, authentically connected, and prospering. When empowered, leaders at every age and stage (parents, students, teachers, supervisors, executives) stand as beacons of growth, guiding and nurturing individuals toward realizing their full potential.

Fostering a Growth & Purpose-Driven Mindset

Central to empowerment is the cultivation of a growth and purpose-driven mindset—a belief in your capacity to learn and evolve over time. No matter where you live and what your circumstances are, you are the one relationship you can't leave home without.

Research and wisdom teachers agree that our mindset is created by a collection of our beliefs—shaped by our family legacy and past traumas —that influence our thoughts, emotions and actions. How you treat others reflects how you treat yourself. A positive mindset is key to unlocking your peak performance potential at any age, and key to staying on track from youth through adulthood. An ancient Chinese proverb, points to this as well: "Be careful of your thoughts, words, actions, habits, and character—these become your destiny." So, changing the way we think can alter the emotional and behavioral patterns in your brain from a self-doubt mindset to an empowering mindset. The shift to positivity creates new possibilities that will support your desired outcomes.

Did you know that your brain can only process positive or negative at one time. Your subconscious mind is responsible for 95% of your behavior and decision making, and it's influenced by the words and messages that you repeatedly feed it. When you wake up in the morning, you have the opportunity to set the tone and rhythm of your day. If you're feeling overwhelmed and continue to tell yourself so, then overwhelm is where you will stay and it will show up in your actions. If you want to change the patterns of your repeated negative behaviors and thoughts, you must first change the messages you tell your subconscious mind. Again, we have a choice in each moment. It's often easier said than done, choosing to respond positively versus reacting negatively.

Affirmations & Visualization

As partners in love and business, we utilize "affirmations and visualizations" daily, in every aspect of our lives, and we coach our clients from families and executives to sports and entertainment celebrities, across public and private sectors, to do the same.

At the start of the pandemic pause, we began repeating a specific desire and goal and each time we said it, we could feel the accomplishment as if it had already happened. We set the affirmation and a "by when" date when we would have a bestselling book and be featured on a TEDx. When we began this process and repetition daily, we had not written a single word or completed an application. After a month, in spite of our doubts, we stayed on track with purpose and committed action and began writing. We left the fear and doubt behind and chose to embrace a messy and imperfect process.

So, 80,000 words later, we submitted a manuscript to an editor. During the back-and-forth review process, we encountered a snag and decided that we would put a hold on the project and went back to square one. Feeling a bit defeated, we continued our daily affirmations. A month later, seemingly out of the blue, we were invited to participate in a thirteen book collaborative series (thank you Habitude Warrior). We said yes, and just months later, we woke up in the location we had visualized, on the by-when-date, hearing the official word that we in fact had our first "bestselling book."

Less than a year later we prepared for our TEDx talk and released our first solo book, "The RFactor." In researching the book we identified four key universal relationship rhythms; Respect, Responsibility, Reframing, and Resilience that stand as cornerstones for every thriving and prosperous relationship. When working in sync, they are empowering catalysts for fostering a relational culture at work and home where individuals feel a connected purpose, valued, and stand accountable.

Respect: Trust & Collaboration

Respect forms the bedrock of thriving relationships and empowering leadership, laying the groundwork for trust and collaboration, be it in a professional team or within a family team. When you are present, and listen from a place of compassion, trust is built as each individual is acknowledged. This creates an inclusive culture where people feel seen and heard and where diverse ideas are valued. Practicing presence, active listening, encouraging open dialogue, and promoting acceptance and diversity of thought are all ways to elevate respect at work and home. Respecting others begins with respecting yourself. What if children were taught first to respect themselves, and then their elders and others?

Responsibility: Clear Communication & Accountability

Empowering leaders recognize that being responsible is not about accepting blame when things go wrong. They focus on the importance of clear communication and accountability, nurturing a sense of ownership in their teams. Vital here is that everyone involved is heard, understands, and agrees on what is expected of them. Along the way, acknowledging wins and evaluating what's working and what's not is also important. Expectations without agreement create pre-mediated resentment. By instilling a culture of openness, curiosity and accountability, teams can move forward collectively, trusting each other and learning from their stumbles and strides.

Reframing: Perspective is Everything

Empowering leaders possess the ability to meet people where they are and support shifting perspectives with positive feedback. They lead with gratitude to reframe obstacles as opportunities for growth and learning. Leading with a gratitude mindset opens the door to appreciation and can shift everything. Reframing also offers an opportunity to face traumas and dramas without letting them define or hold us back. Rather than viewing setbacks as failures, empowering leaders encourage individuals to adopt a positive mindset. They inspire perseverance, empowering individuals to overcome adversity with confidence and determination.

Resilience: Navigating Uncertainty with Confidence

Resilience is the capacity to bounce back after courageously facing inevitable change, adversity and stress. In today's rapidly evolving home and work landscapes, resilience is paramount. By cultivating a culture of empowerment, organizations and families fortify themselves against unforeseen challenges, unlocking untapped potential and driving sustainable success. Empowering leaders equip individuals with the tools and mindset hacks to navigate, adapt, innovate and thrive amidst adversity and uncertainty. Resilience is not a solo job! It takes courage to face the challenge and sometimes even more courage to seek and receive support to navigate through. Vital to resilience is consistently taking action – one small step at a time to move forward.

Empowering Leadership in Action

Empowering leadership encompasses a holistic approach. By fostering a culture centered on the four key relationship rhythms, respect, responsibility, reframing, and resilience leaders empower individuals to embrace their purpose, cultivate a growth-oriented mindset, and navigate challenges with confidence and resilience. Through empowering leadership, organizations can unlock the full potential of their teams, driving innovation, and sustainable success in an ever-changing world.

By promoting respect, encouraging responsibility, embracing reframing, and cultivating resilience, both teams and families will forge deeper connections, achieve collective goals, and navigate challenges with greater confidence and ease. Embracing these rhythms not only enhances productivity and performance but also contributes to overall well-being and fulfillment in both professional and personal spheres. Ask yourself, "Am I choosing the Universal Relationship Rhythms of Respect, Responsibility, Reframing, and Resilience to build a culture of trusting individuals and teams that are prospering and thriving at work and home?"

MARIS SEGAL & KEN ASHBY

About Ken Ashby & Maris Segal: From Mindset to Marketing, Ken Ashby & Maris Segal, a husband and wife dynamic duo, have spent the last thirty-plus years bringing an innovative, collaborative voice to issues, causes, and brands. As entrepreneurs, activists, business strategists, executive producers, coaches, authors, speakers, and trainers, Ken & Maris work with the public and private sectors from boardrooms and classrooms to the world stage. Their leadership expertise in Business Relationship Marketing, Organizational Change & Cultural Inclusion, Personal Growth, Project Management, Public Affairs, and Philanthropy Strategies has been called upon by companies and their agencies. Their experience includes: consumer and financial brands, Olympic organizers, Super Bowls, America's 400th Anniversary, Harvard Kennedy School, Archdiocese of LA and NY Papal visit planners, the White House and celebrities across the arts, entertainment, sports, and culinary genres. With Ken's expertise as an award-winning singer-songwriter, they launched ONE SONG, a songwriting workshop series designed to unleash creativity in individuals and teams.

Their **DRIVE** method: **D**esire, **R**elationships, **I**ntention, **V**ision and **E**mpowerment sits at the core of their companies Prosody Creative Services, ONE SONG, and Segal Leadership Global to set a path for every client to Build High Performing Businesses & Elevate Personal & Professional Leadership for Maximum Impact & a 360-degree Thriving Life!

Author's Website: *www.SegalLeadershipGlobal.com*

Book Series Website: *www.TheBookOfHumanEmpowerment.com*

M.A. FULTS

HAZE GRAY & UNDERWAY

It was May of 1981, and I was about to graduate from the University of Arizona (UofA) with a Bachelor of Fine Arts Degree in Drama Production—not the top of my class, but with a decent grade point average. And I was totally burned out, ready to look elsewhere for 'work,' if only for the short term.

My mother, mentor, counselor, and friend, asked me, "What else have you thought of doing?" I said, with all sincerity, "Joining the Navy." I had always loved the sea, not to sit on sand and bask in the sun, but to be on the water, even though I'd only ever been in a boat on a lake. But something, I cannot say exactly what, something called me.

My Mom's response to the Navy was, "Well, Navy recruiters are on the Mall this week." Being a guidance counselor at the UofA, Mom was well connected to anything regarding the future of graduates. I set my mind to join the Navy and, more importantly, to go to sea.

Physics

The next day I spoke with a Navy recruiter. He was enthusiastic that I would want to join and gave me the necessary information to apply. He was adamant though, even if I joined and went to Officer Candidate School (OCS), there was no guarantee that I would be going to sea. I heard what he said, but I also knew that ships had recently been opened up to women—at least some ships.

So, I began the application process. This included a trip to Phoenix (UofA is in Tucson), to take a basic entrance exam. I remember that one of the questions was something along the lines of "If a truck in motion has a loose box loaded on its bed and has to stop suddenly, what happens to the load?" I answered that the box would go backward, which of course is wrong.

There were a couple of other questions I got totally wrong, to the point where I did not pass. The recruiter, however, was very kind, and said I could take the test again, recommending that I study math and physics prior to doing so. A family friend explained the physics to me: an object in motion will attempt to remain in motion, and the corollary, a stationary object will attempt to stay still, or words to that effect. A few weeks later I retook the exam and easily passed.

No Ships for Women

"Well done—the next step is to get you sworn in and then…wait!" And no, he wasn't referring to "Hurry up and wait," which was what I was told to expect to be the "norm" while at OCS. The first opening for a woman was July of 1982, over one year away. He again cautioned me, though, to not set my heart on a ship, because the billets for women were few and far between, and Naval Academy graduates had first choice.

So, I waited. I got a job delivering pizzas and waited—yes, on customers, too. I attended continuing education classes at the UofA, and waited. Finally, it was July 31st, 1982 and I reported aboard Officer Candidate School in Newport, RI.

Once through Indoctrination week, I began the process of making my mindset, to go to sea, a reality. The Company Officer recommended that I put in a Request "Chit" to be moved from an "1115" Admin Officer designation, to an "1165" Surface Warfare (ship board) Officer designation. I did; it was denied, because there were no ship billets for women expected to be on the Slate Board in seven weeks' time, and there were other women Officer Candidates who may have wanted the same thing.

Academic Excellence

The "Slate Board" was a bulletin board with all the billets available posted for each Officer Candidate to pull from. We would file through in academic order and whatever was on the Slate was what was available. The top billets would go first, so doing well in class was extremely important. Then I heard what could have been the final blow: even if there was a woman-only ship billet, it would be on the Slate for only the first two women who went through.

If, and only if, a ship billet became available, and then, if and only if I was one of the top two women in my class, and then, if and only if those ahead of me did not want to go to sea, would I be able to pick it off the Board. My mind remained set on going to sea, so I had to do well in all my classes—and I did.

I also excelled at the sports, working out in my room every morning prior to reveille, something I'd never done, or even thought to do, before. And, while I've never learned how to run properly, and definitely not for long distances, I could crank out pushups and sit ups, which were the other two fitness test requirements. My fellow Delta Company candidates helped pull me through the mile and half run, and I excelled in the pushup and sit up categories. If only swimming, which I'd been doing since age 6, including competitively, had been an option then, I could have swum the swimsuit off of just about anyone.

As we neared Slate Board Day, I was at the top of my class, but just before finals week, I came down with pneumonia. I made it through the exams; however, my final standing among the women was Fourth. Then we heard that there would be one ship billet for women on the Slate, USS AJAX, a Repair ship. I was told that if the first two women did not want USS AJAX, it would be pulled from the Board. However, because I'd made my desire known, had put in the Request Chit early on, and never wavered from expressing my desire, the billet would return to the Slate Board when I entered the room, and if I still wanted it, I could choose to go to sea.

IF I STILL WANTED IT!? Neither of the two top women desired to go to a ship—still shaking my head on that one, but so grateful! I probably grinned from ear to ear as I pulled that billet off the Board. I was going to sea, I would be a Surface Warfare Officer, drive ships, travel to distant places—I was going to sea.

In May of 1981. I set my mind on going to sea as a US Navy Officer. On November 19th, 1982, I was commissioned with an "1165" designation—I was going to go to sea. I reported aboard USS AJAX on June 2nd, 1983, and we got underway on June 6th.

After being underway for a few days, Captain Ronald Kerslake asked me, "Why did you join the Navy and choose to go to sea?" My response did not shock him, "Well sir, because I had a romantic idea of going to sea. And my limited time underway has solidified that in my mind." He simply smiled and said, "Me, too."

Was that my "Purpose," to go to sea as an officer in the US Navy? After five ships, including one I commanded myself, and a successful twenty-year career, I would have to say, for that season of my life, yes. I am eternally grateful for the experiences I had, and the relationships I formed, while serving as an officer and then as a civilian, for the US Navy Surface Warfare Community. But my Purpose now has changed. Though "service to others" is still front and center, I now help others find and fulfill their purpose for their lives. I am actively involved in helping people toward a better life, and that excites me, very much.

While I can no longer sail as an officer in the US Navy, I still love being at sea. For me there is nothing better than looking around at an empty ocean, with whitecaps forming from prevailing winds; looking up at a sky filled with scattered clouds, or a million shining stars; feeling the salt in the ocean breeze, the sun warming my face; knowing that even without GPS I can navigate a ship from San Diego to Hawaii, and not miss. Yes, I love being Haze Gray and Underway.

M.A. FULTS

About M.A. Fults: Born into an Army family, and with thirty-nine years serving in and then working for the US Navy, means Fults spent many years traveling and living in foreign countries including four years in Teheran, Iran.

She has a BFA in Drama Production from the University of AZ and a MS in Management from Naval Postgraduate School in Monterey, CA. After retiring for the second time in 2022, Fults continued her life-long pursuit of learning, while embarking on her new found passion of Heart Healing, Financial Advising and Life-Coaching. She has been blessed with one son.

Book Series Website: *www.TheBookOfHumanEmpowerment.com*

MARY-FRANCES BUCKLAND

IT'S OKAY TO FEEL ALL THE FEELS

I lay there on the floor, feeling the stark coldness against my hot cheek, hair plastered to my face from the dried snot that ran from my nose completely uncontrolled. My eyes were nearly swollen shut from the torrent of tears that refused to stop flowing. My throat was dry from the simple act of trying to breathe through the screams and whaling which had taken over my entire body.

I ached as if I had just lost a prize-winning fight with the heavyweight champion of the world. This was a pain like none I had ever experienced and, in that moment, when my senses began to return and I realized where I was, I was unsure how to pick myself and my body up off that cold, hard floor.

I often reflect on this day and have come to understand through a lot of emotional work I have done since then, that it was the first time I mourned *my* death. This moment was the death of the *old* me. I had been divorced for nine years at that point, my mother had been gone for five years, and my father had passed a few months prior. Through all of that there was pain, of course.

And I had been processing it appropriately (I thought). I was even creating a new career for myself. My life had seemed to be going rather well. Little did I realize the volcano that had been smoldering within my soul and on this day, the day I found myself on the floor, it erupted and was beyond my control. I had no choice but to surrender to its rage. There was no more ignoring it.

From the moment I rose from the floor that day, I was struggling with trying to figure out who I was, what parts of me were real, asking myself who was I trying to become. For years, I had fallen prey to the judgment of others and crammed myself into a cookie mold of who they thought I was, eventually believing myself to be who they all thought me to be.

But that life-altering moment on my living room floor showed me otherwise and it was time to rise from the ashes and be who I really am. But—*who exactly is that?* The process to discover the real me began that day. I knew that I would need to put in all the hard work to make it possible to see new changes take effect in my life that would build this real me. I recorded:

> *"Embracing my re-birth was like a sculptor sitting in front of a fresh block of clay, endless possibilities and imagination at work. I was in control of the outcome and scared as hell about it."*

Prior to that day, I had enrolled in training classes to become a life coach, completed my Reiki certification as well as hypnotherapy training. Everything I was doing pointed toward a bright new career in front of me, but after I got up off the floor and began to pull myself together, it was clear that I was not as okay as I thought I had been. Again, recording my thoughts:

> *"The masterpiece would start to show its shape and splat! I would take all the clay, form it back into a nice fresh brick and begin again. I entered a continuous lather, rinse, repeat cycle."*

What had I been doing wrong? I put in the work, studying, passing my exams, yet nothing sat well. There was a nagging deep within my soul that, finally, I couldn't ignore any longer because it rose up and took over.

At one point, soon after this life-changing moment, I was approached to be a co-author in the book, *Station 42* with Greg Reid, along with a carefully chosen select number of other authors. Our role was to share our stories to offer guidance to the main character. She was recently divorced and had also lost her mother. This felt like an easy task for me, as her story felt relevant to mine, so I wrote from my heart.

After participating in this collaboration book, I was approached to write my own story, and my book, *Emotionally Scammed: A Lifetime of Decisions Based on Deception*, was born. Writing my own story is when the hard shell that had been surrounding my broken heart began to crack open. I cannot tell you how long I cried, stomped my feet, and pounded the floor while I screamed, wailed and fell apart on my living room floor, more than once. I didn't know exactly what was happening, but it felt like hell rejected me and threw me back to figure it out. I was terrified, but I was committed.

During the process of writing the book, I felt as if there were scattered pieces of me strewn all about, like discarded puzzle pieces and none of it made sense. None of the pieces seemed to fit back into the puzzle I had assembled so many times before. It infuriated me, but also made me curious and I began to pay attention and ask questions I had never asked before. Why was this happening? How can so many pieces of *my* puzzle not fit anymore? I eventually realized those pieces that no longer fit were beliefs that no longer served me. They were paradigms that I no longer wanted to give permission to have control of me; ancestral trauma I no longer wished to claim and pass on.

There were now holes in my puzzle, freeing space for my personal growth. I could fill these holes with the experiences I chose. I realized I could not do this all by myself, so I began therapy and the year it took to write my story was very cathartic. Working with my mentor and life coach, and with consistent counseling and being committed to the deep emotional work, I finally began to see real, positive changes taking place in my life.

Ephesians 4:22-24 describes death and rebirth as this:

"To put off old self, which belongs to your former manner of life and is corrupt through deceitful desires, and renew in the spirit of your minds,

and to put on the new self, created after the likeness of God in true righteousness and holiness."

The Bible refers to baptism as a way of cleansing one's sins and prior life and being born again. Baptism in the water of the Jordan River holds symbolism of rebirth for Christians. The act of being immersed in the water and rising again is seen as symbolic representation of the death of one's old self and being reborn into a new life. Being Catholic, I believe there is one holy baptism for the forgiveness of sins, yet all I had gone through proved I had some grey lines, and I was okay with that. I had the realization that maybe things were not as black and white as I had previously believed.

A few weeks after the reckoning on my living room floor, I was visiting my mother's good friend down in the hollow. I call her Granny. I walked in and sat down, as usual. We were making idle chit chat when, all of the sudden, Granny stopped me and urgently asked, "Have you been born again?" I replied "No." Her question puzzled me for a few minutes. Why would she ask me that? I told her I had not been to church in forever. She asked the question again, adding, "You look like you have been born again." My response this time was profound. "Not in the biblical sense; however, I did release a lot of my past (dying) and was working on the new me (rebirth)." She smiled and said, "I thought so, it looks good on you."

IT IS OKAY TO FEEL ALL THE FEELS!

I was not raised in a home where we were allowed to show our feelings. A child was to be seen and not heard—do not speak unless spoken to. This meant that a lot of my childhood curiosity was not addressed in the healthiest ways. Food became my comfort, my drug of choice. It calmed the panic and made me feel safe. Eating my feelings became a habit that lasted into adulthood.

People may have different coping mechanisms, but they are simply a temporary avoidance. Some will use drugs or alcohol for that momentary euphoria, but no matter what the vice, when the comfort of the escape wears off, reality has twice the impact of the original feelings, combined with the guilt of the coping choice. For me, all those original feelings lurked within my body, and I stuffed them down with food for decades, until that day on the floor when the rage and pain had reached a climactic level and I had no control over it anymore. I had no choice but to surrender to it.

Through the course of my journey to find my real self, I learned that emotional weight is often carried as physical weight. I began working with a coach to identify and process feelings I had not allowed to surface, and as I did the weight began to come off. A truly good coach and mentor also has her own mentor. We are all constantly learning about ourselves and one another.

MARY-FRANCES BUCKLAND

About Mary-Frances Buckland: Mary-Frances is a Transformational coach, specializing in healing wounds from her clients' pasts to achieve a self-actualizing future. Her life lessons have not happened TO her, rather FOR her, allowing her to help clients from experience. She has allowed her past to refine her, opposed to define her. Mary-Frances focuses her energy not only on her healing and growth journey, but she is also helping others on their individual self-guided path as well.

Author's Website: *www.MaryFrancesBuckland.com*

Book Series Website: *www.TheBookOfHumanEmpowerment.com*

MEL REYES

MOVING FROM SELFLESS TO SELFISH

What kind of crap is Coach Mel going to throw at us now? The kind that helps you reshape what, where, and how to focus on what's important: taking back your life and driving towards your goals like your life depended on it! Because it may very well be the case...

And, so, it begins...

This isn't going to be a "kumbaya" moment here, folks. It's just a reality check on what makes us human and how to translate that into finding our purpose and changing our mindsets to elevate everything we do in our lives and careers.

What if I told you that "No one is coming to save you!" or that, "Your efforts to succeed have been a complete waste of time, money, and energy?" Kind of sucks, doesn't it? How many days have you felt like you've punched a clock, hauled ass around town, or constantly thought of what you need-ed to do for others? Then, you crashed face down on your pillow, found yourself drooling on the couch cushion, binge-watching Netflix, or ended up passing out on the train or in the car from exhaustion, only to wake up realizing you didn't do anything YOU wanted to do...

By then, of course, you load up a social app to cheer yourself up. You see another "incredible" accomplishment from your sibling, an elite party your co-worker was invited to, the latest "social influencer challenge" that you can't do, or your friend's "amazing" two-week European cruise. And you sit there saying, "When the hell did my life get so far off track?" "How do they have all this time and money?"

The first step is to fight the urge to drown by comparing yourself to others who have "succeeded" and adopt a mindset that you live in abundance, you can achieve your goals (nutty as they may sound to others), and that with enough focus, energy, drive, and the right tribe, you can do anything! Let's get started!

Learning from Your Past Mistakes

What's wrong with me? That was the resounding question I held in my head for decades. I spent the first half of my life trying to figure out what, apparently, many people already knew. I followed the advice, worked the hustle, and invested time in learning, but I couldn't quite find the golden ticket. I was blessed early on to have a few folks who created guardrails that put me in the right direction, but I was met with more uncertainty or confusion at every step.

Let's take a stroll down the wonderful yellow brick road that landed me where I am today. I spent my early years having a mindset of living in "necessity" drilled into my head. We lived on Government subsidies like Food Stamps, Section 8, Social Security, Medicare, and that scrumptious block of government cheese. By the age of thirteen, we had moved fourteen times, starting in Puerto Rico, then between The Bronx and Brooklyn several times, back to Puerto Rico, and then to a few places in Rockland County, New York.

If you followed the maze of moving, you would think we were on the lam or in the Federal Witnesses Protection program waiting to testify at a big RICO trial. Neither was the case.

At fourteen, I dropped out of wrestling and track to take on two jobs while going to school. Why would I do that, you ask? Because I was wearing hand-me-down polyester bellbottom pants in the mid-80s. There were no Benetton or Izod shirts, no Lee jeans, and, most definitely, no

Adidas shell-top sneakers for me. I made $3.15 an hour at my first job… My shopping was at the Army/Navy Store, where I had clothes on layaway, and I wore them with pride! That's also when I bought my own computer at seventeen… a life-changing decision!

At nineteen, I was left homeless at the end of my sophomore year in college, switched my major, which caused me to lose half my scholarship, and had to work full-time with no car, but I still managed to graduate on time. Later in life, just when I thought I was "thriving," the house of cards I tried to build came tumbling down.

At the ripe old age of forty-two, and the day after waiting a year to have my painfully annoying gallbladder removed, I was "let go" from my job —a job where I had endured a four-hour roundtrip commute to manage the team that built out one of the most transformative digital experiences. Why else was the house crumbling? Because we had just started personal bankruptcy proceedings…

Know When it's Time to Give Up

Not every situation has a solution, not everyone can be saved, and not everyone mirrors your drive. At the core of every relationship, every value that we hold is the need to better ourselves and to improve the lives of others. The instinct to be a friend, a sister, a brother, a mother, or a father is in-grained in us all, from BFFs in primary school to brothers and sisters in college fraternities or sororities and so on. We seek like-minded groups and push forward with shared values. This is where we need to focus our life and career aspirations and ask ourselves, "Am I honoring MY values in what I'm doing for others?" And if not, is it costing me my happiness?

To do this, I had to change my focus from constantly and only giving to others to investing as much time as possible in being selfish so that I could give from a safe place. That meant that I would have to sacrifice time with loved ones, hold others accountable to do more, get up earlier than others, and focus on the things that were important to me. I had to learn how to say "No" at work and at home.

I focused on health, reading, coaching, and mentoring because these defined who I am and helped showcase the level of empathy, passion, and commitment that I'm willing to exert. These character traits are the driving force behind the other pillars of my life, including being a friend, husband, father, leader, and executive coach. I chose to use my life experiences to help "Educate and Elevate" others so that it doesn't take them forty years to figure out what I had to struggle through to be successful.

Take Pride in Knowing You Can Do Anything

For me, coaching and mentoring became my way of giving back. Sharing my experiences comes easily to me; some say I share a bit too much, and some say it's not enough. Either way, I stay true to my ultimate goal, "How can I be of any help?" I came to realize that everyone needs help be-cause I was living proof, but only a few would admit it, and many never ask. So, I'll remind you here that it's okay to be open, vulnerable, and ask for help.

From a life and career standpoint, I look at every opportunity to help folks realize their true skills and align them with their values. I ask folks, how can you merge what you "love" to do with what you "have" to do? We all need a paycheck AND a purpose—if you can put the two together, that's great; if not, then you need an alternate means to fill the gaps. For example, when it comes to pay-ing bills, if you don't earn enough at your current job to live the life you want, then you either ad-just your lifestyle to meet your income, move to an affordable area, take on a second job, or skill up to get a better-paying job.

So, why aren't we doing this with what we feel passionate about? Do you know what you are passionate about? What bothers you so much that you lose sleep over it? Write those down, then assess your skills and experience, and start finding ways to start your quest. DO SOMETHING! Even if it's tiny steps, you'll be moving forward.

I focus on MVE, or the "Minimum Viable Effort" that you can enact to move the needle. If you want something, then do just one simple thing toward that goal—one thing, anything!

Day 1: Start with a Google/LinkedIn search.

Day 2: Select two experts to reach out to.

Day 3: Email or connect with them and ask them for advice. Break it down; you don't have to boil the ocean, just do one small task toward that ultimate goal, EACH DAY, EVERY DAY—NO EXCUSES!

Mel Robbins and many others are huge advocates of the Progress Principle, which calls for small, minimum-viable steps to achieve a larger goal.

"When you tap into the progress principle, one small move forward every day, you're 76% more likely to actually complete what you're working on."
~ Mel Robbins

What Are You Waiting For?

I'm sure you've heard and seen this theme everywhere, from the Couch to 5K app, to company slogans like "Just Do It!" So why haven't you engaged? This is the call to action; this is where you have to realize that NOTHING will change unless you change how you think about what you do. Start by doing one thing toward your goals and taking massive action. Once you find your pas-sion, the progress principle will avalanche into being more active, building a sense of accomplishment, and knowing that you are doing as much as you can to improve the lives around you—most importantly your own.

My college fraternity's motto is "Faciamus," which translates to "We Do." But that was translated to "Let's act!" or "Let's do!" All of these aligned perfectly with my values back then, and I now supercharge with quotes like, "Why not do it now?" "What are you waiting for?" #JFDI (via Heather Antoinetti), and the closing clincher, "How's that working out for you?"

So, I'll ask you to pause and ask yourself, "What one thing are you doing today that's different than what you did yesterday to improve your life?" Stop living in the world of "woulda, shoulda, coulda" and start now!

Now What, Coach Mel?

Let's translate that to your career, family, or relationships. Can you make a dramatic change by pursuing a career in giving? No? Then, can you help others at work, home, church, or temple? Seek out the ways you can give back by volunteering or mentoring. You'll see that you'll be learning, making new connections, and being seen as a well-rounded talent. Being a Go-Giver connects people naturally and, in return, helps you build a valuable network of colleagues. Colleagues who generate ideas, elevate your spirit, and become the positive tribe you need to make a difference.

Once you have a clear view of what you value and what you're willing to do and not do, then you can align those with the values of the companies you want to work for, where you pray, or who you live with. Does their mission and values match yours? Do they foster an environment of learning and advancement? What's important to you should align with where you live, pray, and work.

That's it, folks! This is the end. You made it. Now, go get involved, be authentic, be vulnerable, ask for help, and make sure to recruit others in your journey. You'll feel more fulfilled and benefit from a forward-thinking and positive mindset that targets your passions!

#NoExcuses #CoachMel

MEL REYES

About Mel Reyes: Coach Mel unifies his Puerto Rican roots, having been raised in NY, with his California lifestyle to deliver educational, incredibly entertaining, and motivating, empowering coaching sessions and speeches. His coaching journey spans nearly two decades, a testament to his deep understanding of the craft.

With over thirty years of deep understanding of the IT, Cybersecurity, and Startup landscapes, Coach Mel's training empowers executives to forge resilient teams. He's a mentor and coach who attracts, retains, and develops high-performing talent.

His wealth of experience equips him to guide individuals and teams to new heights and facilitate empowering training sessions.

He takes tremendous pride in volunteering to help nonprofit groups as an advisor, speaker, and mentor and creating his own non-profit to help "Educate and Elevate."

#NoExcuses #CoachMel

Author's Website: *www.ETC.limited*

Book Series Website: *www.TheBookOfHumanEmpowerment.com*

MELISA RUSCSAK
RISING PHOENIX: NAVIGATING LIFE'S STORMS

Navigating Life's Storms to Reclaim Power & Purpose

In a world where shadows whispered tales of dread, my story unfolded, a tapestry woven with threads of turmoil and resilience. Born into the tempest of domestic violence, my infancy was cradled not in the gentle arms of tranquility, but on the turbulent seas of chaos. This maelstrom, a relentless specter, haunted my formative years, casting long, dark shadows over my childhood.

My sanctuary, paradoxically, lay in the silent corners of my existence, where the echoes of discord couldn't reach. Yet, in the eerie calm, the feeling of being an outcast in my own life took root, sown by the hands of a grandmother who dispensed her affection as sparingly as the winter sun shares its warmth. Her love, elusive and conditional, became the chalice I yearned for but could never grasp.

It was in this labyrinth of emotional scarcity that I learned to navigate my world, a silent observer in a play where I never quite found my role. Thus began my journey through the shadowlands, where the light of hope flickered dimly in the distance, an elusive beacon beckoning me to the dawn of my transformation.

The twilight of my youth was a landscape overshadowed by the towering figures of my grandparents, where my grandmother's stern presence loomed large, shaping my world in shades of gray. Her love, if it could be called that, was a currency rare and hard-earned, dispensed in meager allotments that left my heart perpetually bankrupt. Amidst this emotional austerity, school offered no reprieve but a continuation of my solitude, a place where I donned the cloak of invisibility, my voice lost in the cacophony of the unseen and unheard.

By sixteen, the seductive lure of oblivion found me seeking solace in the transient embrace of alcohol, a false friend promising escape but delivering only deeper entanglement in my own web of despair. Life dangled the carrots of escape before me—scholarships to prestigious culinary institutes—yet, ensnared in the thicket of familial obligation and fear, I found myself relinquishing these golden tickets, one by one. It was a surrender not to fate, but to the insidious belief that to rise above one's allotted station was to betray one's roots, a notion as ingrained in my psyche as the DNA that dictated the color of my eyes.

This chapter of my life painted a stark contrast between potential and inhibition, with every hint of opportunity overshadowed by self-doubt and familial loyalty. Choosing to relinquish my scholarships wasn't merely a turning point; it was a retreat into the very shadows I yearned to escape. My life became a delicate dance with fate, each advance met with a retreat, creating a rhythm of struggle that left me both wounded and resilient, poised on the edge of a new beginning.

During those shadowed times, a pivotal event shone brightly: the birth of my daughter. She emerged as a beacon, slicing through the gloom that shrouded my existence. Motherhood propelled me onto an unexpected path, steering me through life's tumultuous waters to shores brimming with both trials and marvels. Her entry into my life infused it with profound joy, a sensation later contrasted by the complexities of a deteriorating marriage with a man not related to her, a relationship marred by previous traumas and ongoing strife.

This era unfolded as a vivid tapestry of contrast, with the vibrancy of new life standing stark against the backdrop of a disintegrating partnership. As time progressed, my once-reliable body became a battleground. At only twenty-eight, the confusion and betrayal I felt as my health spiraled out of control were profound. Strokes ambushed me like nocturnal thieves, ruthlessly robbing me of my vitality and plunging me into a whirlpool of medical turmoil. The familiar landscapes of my life were suddenly alien, reshaped by unseen forces into a world I barely recognized.

As I ventured through this altered existence, each turn revealed new absurdities, transforming the strokes from mere medical events into catalysts for profound change. They heralded a journey of unexpected transformation, awakening a dormant writer within, her voice a whisper in the ashes, waiting for adversity's spark to ignite.

The aftermath of the strokes forged my spirit in adversity's flames. Navigating the surreal landscape of foreign accent syndrome, my existence seemed authored by whimsy, each chapter more unexpected than the last. Communicating in an unfamiliar voice, I traversed a reality both known and peculiar. This alteration in speech mirrored a deeper transformation, signaling that profound change often trails destruction.

Recovery's path was laden with empowerment and challenges, encapsulating the struggle of losing and reclaiming my identity. The endeavor to regain my mobility and speech was a relentless contest with my past, each victory defying the immense odds against me. Life turned into an absurd theater, with my accented speech providing both humor and stark reflection on my predicament.

Within the turmoil of recovery, a robust will emerged. Amidst this tumult, I discovered a latent strength, unearthing a voice long muted by self-doubt. This voice, once suppressed, now echoed with a newfound assurance and intent. My journey became a delicate balance of vulnerability and courage, intertwining moments of despair with revelations of strength.

Healing transformed into an epic journey where humor illuminated the darkest paths, softening the intensity of my battles. Every hesitant step and every oddly pronounced word bore witness to a resilient spirit, a testament to a woman reborn through her trials, not merely enduring them but evolving through them.

Emboldened by this mentorship, I ventured into the world of public speaking and broadcasting, stepping into the light, both literally and metaphorically. The transition from the written word to the spoken one was daunting yet exhilarating, each broadcast a leap of faith, each speech a declaration of my newfound identity. This evolution was not merely about finding my voice but about crafting a message, a narrative imbued with the lessons of my past and the aspirations of my future.

In the fertile ground of this newfound confidence, I sowed the seeds of a new venture, launching a company that was a manifestation of my journey from darkness to light. This business was not just a commercial endeavor but a symbol of renewal and growth, a testament to the power of transformation. As I reflect on the path trodden, from the depths of despair to the pinnacle of self-actualization, the journey resonates with a profound truth: that within the crucible of adversity lies the potential for extraordinary growth and rebirth.

In the crucible of life's harshest trials, I emerged not broken but reborn, a phoenix ascending from despair to triumph. This odyssey of resilience and unexpected fate underscores my journey to reclaim power and purpose, a testament to the indomitable spirit within us all, finding light in the darkest corners.

Strengthened by mentorship, I navigated the realms of public speaking and broadcasting, emerging into a newfound luminescence. Transitioning from pen to podium, I encountered a mix of trepidation and thrill, with each broadcast marking a step towards self-revelation, each address crafting the contours of my emerging persona. This metamorphosis transcended mere vocal expression, molding a narrative enriched by past experiences and forward-looking ambitions.

On this foundation of regained confidence, I cultivated a new enterprise, embodying the transformation from shadowed valleys to sunlit peaks. This venture was more than a business; it was an emblem of rejuvenation and progress, reflecting the profound capacity for change. Contemplating my journey from the abyss of despair to the zenith of self-realization, I recognized a deeper verity: adversity's forge is potent, capable of inspiring remarkable evolution and renewal.

Through life's sternest tests, I was not shattered but transformed, rising like a phoenix from the ashes of desolation to the heights of victory. This saga of resilience and serendipity illuminates my quest for empowerment and significance, affirming the relentless power of the human spirit to uncover radiance amidst the gloom, guiding us all towards the dawn of our own renewal.

MELISA RUSCSAK

About Melisa Ruscsak: M.L. Ruscsak, a survivor turned trailblazer, embodies the essence of transformation. From navigating personal cataclysms to becoming a celebrated author and CEO, her journey is a riveting tale of resilience and rebirth. M.L.'s narrative isn't just her own but a beacon for anyone seeking to transcend adversity. Her books are not merely pages but lifelines of hope and empowerment.

As the founder of Trient Press, she champions voices that echo her indomitable spirit, illuminating paths for others in their darkest hours. Engage with M.L.'s inspiring journey and discover how you, too, can rise from the ashes of hardship to claim your purpose and power. Continue the conversation and explore the depths of M.L.'s transformative odyssey at *www.MLRuscsak.com*, where every story is a step towards collective empowerment and individual triumph.

Author's Website: *www.MLRuscsak.com*

Book Series Website: *www.TheBookOfHumanEmpowerment.com*

MICHAEL MASTROMATTEO
FINDING EMPOWERMENT THROUGH ADVERSE TIMES

In finding empowerment, I first needed to find my purpose. In my youth, while I was discovering what values meant most to me, I realized I wanted happiness to be my main goal in life. Maybe a bit naive and Polyanna-ish, but it made sense to me. What's better than being happy, optimistic, and content in everything you do!?

To achieve my goal of happiness and still move towards personal growth and success, I focused on doing what brought me joy in life while making sure every step in life was a step higher than the last. This philosophy has worked well for me most of my life.

I loved playing and performing music. It not only made me happy, but I could see how it brought joy to others as well. I found my purpose.

I made a career out of playing piano. First, while in college performing in restaurants during the week and in bands on weekends, I didn't make a lot of money—but I was making money and doing what I loved. An added bonus was that performing in fancy restaurants did offer me a better cuisine than eating Top Ramen like many of my classmates! After college, I went on to perform on cruise ships, hotels, and pubs up in Europe and Scandinavia.

When I returned home, there was a multi-venue entertainment complex opening up in Sacramento. One of the venues was a "Dueling Piano

Bar," where I auditioned and got the gig! As bars open and close for various reasons, the gig ended. There was still plenty of work as many dueling piano bars were opening up all over the country. This afforded me the opportunity to move round and experience life many places.

While performing in Orlando, I met a stunningly beautiful girl. We hit it off right away. Every moment with her was fun! We fell in love and started a family. To do this right, we needed to become more stable and make more money. I saw how many of these dueling piano bars were making substantial profits. In staying with my principle of making each step in life better than the last, we found some investors and opened our own Dueling Piano Bar.

I had some experience in this. I grew up in the restaurant business as my family had a restaurant, ice cream parlor and delicatessen. (I didn't realize it while I was growing up, but my father being a business owner in our family-run business empowered me with the mindset to be an entrepreneur!)

We had some success but, as I mentioned earlier, many bars close for various reasons and, unfortunately, ours didn't make it. Here I was, back on the circuit, working for someone else—now with a wife, a new baby, and another on the way.

This was a temporary setback. I still had the entrepreneur mindset! I also had a greater purpose, to provide for and to keep my new family happy.

Another opportunity I discovered was that many of these dueling piano bars, as a side hustle, were also sending teams out to perform dueling piano shows for corporate events, weddings, fundraisers etc.. We decided to create a business solely focusing on this aspect of the business.

This was actually a much safer business plan, with none of the hassles and expenses of running a bar and restaurant. My wife did the marketing, and I handled all the logistics of producing the shows. We also consulted restaurants, night clubs, casinos etc., who wanted the concept for their venues. We would set them up with the pianos, sound system, and performers and get commissions for these ongoing performances.

This worked well for our young family, also. We were making really good money for the first time in our lives! We decided to homeschool our girls, giving us the opportunity to stay together all the time. We could afford to buy a beautiful house, and we purchased a RV so when we got shows or were setting shows up in venues for ongoing performances, we could stay together. Though this lifestyle was a bit unconventional, as compared to parents with a 9-5 job and the kids stuck in school five days a week, it offered us a lot of freedom to travel and we shared many amazing adventures together. Life was great!

The Trifecta of Tragedy

1. Marriages all have their ups and downs. The stress of raising a family and running a business started taking a toll on us. I thought this was just a difficult a phase in life we had to work through until the girls grew up and we could send them off to college. I really don't want to go into the details about this, but the arguing started. The fighting got worse and she started using the girls as her little pony soldiers to gang up on me and justify her issues!

Things quickly escalated from really bad to unbearable. They finally threw me out of the house. I thought we needed a cooling off period. I didn't think at the time that it would be permanently.

I moved into my mom and dad's house with only the shirt on my back and a van full of music gear so I could continue to work.

2. Four months after I moved into my parents' house, my father passed away. I was completely crushed as I had lost my family and now I'd lost my dad. I looked at the fact that I was able to spend the last four months of my dad's life as a blessing.

3. Four months after my father passed, Covid hit! Gavin Newsome was on the news saying, "We're in a complete shutdown; all events and gatherings need to be canceled!" We're in the event industry. It completely shut down our business!

In a matter of eight months, I went from having a beautiful family, a successful business, and a wonderful life to suddenly being locked down, isolated, alienated from my children, grieving over the loss of my father, and caring for my mother. It was just too much to process. We were living the "American Dream!" What just happened?

One of these traumatic events is enough to overwhelm someone, but all three in such a short time! The shock of this all sent me into a world of numbness. How was I to cope? I lost my purpose. I had to create a whole new mindset to survive.

My family was the number one priority in my life. It inspired me to want to be the best version of myself, bringing purpose, love, personal growth, and so much more. My father taught me that, in order to take best care of your family, you have to have your priorities in order.

First God, then self, then family. God—to give you spiritual wisdom and strength. Self—because if you don't take care of yourself first, you're no good to anybody else. Family—your legacy, purpose for living, to create, elevate, and empower amazing people; to guide them so they make the world an amazing place for themselves and for all of us to share.

Pulling Yourself Out of the Abyss of Numbness & Developing Empowerment through Difficult Times

Experiencing the loss of a parent, divorce, the shutdown of a business, and parental alienation are all significant life challenges that deeply impacted my sense of empowerment and well-being. Parental alienation is what hurt the most. You can always make more money. You can grieve and find a sense of closure after the loss of a parent. The same is true with divorce. The pain of parental alienation is comparable to the death of a child with absolutely no closure unless you can somehow reconnect.

Here are some strategies that I discovered to help me regain empowerment through difficult times.

1. Seek Support: You can't do this on your own. I'm fortunate enough to have a wonderful family and group of friends to talk to. Then I found a good counselor to try to help me make sense of this all. I joined a parental alienation support group. Talking with others going through a similar situation not only helped me not feel alone but helped change my mind set through education. I met Erik Swanson, who inspired me to join his mastermind group. Surrounding yourself with a group of amazing people, being a part of a diverse group where everyone involved is there to mastermind, support each other and lift each other up is nothing more than incredible! As they say, "You are who you surround yourself with."

2. Self-Care: I learned I needed to take care of myself physically, mentally, and emotionally, making sure I was getting enough rest, eating healthily, and engaging in activities that bring me joy and relaxation. Self-care practices like meditation, exercise, or hobbies helped reduce stress and increase feelings of empowerment.

3. Focus on What You Can Control: It's natural to feel overwhelmed when facing multiple challenges, so I worked in finding focus on the things I could control rather than dwelling on what I couldn't.

4. **Educate Yourself:** I was dealing with parental alienation and divorce. Educating myself in parental alienation helped me not only me make some kind of sense of why my children, where once we were very close, they no longer wanted me to be a part of their life, but it also gave me tools on how to cope and hopefully reconnect someday.

In divorce, educate yourself about your legal rights and options. Boy—I made a lot of mistakes here! Family court is difficult. Make sure you get the right lawyer! There are some unscrupulous lawyers out there that take advantage of families in crisis for profit! Understanding the legal process and seeking guidance from professionals can help navigate these challenging situations more effectively.

5. Practice Forgiveness: Forgiveness doesn't mean condoning the actions of others, but it can release you from the emotional burden of anger and resentment. Forgiving myself and others involved became a powerful step towards healing and reclaiming my sense of empowerment.

6. Focus on Personal Growth: I used this period of adversity as an opportunity for personal growth and self-discovery. I reflected on my values, strengths, and aspirations, and reconsidered how I needed to reinvent myself to cultivate resilience and thrive in the face of adversity.

7. Stay Connected to Your Parent's Memory: While my father is longer be physically present, I keep his memory alive by cherishing the moments we shared and honoring his legacy. I do this by finding meaningful ways to commemorate him, whether through rituals, keepsakes, or sharing stories with loved ones.

8. Seek Meaning & Purpose: I found meaning and purpose in experiences by channeling my energy into activities or causes that align with my values and passions.

Things are getting better for me. The wounds have healed but the scars remain. After five years, I'm reconnecting with one of my daughters and the business is getting back on track.

I realize I never lost my core purpose. It is to love my children and provide even while being shut out of their lives. My new mind set it to be unstoppable.

I hope some of the things I've learned and shared in this chapter can help some of the readers who may have experienced similar traumatic experiences heal as well.

Don't dwell in the darkness. Become a lighthouse and SHINE!

MICHAEL MASTROMATTEO

About Michael Mastromatteo: Michael Mastromatteo is a multifaceted individual whose passions and talents span a wide range of fields. As a father, he brings the same dedication and creativity to his family as he does to his professional endeavors. A skilled pianist and composer, Michael's love for music is evident in his work as a producer and entrepreneur. He is the CEO of 2 Grand Entertainment, a company that reflects his commitment to excellence in the entertainment industry.

Beyond his work in music, Michael is also an accomplished author and educator, sharing his knowledge and experience with others to inspire and empower them. His work is characterized by a blend of artistry and business acumen, making him a respected figure in both the creative and entrepreneurial communities. Discover more about his journey and projects at *www.2GrandEntertainment.com*.

Author's Website: *www.2GrandEntertainment.com*

Book Series Website: *www.TheBookOfHumanEmpowerment.com*

MICHELLE MARIE SHOCKLEY

THE USELESSNESS OF AN ARROGANT MINDSET

What does arrogance have to do with mindset? Unfortunately, there are many types of destructive or even self-destructive mindsets; arrogance is one of them. Often in my life I was arrogant—I mean horribly arrogant.

Can you imagine having this mindset, even if unconsciously? Can you imagine how painful this could be for the individual at the receiving end of this mentality? We can surely cite numerous examples of individuals who obviously look down on other human beings; however, have we ever considered that there may be a deeper, existential meaning?

Merriam-Webster defines arrogance as *an attitude of superiority that shows itself in an overbearing manner or in presumptuous claims or assumptions*. My definition includes that, but also an act of not sharing love with other individuals because one deems them as being unequal. In self-reflection, I would say that I was exceedingly judgmental. Today, I am quite ashamed of this mindset I had. Reaching the point of reflection and correction is an arduous journey, but once the process was completed, I was more at peace with my fellow man.

Let us look at arrogance within the framework of Christianity. I have been a Christian since I was nine years old. Have I always behaved in a Christian-like manner? No. I am a sinner in need of a Savior. Would I like to behave as a Christian should behave? Yes. Still, wanting and doing are two different approaches to life. We all know individuals who want to succeed; we also know outstanding examples of people who do succeed.

Arrogance is unfortunately the chosen primrose path I followed while *"wanting"* to behave as a Christian should. My *"My-sin-is-not-as-large-as-his-sin"* arrogant mindset said everything! I judged people by how they acted, by what they wore, if they drank or seemed to party too much.

In my own family, I have been arrogant towards a particular relative who had substance abuse issues, mental issues, and, years ago, even a criminal record. She only completed her GED and has had no vocational training. I lived my life on the straight-and-narrow, graduating as Salutatorian in high school and then completing my bachelor's degree at Indiana University, followed by my German accounting certificate in Wiesbaden, Germany.

Not having toyed with drugs and alcohol, while doing well in high school and college must be enough of a reason to prove that I am better than she is. Right? I was a better Christian, was I not? Sadly, this type of "Christian" is why people turn their back on the church. As an example, in John 8:7 (KJV) Jesus said: *"...He that is without sin among you, let him first cast a stone at her."*

My sins were indeed greater than her sins because I was in a position to lift her up and I did not. Instead, I looked down upon her and her lifestyle. I even took this further and "proved" to others that I was better than she was. I was dramatic, even sensationalistic, concerning her many mistakes. My friends would always ask about the newest updates of this relative and I would encourage their curiosity them information. How hideous was this behavior!

What this relative needed was love and compassion. In Philippians 2:3 (NIV) Paul wrote: *"Do nothing out of selfish ambition or vain conceit. Rather, in humility value others above yourselves."* Withholding much needed love from this relative was not only detrimental to her, but also to me. I viewed our tense relationship as "duty" because we were related, but no more than that. Acting this way and perpetuating a useless, arrogant mindset, caused me to miss the chance to show her compassion; I repeated this sin against others and my relative continually and had, for years, no metanoia.

Once, I heard a story about a man who had died, went to Heaven, and returned to his body. He said one of the questions he was asked in Heaven with regards to his worthiness to enter Heaven was: *"How have you expanded your capacity to love?"* With the self-destructing characteristic of arrogance, I believe I reduced my capacity to love instead of expanding it.

This gentlemen went on to say, "Hell is looking back at your life and seeing all of the times you withheld love from other people." Have you ever considered that arrogance could be standing in your way of a higher fulfillment? At some point in time, I realized, I needed to make a change.

How did I deal with this attitude? First, to correct an inept mindset, I had to become aware of it. I believe, as children, we compared ourselves with other individuals, especially in America where we were in constant competition with our classmates—or at least it was like that in the 1970s and 1980s. There is, of course, healthy competition; however, please consider that the champion team from today may be the losing team tomorrow.

Life is an intricate weaving of individual moments; all situations or stages in life are temporary. Comparison leads to jealousy and envy while setting into motion a downward spiral. I think the metanoia came once I began experiencing arrogant behavior towards me in Germany. On the receiving end of the pain, I realized how I was judging others.

Secondly, I had to be willing to correct my unacceptable mindset. Arrogance is unacceptable, not only to societal norms, but also from a Christian perspective. Did living with an "arrogant chip on my shoulder" help anyone? No, it did not. It hurt me and all the individuals with whom I denied sharing God's divine Love. Being willing to change was the beginning of the unfettering of the bonds to arrogance. Of course, I was willing to make the change, but could I follow through with the plan—or would the bonds clasp tighter around me?

The third step was to make the conscious decision to actively change my negative mindset. To go back to the thesis that one of our purposes on this Earth is *"to expand our capacity to love,"* would I be able to look at my fellow man without being judgmental? How often in my life had I placed labels on people or felt that I was superior to them?

While my children were young, many mothers made comparisons as to how smart or how athletic their children were. I eagerly joined this ridiculous comparison game and was convinced that my children were smarter, cuter, more athletic, more Christian, etc., than their classmates were. How pride came before my fall!

Fourthly, I had to implement the change process steps. I began showing compassion when I saw someone who was less fortunate than myself. Each time the thought came, "Better him than me," I replaced the idea with the thought, "That is a child of the Living God." When a thought came, "He is driving a junker of a car," I replaced it with, "He is doing as well as he can."

I needed to practice humility. From this insight, I began to treat every person I met with respect—at least to the best of my ability at that moment in my development. While working in the HR and Payroll department at a production facility, I decided to treat every employee who walked into my office with even greater respect and appreciation than was expected! It did not matter if he worked as the green keeper, the general manager, the production worker, or the union president, each person was treated as if he or she were the most valuable employee in the company.

This made a difference in their life and in my life. In the work life of several employees, I was able to help them out of embarrassing financial situations. In my life, I felt better that I was somehow being a positive influence instead of a difficult co-worker.

Retrospectively, being arrogant had a deeper religious meaning for me than I first realized. Once I delved into the flaws of being arrogant and judgmental, I had the epiphany on how I would like to be treated: kind-heartedly with respect and appreciation.

One of my personal sayings is: "Be generous in order to receive generosity." This is based on The Golden Rule from the Bible: "Therefore all things whatsoever ye would that men should do unto you, do ye even so to them...." Matthew 7:12. Only by respecting and appreciating other people could I hope to receive respect and appreciation. This would be my chance to expand my capacity to love and to defeat the uselessness of an arrogant mindset.

MICHELLE MARIE SHOCKLEY

About Michelle Marie Shockley: Born in rural Tennessee, Michelle lived in Mississippi and Michigan before her mother and step-father settled down in Southern Indiana. She lived there until the age of twenty-four when she moved to Germany in 1994 to marry her college sweetheart. From the marriage, Michelle has two children: Alexa, who lives in America, and Carsten, who lives in Germany.

After twenty-two years of marriage, Michelle separated from her German husband and decided to remain in Germany where she today has her own business as an interim manager, trainer, and public speaker. Michelle has been training sport clubs, companies, and executives in Martial Arts, Aerobics, English and Human Resources topics. She enjoys traveling and reading.

Michelle has a bachelor's degree from Indiana University in German language (B.A.) and a vocational certification as "Steuerfachgehifin" (tax accountant) in Germany.

Author's Website: *www.MichelleMarie.world*

Book Series Website: *www.TheBookOfHumanEmpowerment.com*

NANCY DEBRA BARROWS
FROM PAIN TO PURPOSE

. . . .

How often do you find yourself staring at the clock, wondering where the day has gone, or reaching mid-afternoon only to realize you haven't eaten? If you can relate, you're not alone. Our daily demands keep increasing, and amidst the hustle of modern life, it's easy to lose sight of what truly matters. We chase success, wealth, and recognition, yet often feel frustrated, unfulfilled, burnt out, and disconnected.

I know this scenario intimately because I lived it. Exhaustion that sleep couldn't fix became my norm. My days were packed, leaving no energy for socializing. I kept pushing myself, thinking, "If I can just get past this…" But the more I pushed, the deeper I sank. Eventually, my body and mind demanded I stop. I couldn't continue.

Our resources are limited, both internally and externally. If we don't use them wisely and intentionally, we lose balance and all sense of purpose, contentment, and joy. We live in a culture that celebrates the "work more, do more" mentality. We're lured into believing burning the candle at both ends is admirable. But living happy, healthy lives involves thinking, "What can I do less of? What can I say no to? Is this adding to or detracting from my happiness?"

This shift in mindset is the first step toward true transformation.

A deeper, more meaningful path lies ahead—one guided by purpose, intention, and mindset. Embracing purpose and understanding the interconnectedness of mindset transforms our lives, leading to greater fulfillment, connection, and joy.

A growth mindset allows you to see challenges as opportunities for growth and views failure as a steppingstone to success. Shifting to this mindset transformed my life, helping me see every setback as a lesson and every challenge as a chance to grow stronger.

Imagine you're an adult who never learned to tie your shoes properly. You've always relied on slip-on shoes or someone else to tie them for you. One day, you decide it's time to master this basic skill.

At first, you struggle. The loops and knots are confusing, and your shoes keep coming undone. Instead of giving up, you keep learning. You watch videos, read articles, and practice different techniques. Eventually, you discover a new method—the "Ian Knot"—that is faster and more secure. Over time, it becomes automatic.

You could have given up, but your determination led you to success. Your mindset was open to learning, embracing mistakes as part of the process.

In essence, your mindset shapes how you perceive, pursue, and realize your purpose in life. A growth mindset empowers you to approach your journey with resilience, adaptability, and a sense of possibility, enabling you to realize your full potential and make a meaningful impact in the world.

At a young age, I experienced sexual abuse—a traumatic event that left deep scars. For years, I wore a mask, hiding my true self and burying the pain. The weight of the trauma was suffocating, and I felt lost, ashamed, and disconnected from my own world. I carried a heavy burden, pretending to be okay while my inner world was in turmoil.

However, there came a pivotal moment when I decided I would not give my abuser one more second of my life. He had already taken too much. Surviving each day was not enough. I needed to change my mindset to reclaim my life and find a deeper sense of purpose. Through hard work, therapy, support, and self-reflection, I began to shift my mindset and perspective. I learned how to thrive and how to help others do the same.

Your experience doesn't need to be the same as mine. Living life and being human can leave us in a place of depletion and despair. I chose to embrace gratitude—not for the abuse itself, but for the strength I found within to overcome it. This shift allowed me to see my experiences as the foundation of who I am and what I'm meant to do. The work brought me to a place where I finally met the real Nancy Debra Barrows, unmasked and unburdened.

I stopped trying to outrun my story and invited it to walk alongside me, harnessing the lessons learned to grow as a person and eventually start my business, "The Chick With The Toolbelt," where I partner with clients to transform "surviving into thriving." By sharing my story and encouraging others to remove their masks, I discovered my true purpose: to guide others towards self-empowerment—mindset and purpose.

At the heart of living with purpose lies the question: Why? Why do we do what we do? What drives us, inspires us, and gives our lives meaning? Discovering your why is a deeply personal journey that requires commitment, self-reflection, introspection, and soul-searching. Explore your passions, values, and aspirations. What makes your heart sing? What brings you a sense of fulfillment and joy? Your 'why' is the compass that guides your actions and decisions, leading you towards a life of purpose and significance.

Mindset shapes our thoughts, actions, and ultimately, our destiny. Gratitude, in particular, has numerous psychological, emotional, and physical benefits, including improved mental health, better relationships, and increased resilience. Gratitude is more than just saying "thank you." It's a deeper appreciation for the moments, people, and experiences that bring value and joy to our lives. When we practice gratitude, we acknowledge the goodness in our lives and the sources of that goodness.

Incorporating gratitude into your daily life can transform your mindset and enhance your overall well-being. Here are some practical activities to help you cultivate mindful gratitude:

- **Gratitude Journal:** Each day, write down three things you are grateful for. This practice helps shift your focus from what's wrong to what's right.

- **Gratitude Letter:** Write a letter to someone who has positively impacted your life. Expressing gratitude lifts your spirits and strengthens your connections with others.

- **Mindful Appreciation:** Spend a few minutes each day observing your surroundings and appreciating the beauty in everyday moments.

- **Gratitude Jar:** Keep a jar and write down something good that happened each day. Over time, you'll accumulate a collection of positive moments to look back on.

- **Gratitude Meditation:** Spend a few minutes focusing on things you are grateful for.

Living with purpose and cultivating a positive mindset doesn't exempt you from challenges or setbacks—it arms you with tools and perspective to navigate adversity with resilience and mindfulness. Embrace the power of mindfulness to anchor yourself amidst life's storms and cultivate a sense of calm and clarity.

Whether it's sharing a smile with a stranger, lending a helping hand, or savoring nature's beauty, every action holds the potential for purpose and meaning. Savor the simple joys of life, and cultivate gratitude for the small blessings, knowing they are the building blocks of a purposeful existence.

Practicing gratitude during difficult times can help you find silver linings and maintain a positive outlook. Here's how to embrace gratitude in the face of adversity:

- **Focus on Growth:** Reflect on how adversity has helped you grow or develop new strengths.

- **Appreciate Support Systems:** Recognize the people who have supported you during hard times.

- **Find Lessons in Challenges:** Look for the lessons or opportunities hidden within difficult experiences.

- **Practice Self-Compassion:** Be grateful for your own efforts and progress, no matter how small.

In my own journey, gratitude played a crucial role in my healing process. Initially, it was challenging to find anything to be grateful for amidst the pain of my past. However, as I began to practice gratitude regularly, I noticed subtle shifts in my mindset. Gratitude helped me reframe my past. Instead of viewing my experiences solely as sources of pain, I began to see them as catalysts for growth and transformation.

Embracing purpose and mindset is a transformative journey that requires courage, commitment, and resilience. By uncovering your why, aligning your actions with your intentions, and cultivating a gratitude mindset, you can create a life filled with purpose and fulfillment.

Remember, your experiences become the foundation for helping others on their journey. Your story is powerful and inspiring—a beacon of hope and inspiration. Embrace the journey of self-discovery, knowing that every step forward brings you closer to a life of greater meaning and joy.

With purpose and mindset as your guides, the possibilities are endless. Here's to a life filled with purpose, passion, and boundless potential. The world is waiting for your unique gifts and contributions. Are you ready to embrace the adventure?

NANCY DEBRA BARROWS

About Nancy Debra Barrows: Nancy Debra Barrows, renowned as the Queen of Engagement, is an accomplished keynote speaker and her achievements span numerous accolades, including five-time recognition as a LinkedIn Top Voice in thought leadership, public speaking, communication, personal coaching, and personal branding.

Being named one of the Top 50 Most Impactful People on LinkedIn, a Top 250 Rising Stars and Influencers to Watch on LinkedIn and as one of the platform's 50 Most Inspiring Connections out of 1 billion users. Nancy is a seven-time #1 international bestselling author. Additionally, Nancy serves as the COO & Chief Engagement Officer at Voice Your Vibe and is the producer and co-host of Voice Your Vibe Live, featuring award-winning shows broadcast in over 120 countries, winning accolades such as the Best Live Festive Show at the IBMTV Awards.

Through her work on Voice Your Vibe's groundbreaking masterminds and heart-centered leadership programs, Nancy has helped countless C-Suite Executives and Entrepreneurs globally to shift their mindset to see they have a powerful voice, get clear on their vision, show-up and embrace their role as an elite thought leader!

As the Chief Excitement Officer/Founder of The Chick With The Toolbelt and creator of the #RadiatingReal movement, she champions the ethos of authenticity, encouraging individuals to embrace their true selves, unmasked, and bask in the unconditional love and acceptance they deserve. She is a dedicated Cat Momma, Native New York'er, lover of carrot cake and does not accept apologies for LIVING life and being human.

Author's Website: *www.VoiceYourVibe.com*

Book Series Website: *www.TheBookOfHumanEmpowerment.com*

NEETU PRABHU

MONEY, PURPOSE, & MINDSET

Have you ever dreamt of a world where your heart is always full, your days are brimming with life, and your bank account is overflowing with money? A world where you carry love in your heart, your health is at its peak, and wealth simply overflows? Abundance fills every moment of your being, all day, every day. Is this your existential truth, or is this still a long-lost yearning desire?

In over a decade of my experience in the financial industry, I've seen the complete spectrum: those scrambling for money and those with multimillions who are yet unhappy, unfulfilled, and unsettled. The real cause of suffering is unfulfilled desires and ignorance of your true nature. You can and must resolve any and all of these issues and discover your true joy. It is absolutely your birthright and the purpose of your life to do so!

Understanding Purpose

Your purpose is not a distant echo waiting to be discovered; it's a song that's been playing in your heart since the beginning, waiting for you to tune in and listen. So quiet down, will you? Hush and listen. Find the courage to be uniquely you. Start by asking yourself what brings you joy, what activities make time stand still, and what you would do even if you weren't paid for it. But finding your purpose isn't just about recognizing what you love—it also involves understanding how it can serve others.

Long ago, I acted as though angels were supposed to sing or God was supposed to scream through a loudspeaker, telling me what I was supposed to do. This made making decisions feel very scary. What if I make a huge mistake? What if everyone laughs at me? What if I fail? I became aware of my thoughts, shifted my mindset, rearranged how I looked at it, and said, "It's okay, honey, it's safe to make mistakes. It's safe to live. It's safe to simply be me."

The pressure was largely me pushing myself. I would find myself in flight, fright, or freeze mode. I'd self-sabotage and kill my own dreams. How many of your dreams and desires are stillborn? What is still tugging at your heart? Your desires that rise from you are full of promise and potential, and then—you kill them!

The pressure is always simply our own doubt and our fear holding us back and making us feel frozen and paralyzed by decisions. When we believe that one wrong decision could cause some sort of massive chaos, it makes it impossible to follow our hearts and to do what we truly want. So, remember—it's your purpose; it's your calling. Others may or may not understand it. They don't need to. Only YOU need to get it, to begin with.

And those who believe in you will join forces with you. You have the power within. You create the snowball, the avalanche, the massive fire, and the whole world will come to watch and celebrate you. Will there be haters? Maybe. Just remember to keep your heart soft and your skin thick. Remember your why—the one that makes you cry—and allow yourself to shine as YOU.

Major Spoiler Alert: Don't... Chase... Money!

That's you stemming from lack, and that is more of what will be placed in front of you. You may or may not have come from wealth. Yet, when you tune in, tap into, and turn it on, wealth will come through you and to you. The outside world is a mere reflection of your own inner stories about yourself. What is the story you are telling?

For many, the story of money is tinged with unease—an inherited discomfort, a whispered legacy of scarcity that echoes through our choices and fears. I know this path well, for it was once my own. From a modest upbringing where each penny was a prisoner of necessity, I journeyed through shadows of doubt and mountains of hope to a place of understanding.

We all carry old tales about money—stories handed down through generations, often laced with caution and restraint. These narratives can confine us, keep us from the abundance that is our birthright. It's time to unravel our old narratives that we keep repeating on a loop. It is time to ask ourselves: Are these stories serving us, or are they keeping us from realizing our true potential? This questioning is the first step toward liberation from financial fears and limiting beliefs.

Shifting Your Mindset

- **Transformation Begins with the Core Belief:** You are Enough. This mindset is crucial as it underpins every step towards financial and personal empowerment. It shapes how you perceive challenges and opportunities alike.

- **Embrace Change with Self-Love:** Personal development is not about fixing what's broken but enhancing your life from a place of completeness. Acknowledging that you are enough allows you to approach changes with confidence and creativity.

- **Transform Fear into Action:** Common fears, such as inadequacy or financial insecurity, often obstruct our paths. Addressing these fears directly reduces their influence, enabling a proactive approach to life's challenges. It is about time we recognize and shake off the old tales of financial constraint that have haunted our lives. We recognize the patterns we've inherited—the notions that money is scarce, that bills are a burden, and that financial management is inherently stressful. These are not absolute truths; they are merely stories that can be rewritten.

- **Recognize Your Power:** Your intrinsic power is independent of external circumstances. It's a reservoir of potential, capable of influencing both your life and those around you. Embrace this power, especially during challenging times, to maintain momentum towards your goals. Start by dismantling all limiting beliefs. Scrutinize the stories you've told yourself about money. It's time to rewrite these narratives and adopt a new mindset where money is seen as a tool for creating abundance, not a source of endless worry. Now, while all this is not going to happen overnight, this is me helping you see—this is possible. This is the way it's meant to be; you are inherently free.

- **Live in Seasons:** Life moves through cycles, and recognizing these can enhance your adaptability and resilience. Each season brings its own set of challenges and opportunities—navigating these wisely aligns your actions with both external circumstances and internal growth. Release the fight with your current circumstances. That's only creating more resistance. Start with acceptance. Forgive and let go of whatever is not serving your greater good. Focus all your attention and energy on creating new circumstances that will make the old ones obsolete.

- **Allow Your Desires to Evolve:** As you grow, so do your desires. Allow yourself to grow. You will find your flow.

The Power of Transformation

Each step on this path is a step toward a greater self—a self that understands the profound connections between our financial health and our emotional and spiritual well-being. As we change our beliefs about money, we also change our lives, opening doors to new possibilities and new joys.

Redefining Wealth

True wealth is about more than numbers in a bank account; it's about the richness of our lives and the impact we have on others.

Refine your purpose. Reset your mindset.

Rest in your true self. Remember your desires.

Rekindle your fire. Restart your life.

A Call to Your Heart

As these words echo in your mind, let them resonate deeply within your spirit. This is more than an invitation; it's a beckoning to journey into the very core of your being. What stories have you woven about wealth and your worth? Dare to unravel them, thread by thread. What if rewriting these tales is your gateway to not only material abundance but a profound, soulful awakening?

Reflect on this: your financial story is a mirror of your deepest self. What does it reflect about your fears, your dreams, your values? What stories about wealth and self-worth are you holding onto, and how might changing these narratives transform your life? As you reflect on your financial journey, what profound truths does it reveal about your deepest desires and fears? Are you ready to heed the call of your heart and step into the life you were destined to live?

This chapter closes here, but your story is just beginning. It's a narrative brimming with potential and awaiting your bold strokes. Will you step forward? Will you transform not only your destiny but also inspire a cascade of change in the lives you touch?

Step into this realm of transformation, where every question is a key and every dream a destination. Let your heart lead you to the life you are meant to live.

NEETU PRABHU

About Neetu Prabhu: Neetu Prabhu, Founder and CEO of Unity Wealth Strategies, is a distinguished wealth strategist serving ultra-high net worth clients and business owners. She specializes in wealth building, legacy planning, and multigenerational wealth transfers, utilizing tax-free income strategies to revolutionize her clients' financial futures. Neetu is recognized for her fiduciary excellence and ethical service, earning accolades like the prestigious Million Dollar Round Table, Court of the Table award, and multiple honors for her impactful decade-long tenure in financial services.

Beyond her professional endeavors, Neetu is passionately committed to empowering single moms and survivors of domestic violence. A philanthropist at heart, she champions financial literacy for women, acting as a guiding force to foster independence and resilience. She is also a multi-time #1 Amazon bestselling author and a featured speaker alongside notable figures like Brian Tracy and Erik Swanson.

Author's Website: *www.LinkedIn.com/in/NeetuPrabhu*

Book Series Website: *www.TheBookOfHumanEmpowerment.com*

NICOLE KERNOHAN
TRANSFORMING ADVERSITY: A JOURNEY OF HEALING & GROWTH

. . . .

Don't tell me the sky is the limit when there are footprints on the moon" might as well be my motto for life.

Twenty-two years ago, life threw me a curveball, altering my path in ways I could have never imagined. It was a medical crisis that I still remember vividly, as if it happened just yesterday. I lost the functionality of the right side of my body, finding myself essentially paralyzed in my right arm and leg. This sudden turn of events thrust me into uncertainty about my future mobility and independence.

At that time, I was in my fourth year of university, pursuing a degree in Business Administration. Until then, life seemed like a series of exciting adventures; I was on the brink of graduation, looking forward to stepping into my career. I was an A student, healthy, surrounded by great friends, engaged in volunteering, working part-time—simply put, I was happy.

However, beneath this seemingly perfect surface, there was a deep challenge: my intense perfectionism and unreasonably high expectations for myself. I juggled multiple commitments, spending endless hours studying and obsessing over achieving perfection, feeling overwhelmed by the pressure of maintaining an impeccable academic record. Looking back now, I realize how unnecessary and detrimental that level of stress was; but in the moment, it felt all too real.

The onset of tingling and numbness in my right hand and foot prompted me to seek medical attention, and, soon after, I found myself admitted to the hospital. Over the course of a few days, the symptoms progressed until I was completely paralyzed on the right side.

Despite the grim prognosis from the doctors, who were uncertain about the possibility of my regaining functionality, I chose to anchor my hopes in faith rather than giving in to fear. When they told me, "Nicole, you may or may not regain functionality, and we can't guarantee another episode won't occur," I accepted the diagnosis but refused to accept their prognosis. Instead, I embraced an unwavering belief that I would fully recover and lead a vibrant, healthy life. This belief became the guiding force behind my subsequent actions and decisions.

That episode of Multiple Sclerosis became a pivotal moment in my life. Rather than descending into despair, I approached the challenge with an unwavering belief in possibilities. I was convinced that if one approach didn't work, I would try another, and another, and another until I found what worked for me. My optimism was infectious, impacting not just myself but also those around me—friends, family, peers, and even the healthcare professionals and natural health practitioners I collaborated with.

I never uttered the words "I can't" or "I've tried everything" or "There's no hope." To me, hope was a tangible, powerful force driving me forward. Some feared that my hope was misguided, but I don't believe in "false hope." Anyone who has achieved something significant or overcome great odds did so because they held onto hope, however slim it may have seemed.

Hope is what keeps the flame burning inside, propelling us to keep moving forward. This attitude gave others confidence in me and built their belief in me, and many became great encouragers and supporters!

In the months and years following that health crisis, my thoughts and actions underwent a profound transformation, altering the course of my life in ways far beyond my physical health. I changed my diet, took supplements, embraced relaxing activities like yoga and nature walks, and learned to slow down while still being passionate and driven towards my goals.

What I've come to realize, especially in retrospect, is that the most crucial aspect of my recovery wasn't the specific health protocols or actions I took—though they were undeniably important. It was my mindset that laid the foundation for healing. My perspective of myself and the potential and possibilities for my life, my self-image, self-confidence, belief, and faith in myself and others, as well as my determination and resilience. These are just a few of the deep-rooted facets of the mind that created the environment for powerful actions.

Our minds possess incredible power.

Through my journey, with years of study and training in positive psychology and working with many clients, I've learned that our results in life, health, and business aren't merely a reflection of our actions but rather the energy or feeling behind those actions. My unwavering faith and optimistic outlook not only changed how I felt about myself and my life but also put me in a state of calmness, confidence, and gratitude for the opportunities to heal and stay healthy.

This perspective not only helped with my physical recovery but also made it easier for me to stay consistent with each new strategy I tried. I didn't complain about failed attempts; instead, I saw them as steps toward success. Failure at a method didn't mean personal failure; it simply meant that particular approach didn't work. This strong self-image allowed me to bounce back quickly from setbacks without losing sight of my ultimate goal, which, to me, defines true success—pursuing a meaningful goal with unwavering enthusiasm, despite the obstacles along the way.

Understanding this fundamental truth has empowered me to apply it not only to my health but also to other aspects of life and business. Our minds, indeed, are incredible!

So, what does this mean for you? Allow me to pass along a few empowering takeaways:

1. **Embrace Possibilities with a Positive Mindset:** Believe in your potential to overcome challenges and achieve success, and let that belief guide your actions and decisions. Catch your perspective if it is limiting you and choose another point of view that feels better and inspires you to keep going.

2. **Embrace Challenges with Determination & Cultivate Resilience in Your Actions:** View setbacks as opportunities for growth. My father-in-law always said, "It's not a problem—it's an opportunity for a solution!" Choose to keep moving forward with renewed enthusiasm.

3. **Elevate Your Journey with Empowering Connections:** Surround yourself with individuals who uplift you, believe in you, and encourage you. Jim Rohn famously said, "You are the average of the five people you spend the most time with." Choose people who inspire you to be your best self and support your journey to success.

   A strong supportive community helps you navigate challenges and failures with resilience, seeing setbacks as opportunities for growth and motivating you to keep moving forward. Surround yourself with empowering people who inspire you and push you!

Life is a series of moments, some challenging and others exhilarating, each offering a chance for growth. Choose faith in yourself and the endless possibilities ahead. Trust in your ability to adapt, learn, and thrive. Ultimately, it's not the challenges themselves that define us, but our response to them. Dare to dream big, push your boundaries, your "comfort zone" and your "familiar zone," and believe that anything is possible!

NICOLE KERNOHAN

About Nicole Kernohan: Nicole is a High-Performance Coach, Speaker, Partner with the international coaching company, Elevated Worldwide. She trains and empowers entrepreneurs and business leaders to own their choice and change their perspective leading to true transformation in business and life.

After an episode of MS partially paralyzed her in 2003, she began the in-depth study of the mind and body and has lived healthy for over twenty years. She also has twenty years of experience in business development, business strategy, and operations through entrepreneurship and corporate ventures.

Contact Nicole on Social Media:
Instagram: *www.instagram.com/NicoleKernohan*
Facebook: *www.facebook.com/Nicole.Kernohan10*

Author's Website: *www.NicoleKernohan.com*

Book Series Website: *www.TheBookOfHumanEmpowerment.com*

ONIKA SHIRLEY

EMPOWERING YOU: A JOURNEY OF PURPOSE & ACTION

In a world filled with challenges and obstacles, it is essential to understand the true purpose of human empowerment. Through my life's work, I have dedicated myself to inspiring and uplifting others to reach their full potential.

My journey towards understanding human empowerment has been one of self-discovery and growth, driven by a desire to make a positive difference in the lives of others. Through my actions and the values that guide me, I have come to realize the transformative power of empowering individuals to believe in themselves and unlock their true potential. This mindset has become the foundation of my personal brand, one that is built on authenticity, integrity, and an unwavering commitment to bringing about positive change in the world.

It is not enough to simply speak of empowerment; true change comes from action. I have always believed that actions speak louder than words, and it is through my actions that I strive to lead by example and inspire others to do the same. Whether it is through mentorship, advocacy, or simply lending a listening ear, I am dedicated to empowering individuals to take control of their own lives and make a difference in their communities.

My journey has taught me that true empowerment lies in recognizing the potential within ourselves and others, and in fostering a mindset of growth, resilience, and compassion. By sharing my own experiences and lessons learned along the way, I hope to ignite a spark within others to embrace their true purpose and contribute to a more empowered, united, and inclusive society.

As we navigate the complexities of life and strive to make a positive impact, it is essential to cultivate a sense of purpose and a strong mindset that fuels our actions. Through my work and dedication to human empowerment, I have witnessed the transformative power of individuals coming together to uplift and support one another. It is through this collective effort that we can create lasting change and build a more inclusive and equitable society for all.

In the face of adversity and challenges, it is our unwavering belief in the potential of every individual that drives us forward. By embracing a mindset of empowerment and taking meaningful action, we have the opportunity to inspire others and create a ripple effect of positive change that extends far beyond ourselves. Together, let us continue to share our true purpose and mindset about human empowerment, knowing that our actions have the power to shape a brighter future for generations to come.

"Empowerment is not about giving people power; it is about unlocking the power they already have within themselves."
~ Barbara Gilder

Throughout my journey as an author, a leader in my career, and a source of inspiration for many individuals, I have witnessed the transformative power of empowering others to believe in themselves and pursue their dreams. Over the years, I have dedicated myself to motivating individuals to take action, even when they may have doubted their own abilities.

By instilling a sense of self-belief and challenging individuals to overcome self-sabotage, I have seen firsthand the incredible impact that empowerment can have on unlocking one's full potential and propelling them towards success.

I want to break down barriers and empower individuals to go after their dreams with unwavering determination and confidence. The power of inspiration and motivation cannot be underestimated. As individuals strive to achieve their dreams and overcome hurdles along the way, it is often the spark of inspiration and the drive of motivation that propels them forward. By instilling a sense of belief in oneself and fostering unwavering determination and confidence, individuals can break down barriers that once seemed insurmountable.

It's time to reach new heights, conquer your fears, and pursue your dreams with a renewed sense of purpose and resilience. Together, let us discover the incredible potential that lies within each of us when we are inspired and motivated to take action towards our goals.

I invite you to reflect on a time when you felt truly inspired and motivated to pursue something meaningful in your life. Perhaps it was a moment of clarity when you realized your true passion or a spark of inspiration that ignited a fire within you to push past your limitations.

For me, this journey began when I was faced with a daunting challenge that seemed insurmountable. Doubt and fear crept in, threatening to hold me back from pursuing my dreams. But then, something shifted. I found inspiration in the stories of others who had overcome similar obstacles and achieved extraordinary success. Their resilience and determination fueled my own sense of purpose and gave me the courage to take the first step towards my goals.

As we travel further along this path, let us not forget the power of motivation in propelling us forward. Whether it be the encouragement of a mentor, the support of loved ones, or the satisfaction of small victories along the way, motivation plays a crucial role in keeping us focused and dedicated to our journey.

Together, let us embrace the challenges that lie ahead with a sense of determination and optimism. Let us draw strength from the stories of those who have walked this path before us and find inspiration in the limitless potential that resides within each of us. I want to share a little about my journey with you. At the age of nineteen, I faced two life-changing car accidents that left me with physical limitations, particularly in my leg. It was a challenging time, but I knew I had to dig deep and find the strength to keep going.

During this difficult period, I found inspiration and motivation in the incredible words of the legendary Les Brown. His messages of hope, perseverance, and self-belief resonated with me and sparked a fire within me to pursue a career in speaking, coaching, and mentoring. Even though Les Brown was a virtual mentor to me, his guidance and wisdom played a crucial role in shaping my path forward.

Through my own experiences and the lessons I learned from mentors like Les Brown, I discovered the importance of staying motivated and focused on my goals, no matter the obstacles that may arise. My journey has taught me that with the right mindset and determination, anything is possible.

With Les Brown's powerful words echoing in my mind, I have embraced my calling as a speaker, coach, and mentor with passion and purpose. I believe that my story is a testament to the power of resilience, determination, and unwavering self-belief in overcoming challenges and achieving greatness.

I hope that my experiences can inspire and motivate you in your own pursuits. Remember that with perseverance and belief in yourself, you can overcome any obstacle and reach for your dreams. Let's shift our focus! I want to provide you with some actionable steps you can take to harness your own inspiration and motivation to overcome challenges and pursue your dreams:

1. **Identify Your Sources of Inspiration:** Take some time to reflect on what truly inspires you. It could be a person, a quote, a book, or a personal goal. Surround yourself with sources of inspiration that uplift and motivate you to keep going, especially during tough times.

2. **Set Clear Goals:** Define your goals and break them down into smaller, manageable steps. Having a clear vision of what you want to achieve will help you stay focused and motivated on your journey.

3. **Create a Support System:** Surround yourself with positive and supportive individuals who believe in your potential. Seek out mentors, friends, or family members who can offer guidance, encouragement, and motivation when you need it most.

4. **Practice Self-Care:** Taking care of your physical, emotional, and mental well-being is essential for maintaining motivation and resilience. Make time for activities that bring you joy, relaxation, and rejuvenation.

5. **Embrace Failure as a Learning Opportunity:** Understand that setbacks and failures are a natural part of any journey. Instead of letting them discourage you, use them as valuable lessons to learn and grow from. Stay resilient and keep pushing forward.

6. **Stay Consistent & Persistent:** Consistency is key to achieving long-term success. Stay committed to your goals, even when faced with challenges or setbacks. Persistence and determination will help you overcome obstacles and reach new heights.

7. **Celebrate Your Victories:** Acknowledge and celebrate your achievements, no matter how big or small. Recognizing your progress and accomplishments will boost your confidence and motivation to continue pursuing your dreams.

By incorporating these actionable steps into your life, you can harness the transformative power of inspiration and motivation to overcome challenges, stay focused on your goals, and pursue your dreams with renewed purpose and resilience. Remember, you have the potential within you to achieve greatness—believe in yourself and keep moving forward.

"Through the wreckage of adversity, I found the strength to rise, the courage to persevere, and the determination to walk in my purpose, undeterred by the scars of the past."
~ Dr. Onika Shirley

DR. ONIKA L. SHIRLEY

About Dr. Onika L. Shirley: Dr. Onika L. Shirley is the Founder and CEO of Action Speaks Volume, Inc. She is a Procrastination Strategist and Behavior Change Expert and is known for building unshakable confidence, stopping procrastination, and getting your dreams out of your head and into your life. She is a Master Storyteller, International Speaker, Serves in Global Ministry, International bestselling author, International Award Recipient, Serial Entrepreneur, and Global Philanthropist impacting lives in the USA, Africa, India, and Pakistan.

Dr. O is a Motivational Speaker and Christian Counselor. Dr. Onika is the Founder and Director of Action Speaks Volume Orphanage Home and Sewing School in Telangana State, India, and Action Speaks Volume sewing school in Khanewal and Shankot, Pakistan. She founded, operated, and visited an Orphanage home in Tuni, India, for four years and supported widows in Tuni, India.

She is the founder of Empowering Eight Inner Circle, ASV C.A.R.E.S, ASV Next Level Living Program, and P6 Solutions and Consulting. She has served for 13 years as a therapeutic foster parent. Of all the things Dr. O does, she is most proud of her profound faith in Christ and her opportunity to serve the body of Christ globally.

Author's Website: *www.ActionSpeaksVolumes.com*

Book Series Website: *www.TheBookOfHumanEmpowerment.com*

ROBERT BAUTNER

ROSES ONLY BLOOM IN THE FERTILIZER OF LIFE

Suffering Creates Your Path to Success

Mentorship has been one of the most profound and transformative roles in my life. Beyond simply fulfilling its responsibilities, it's been both a privilege and an opportunity to lead others toward reaching their fullest potential while also growing myself.

After sharing my journey in these books, mentorship has served as my compass throughout—from mothering my daughters to professional dentistry practice management, employer responsibility responsibilities, community outreach initiatives, and volunteerism roles; it remains a testament to faith as an unyielding strength of mine.

Mentor & Mentee Roles

In my experience, one of the hallmarks of successful mentorship relationships is their reciprocal nature. While I've had the honor of mentoring many over time, I also benefitted greatly from being mentored myself! Effective mentoring relationships require mutual respect, trust, and an aim of personal and professional growth as key ingredients of their foundation.

My journey began with my parents as my initial mentors. They instilled within me the values of hard work, perseverance, and faith—values that continue to influence every aspect of my life today. Later in my career journey, I encountered mentors who helped develop my technical dental abilities and also encouraged me to view patients holistically as individuals rather than simply symptoms to treat. Not only were these mentors people who inspired me to strive for excellence in my work and practice, but many of them became more than just mentors and acquaintances—some even peers, colleagues, and my closest allies.

Faith is Our Guide

Faith has always been at the core of my life, providing strength, guidance, and an overall sense of direction and purpose. When serving as a mentor myself, my faith serves as the cornerstone for leading and supporting others. Mentorship, to me, extends far beyond professional achievements—it involves supporting growth while inspiring individuals to realize their full potential with honesty and kindness.

Although my professional path has not led me to learn more about the life and journey of Dr. Wayne Dyer's teachings, I've learned that some of his teachings align with my beliefs and experience, which resonated deeply with me, particularly his belief that our positive thoughts do shape our reality. I can attest firsthand how positivity influences those around us—it has more significant influence than we can even begin to measure, and that encourages others to adopt similar mindsets, as evidenced by my experiences and observations.

Furthermore, his ideas surrounding frequency positively aligned closely with my faith-based experiences, which helped keep my optimism strong throughout difficult situations.

Mentorship as a Path for Personal Growth

My life exemplifies the transformative power of mentorship. While facing challenges posed by working in an industry dominated by men, mentors helped me navigate those waters with insight from not just technical expertise or business acumen but also resilience, adaptability, and staying true to one's values.

Starting my dental practice at Williamsburg Center for Dental Health was one of the biggest leaps of faith I ever took. It challenged all that I knew and my ability to mentor others. Over time, as my practice developed, I became an advisor and mentor to my team members, teaching them all aspects of dentistry while simultaneously creating an atmosphere of respect, kindness, and excellence within our clinic environment.

Environment & Mindset—Examining Their Interrelations

Environment plays a pivotal role in mentoring. Fostering an encouraging, caring atmosphere at my dental practice is paramount for growth—both for me and those I mentor. Through hard work on both sides, we have succeeded in cultivating an atmosphere in which patients and staff feel supported while operating with positive intentions in an encouraging community—ultimately leading to remarkable achievements!

This philosophy extends to patient care as well. Every interaction I have with patients presents me with an opportunity to mentor, educate, and empower them regarding their oral health needs and well-being. I learned this holistic approach from my mentors and am proud to pass it on to my team and peers daily.

Faith as My Foundation of Mentorship

Faith and mentorship philosophy have always been at the core of my life. Belief in an all-powerful higher power has given me the strength to face my challenges head-on and guide others through their difficulties. Not only am I spiritual in private matters, but my beliefs also guide my decisions and actions across work environments and relationships.

Much like Dr. Wayne Dyer's words about aligning oneself with positive frequencies, faith, like frequency, enables me to keep a positive and hopeful mindset even during challenging times. My role as a mentor requires not only imparting technical knowledge and professional experience; I am also accountable for imparting purposeful, faith-filled enactment to those I mentor.

Mentorship in My Family Life

As the mother of three daughters, I have taken on the additional role of mentor at home. Through hard work, faith, and compassion-instilling parenting philosophies taught to me by my parents, I strive to instill these same qualities in them, too. Balancing my professional responsibilities alongside motherhood has been challenging but has always seemed complementary rather than conflictive.

My daughters have witnessed me establish a successful business venture while managing the challenges associated with professional life and remaining firm in my faith. Through my example, I hope to have taught them what it means to be a leader, mentor, and person of integrity while drawing strength from learning from them through resilience, creativity, determination, and inspiration. Nothing is more important to me than empowering them with these life experiences.

Scaling My Mentorship Beyond My Professional Sphere

My dedication to mentorship extends far beyond the walls of my dental practice. Through mission work in Honduras and El Salvador with Orphan Helpers and volunteer activities at Williamsburg Community Chapel, I've used my talents and resources to make an impactful difference in people's lives. These experiences have reinforced my faith in mentorship's capacity for transformation while revealing new understandings about compassion, humility, and service.

Through these experiences, I have come to appreciate that mentorship should not be seen as hierarchical but relational. My goal as a mentor, whether mentoring young people in Honduras or helping my colleagues achieve their full potential, is always empowerment-based. My approach stems from my faith, which teaches that all individuals possess great value; our purpose here on Earth should always be service and upliftment.

Leaving a Legacy Through Mentorship

Mentorship is not simply a role but represents an invaluable legacy that my mentors have left me. Their impactful influence was immense for my development as an individual, and thus, I am committed to passing that legacy onto future generations through mentorship. Mentorship means living purposefully, guided by faith, and contributing positively to society.

My mentors have helped shape who I am today, and I continue to honor their legacy by mentoring others with equal dedication, compassion, and integrity. For me personally, success should not only be defined in terms of what one achieves for oneself but also by what one helps others accomplish.

Mentorship has been an exciting journey involving faith, leadership, and positive influence. It has guided me through life's many obstacles while molding me into the leader and mother I am today and creating positive change for others around me. Thanks to faith, I found the strength to overcome the barriers while giving those I mentor an environment where they could excel; through mentoring legacy, I hope my words continue inspiring future generations with positivity.

We can change how we perceive things and what we perceive them. As an educator, mentor, and leader, I have witnessed this truth firsthand. I encourage you to accept each step with faith, positivity, and an aim toward serving others in need.

ROBERT BAUTNER

About Robert Bautner: Robert is an author and businessman. When he isn't writing, he is caring for his clients' horses on his property in a beautiful mountain valley of Utah. He encourages people to look at life through a new lens, particularly people who are struggling with differentness.

His life's work is turning negatives into positives and viewing it all as a journey of authenticity and grace. His dream is to share this perspective with his readers. His first book, *Stop Your Crying*, is a powerful and poignant story of how one autistic boy overcame the trauma of abuse and achieved all his dreams.

His second book, *The Wolf Cycle*, is an entirely new way of looking at relationships and personality. It uses the unlikely tale of The Three Little Pigs as an allegory to explain how our brains are wired, how we relate to each other as brothers or as wolves, and how we can all learn to build a better house. These works and more can be found on his website *www.RobertBautner.com.*

Author's Website: *www.RobertBautner.com*

Book Series Website: *www.TheBookOfHumanEmpowerment.com*

RONALD TREMBLAY
LATE FOR BREAKFAST

In the first couple of years of my life, I learned quickly who fed, cuddled, protected and loved me. I experimented with taste. I would try to eat anything—rocks, dirt, carrots, bugs, you name it. I discovered sweet, sticky, awful, and dangerous. My mom and dad guided me with "no," "yes," "good boy," and "bad boy." The tone of their voices was always one of love and good intention. They taught me trust.

As I grew and discovered the mirror, I saw a lucky little boy, yet maybe not in those words. My experience as a child was exciting. Dad taught me to row, sail, and fish on our adventures on the ocean. My dad taught me how to use tools properly and safely. As I began creating things out of wood, metal, or leaves, I developed a strong hand-eye-coordination ability.

Life was middle class; I was the oldest of three. My first experiences were my parents' first, too. They were generous with love and time. My mom did not like that my dad bought me the best toys and all my friends wanted to play at my place. My family home was the hub of the neighborhood. It was a childhood of wonderful experiences—or was it?

In my daydreams, everything was possible. I could fly, and sometimes that meant falling from a tree in the attempt to fly, or when I burned four fingertips on one hand in the discovery of a hot stove top.

I was seven when, as usual, mom was calling for me to come to the kitchen for breakfast. "It's going to get cold, and you are going to be late for school." I was in my room, playing. My dresser was the center of my imaginary universe where I played with my toy cars and boats, daydreaming alone. Being seven was great.

When I did not respond to her many calls to breakfast, she did what she always did. She came and got me. Until, one day, it was different. She stepped into the room, with a raised fist, screaming, and swiftly landed a backhand to my head. I went flying and hit my head on a bedpost and crumpled to the ground. With a trickle of something running down my nose, I looked up to see my mother wailing in remorse, as she bent down to inspect the damage to my face. Everything shifted in that moment.

My nose was split, and mom did what she always did; she took care of me, taking me to the hospital for stitches.

Late for breakfast—little did I know that would change my life.
This experience was not like looking in the mirror. There was something behind the surface that jumped out and scared my seven-year-old mind and imprinted powerful decisions that would take me decades to understand, all in a split second. This was unknown to my conscious mind at seven-years-old.

When I graduated from high school with not enough credits to attend university with my buddies, I went to work in my family's auto service business, fixing cars. I have never left the trade. I became fully licensed at twenty-four, manager at twenty-five and owner of the third location at twenty-six. Alongside that, I married at twenty-one-years old, had three sons and a daughter, divorced at thirty-eight, remarried at forty-two to the true love of my life with no additional children.

During all that, at twenty-nine, I was so stressed out that I began attending personal discovery and empowerment training to hopefully learn how to reclaim my happiness, which I was so sadly lacking. My life looked good from the outside, but a huge hole was in my heart that I did not understand. I thought I was doing everything right, but nothing truly made me happy.

My search was tireless and personal, difficult at times and my first marriage paid the ultimate price: divorce. The journey of introspection through many personal trainings over the years proved beneficial for me finding my happiness. That seven-year-old moment with my mother continues to come up and gives me great value and understanding of my mindset and purpose. I was able to forgive my mother and have a close connection with her for the rest of her life. My personal search was worth it.

I now understand, in that moment at seven years of age, my seven-year-old mind had a profound life altering experience, witnessing a full-grown adult woman (my mother, who I loved) express full-on rage and, in a split-second, change to deep remorse, left a very clear and permanent imprint on my memory.

Looking back through all the lumps and bumps, wins, and challenges in my life, I have been able to uncover the meaning I made up about that moment and how that has guided my life. I now understand that, at seven years of age, I made some very big decisions, in the moment that I witnessed my mother's emotions change in a split second, and these decisions have been quietly operating in the background ever since, much to my surprise.

- Do not trust women; their emotional capacity is frightening (this did not work in my first marriage).
- It is my dad's fault, for being at work all the time (this led me to learn how to accept my dad and forgive him).
- Having fun is bad (this gave me a critical eye).
- I must protect my siblings from my mother when dad is not home (that was hard to let go of and acknowledge their unique skills and talents).
- I better do what I am told, especially when taking directions from a woman, or I could be killed (being a slave to another is hard when I did not know why. It is easy to serve now that I know my why).

Looking in the mirror and seeing past the surface reflection is worthy work to do, as it turns out. Those decisions can be changed with reasonable ease when you're an adult. But when your brain is seven years old, not so much. What's really challenging is when your brain is operating with a seven-year-old set of instructions and you are physically twenty-one or thirty, or forty, or fifty, or sixty or seventy, or even eighty-five.

Depending on the childhood decisions that are still being held true in your brain, life can be a struggle for you, and everyone in your life. It can take a significant amount of faith and trust in yourself and others to sift through the thoughts to reveal where they came from for the possibility of changing those decisions can occur. This is the work of purpose and mindset.

Evan in my sixties, I am stunned by the power our minds have to create the life we have. There is a lot to be gained by taking responsibility for everything that has occurred in your life, no matter how difficult it may be to do so. Our thoughts create our purpose and mindset, which creates what we experience in life. Find a way to thank the universe for bringing your life to you, for you to learn and grow to be the amazing person you are today.

More value can be created in life by focusing on how we are being, allowing that to guide what we do and that generates what we have in our lives. Be—Do—Have.

Focusing on how we are being first before choosing the actions to have what we have creates results of a much deeper meaning.

A few years back, I came into an inheritance. I took care of some nagging financial things then built the workshop I always wanted. It got out of control, of course, and became a two-story, three bay with mezzanine heated building that looks more like a 3,900 square foot house than a garage. During the construction, I would often stand in the middle of the cavernous unfinished space and ask myself: "What am I doing?" I would stand there in bewilderment, with no reasonable answer from my thoughts.

My friends loved it, the construction workers were envious, and my wife's friends often said to her, "Why are you letting him do that? Are you crazy?" She would reply, reluctantly, "It is his money."

Then one day, a couple years after the building was complete and all my stuff was set up—cars, boats, projects, tools, machinery, supplies, everything I could possibly want—I came home after a great weekend with friends camping in the woods, drove onto my property with the view of my private shop and home a couple hundred feet away and BOOM. It came to me.

Like the flash I experienced when I was seven, except on this day, I was sixty-one. The shop I built is an adult version of my dresser from when I was seven. What? How can this be? Everything that was in that building would take me years to complete; every item was a dream waiting to be completed.

Most of the time, I would move stuff around, re-arranging things, and that was the most satisfying for me, just moving stuff around, thinking about what the items could be like when complete. Up to that point, I was mostly staging, not doing, or completing much. But I was happy as could be just moving and staging all that stuff. That is what disturbed me the most.

The dresser I lost at age seven had come back to get me, in my sixties.

Today, I am completing projects at a rapid rate and enjoying the use of them or selling them and moving on to bigger and better things as a grandfather to five.

My message is this: There is no detail in your life that does not matter. Everything, everything, everything that occurs in your life matters. Learn the lessons and grow.

No matter what, always respect the playful, innocent promise that you have always been. It is never too late to look behind the surface reflection in the mirror and embrace your deeper truths. The truth always sets you free.

RONALD TREMBLAY

About Ronald Tremblay: Born in Vancouver, B.C. Canada, into an automotive service family, Ronald grew up around cars and boats from birth. His family lived on a large sailboat through his high school years, which included extensive coastal cruising and sailing adventures on the B.C. coastline. He fathered three sons and a daughter from his first marriage that ended after seventeen years.

He participated in many personal growth workshops, leadership, and business training over his years. While still operating his third-generation automotive shop in Vancouver, he also spent eight years as a freelance trainer for hundreds of shop owners across Canada to implement systems and procedures he learned from his family business and Total Automotive Consulting and Training.

His knowledge increased business productivity, profit, and reduced stress for their customers and staff. He now lives on a five-acre dream property with his second wife, Ruth, of twenty-one awesome years, admiring life, and connecting with family, including five grandchildren, and chasing his passion for transforming peoples' experience of life with his second wind and renewed purpose after handing over his business to the fourth-generation leadership, an eighty-six-year legacy and growing.

Author's Website: *www.RonaldTremblay.com*

Book Series Website: *www.TheBookOfHumanEmpowerment.com*

RUTH TREMBLAY
OTHER MOTHER

I was living the unseen baggage of loss, poor boundaries, no vision, or real purpose, just a dull ache in my heart.

I longed for the 'idea' of security, love, acceptance, family—all of it.

I did not know that I was sabotaging myself because I was living and making choices guided by feelings, which were fluid and changing. Not a good foundation. I was not questioning how I was treated because my spirit was so sad and broken; I just gave my heart away.

The relationships chipped away at my heart—guys not keeping their word, not being their word. Looking back, them not meeting my family should have been a red flag. Again, no foundation. Imagine making excuses for poor behavior from someone who didn't want a relationship with me! For whatever reason, I made that behavior okay because I repeated it. I made excuses for them, and the experiences brought me no closer to love. Life was happening to me.

When I was a young woman, there were no conversations, TV shows, books, nothing mainstream that spoke of feelings, dreams, visions, personal space, or boundaries. Just like the movies where a woman is searching for love or wanting to get married—I had found just that, wanting and searching. I was looking for the answer outside of myself. The inside conversations were not helping either. They were like trying to Google "What is love?" and "How to find love?"

No Boundaries = No Foundation for Relationship

One day, I chose something new and unknown. I heard a woman say, "I looked at all the failed relationships in my life, and the only thing in common with them was me." It shook my core; she had just described my life.

My journey had begun; life would never be the same. I searched for books and attended a Women's Weekend. I discovered how to create deep, trusting relationships with women, and that my power comes from within. I discovered things that work and don't work in relationships; how men and women differ in relationships. My experiences had become my story, and I believed them.

I will be forever grateful for the gift of the book, "Codependent No More" by Melody Beattie. I discovered I was co-dependent! She describes co-dependency as:

1. Putting responsibility in the wrong place.
2. Neglect themselves in favor of others.
3. Co-dependents can't see themselves.

With each discovery, I became more curious about my transformation. I was beginning to truly love myself.

Then, my mother, Patricia, died. She had a quiet, peaceful death at home. I did not know then that the lessons I learned as I moved through the grief would be the foundation of strength for my own experience with cancer. Today, I can weave strength, beauty, love and loss into the experience of her death.

A family member came to the house shortly after her passing to assist me in sorting through her clothes. Mom did not have much, yet I have no memory of scarcity. Just enough. When we opened the last dresser drawer, we were surprised by what we found.

Inside were books, dolls, and toys to give to children 'abundance.' The impact of that experience formed part of my foundation.

Minutes after mom passed, we found a monarch at the door; it too had died. I believe it was a sign from mom, and she was sharing a message that her spirit would be close. Whenever I see a butterfly, I speak the words out loud. "Hi, Mom. Thanks for the visit. I love and miss you. You did your best and taught me what you knew. The world is different, and I have shifted my mindset." All of these experiences were having an impact on my choices.

What would it look like in twenty years? How would I describe the man, my partner, the vision of my life? What was important? I spent time contemplating some ideas from childhood and movies—funny, strong, athletic, romantic.

They were not words that would describe the 'foundation' of lifelong relationship. I had known Cancer, and it was not funny. If I chose funny, and he was no longer funny, it would unhinge the foundation of our relationship.

1. He has men in his life.
2. Faith in a higher power.
3. The family unit is important.

Without explanation, each of these is a deal breaker for me if he does not have these qualities.

The world was looking different, with clear boundaries.

Another step forward: I looked at the Vision of my life and created a path for myself; I wrote a letter to my mother from the future, sharing with her what my life looked like.

"My husband and I adore each other. We have an intimate, trusting relationship. Our lives are in harmony. We are soul mates. Our family is healthy; the children are happy and successful because of our strong marriage. We are proud of them. My life is blessed." This is part of my Vision.

My purpose became clear: Two words—love and family.

Twenty minutes later, I walked across the street and would bump into the man that would later become my husband. We had known each other for years. It turned out he was living nearby due to a divorce.

He has men in his life, he has faith in a higher power, and the family unit is important to him.

The two of us began dating. There were six of us intertwined in parts of the relationship, including four young people who had also experienced divorce. We created a foundation that would include the idea that I would never discipline them; they have a mother and a father for that. I chose to love and to be the "keeper of secrets and things they wanted to share."

Building trust and boundaries and never speaking badly of their mom were imperative for them to experience a happy, loving relationship. It was the best toughest thing I have ever stepped into, Purpose and Vision.

After we married, it was a surprise how quickly friends used the term stepmother, or that strangers would assume I was 'mom' when we were out. As the kids felt the need to defend their mom, I knew we needed another choice. Stepmother didn't fit as I was not stepping into motherhood. Remembering the dresser and my mother, I felt abundance, love, and family. I had become their Other Mother.

Every time a butterfly appears, there are now six of us who say, "Hi Patricia," "Hi, Ruthie's mom," and, "We love you."

"Our deepest fear is not that we are inadequate. Our deepest fear is that we are powerful beyond measure. It is our light, not our darkness, that most frightens us. We ask ourselves, who am I to be brilliant, gorgeous, talented, fabulous? Actually, who are you not to be? You are a child of God. Your playing small doesn't serve the world. There's nothing

enlightened about shrinking so others won't feel insecure around you. We are all meant to shine, as children do.

We were born to make manifest the glory of God that is within us. It's not just in some of us; it's in everyone. And as we let our own light shine, we unconsciously give other people permission to do the same. As we're liberated from our own fear, our presence automatically liberates others."

~ Marianne Williamson—*A Return to Love*

RUTH TREMBLAY

About Ruth Tremblay: Born in West Germany into a military family, she followed her father's footsteps and served in the Air Force. She was an Assistant Air Traffic Controller, and an Enforcement Office for the National Revenue Agency. She would describe her employment history as being in service.

After becoming a mother again, she was diagnosed with stage 3 colon cancer and stage 4 metastatic liver cancer. Working to advocate for early detection, as well as studying the healing powers of Visualization. If asked, her biggest accomplishment is her successful marriage, with Ronald, and the relationships created with four amazing young people who have grown into loving, generous people who are all parents themselves.

Book Series Website: *www.TheBookOfHumanEmpowerment.com*

SAMARA BETH SCHWARTZ

PURSUE THE NEW: UNLEASHING POTENTIAL WITH LIL' BAMBOO

They call me Lil' Bamboo, a nickname that might sound delicate but symbolizes an extraordinary resilience. This resilience wasn't just born out of my experiences; it has been passed down through generations, from ancestors who survived unimaginable horrors to the challenges I face in the modern world. This is my story, our story, of unyielding strength and the profound search for purpose.

Imagine being a child, tasked to interview a Holocaust survivor for a school project, and your own grandparent, marked by the horrors of her past, guides you to another survivor because the pain and embarrassment is too raw for her to recount. That was my reality. I watched in painful silence as my Bubbye's friend recounted her harrowing tale, mesmerized by numbers tattooed on her arm, a vivid lesson in resilience etched in my mind forever.

This history wasn't just about survival; it was about the ability to thrive against all odds, to build anew from the ashes of destruction. My grandparents, after enduring the unthinkable in Auschwitz, built a life from scratch in America, their spirit unbroken, their determination unyielding.

On 9/11, my husband was at the Pentagon, and I was in New York City. In those terrifying moments, watching buildings crumble, my world tilted. But amidst the chaos, my mindset was my fortress. I chose to focus on hope, on rebuilding, on priorities and lessons we could carry forward. This crisis, like the stories of my grandparents, taught me that fear does not have a place in the heart of the resilient.

My life as a military spouse, moving from place to place, constantly adapting and reinventing; selling and donating my belongings; and moving my businesses, was like the bamboo bending in the wind but never breaking. Each new location was a test of my ability to find purpose, to create something meaningful despite the upheaval.

Aikido Master Kenyo Furuya said, "We must be ever ready to move in our lives, and not become too comfortable in one state for too long. When we become complacent, we stop growing. Through strong practice, we remain ever ready to accept new challenges and new opportunities for love and growth." Using the metaphor of bamboo, which is noted for its strength and hollow structure, we understand that a mind cleared of clutter can similarly enhance our character.

The most profound test of my resilience came with the devastating loss of my son, who had Giant Omphalocele [om-fãloh-seel], a rare condition where his liver, intestines, and stomach were in a membrane protruding from his naval. He also had a hole in his heart and 10% lung capacity. He didn't have much of a chance. Holding him lifeless for three hours in my arms, feeling guilt and loss, plunged me into depths of sorrow and depression, the likes of which I had never known.

At the same time, I was navigating life with my younger son, who was five at the time, and diagnosed with autism at thirteen months old. The dual challenges of grieving one child while tirelessly advocating for another taught me the deepest meanings of resilience and hope. I learned to embrace each day's joys and challenges with a renewed spirit, finding strength in the supportive community around me and the therapeutic power of sharing my story.

A year after losing my son, my daughter was born a preemie and she survived years of complications from salmonella poisoning, frequenting hospitals and doctor offices. Somehow, I managed to run my booked-solid events business, while raising two amazing children. I kept picking myself up and taking massive action. Again and again. Within three years, my events company became one of the top event planning companies in Houston, Texas, winning national awards, featured in magazines and press interviews.

I went from being well-known to being unknown, again, when we had to move my family to Vancouver, British Columbia. Five years later, we moved to Arizona.

When life threw the devastating curveballs of a divorce after a twenty-two-year marriage, personal loss, and a business closing during the pandemic, my purpose became my anchor, guiding me back to a path of abundance and philanthropy, inspired by the entrepreneurial spirit of my forbearers. It was far from easy. I hit the lowest point of my life and wanted to end it, but the universe put people in my life that helped me rise back up to the resilient person I was meant to be.

I have lost jobs in economic downturns and hurricane disasters, started new companies and moved businesses across the country and internationally. As I ventured into community leadership, I found new ways to channel my experiences into helping others. Organizing charity events and spearheading community outreach programs became not just a way to give back but also a path to healing. Each event planned, every dollar raised for charity, reinforced my belief in the power of community to transform lives.

In the quiet moments of reflection, I've looked into the mirrors that my friend, Rabbi Allouche, spoke about when they said, "The physical and the subconscious. What do I see? Not just a reflection of myself but of all those who came before me. My soul, a divine flame, fueled by their experiences, their victories over darkness. It's a powerful reminder that we are not defined by the traumas of the past but by how we rise above them."

My journey through life's storms has taught me the true essence of resilience. Like the bamboo, I have swayed but never snapped. I share my story not just to tell you about my life but to inspire you to discover your own strength, your own purpose. Together, we can continue to bend, adapt, and thrive, no matter what life throws our way.

As a Business Coach, here are some tips:

1. **Find Your Roots:** Dig deep into your family history. Understanding where you come from can provide a strong foundation and a clear sense of purpose. Create a roots project by researching your genealogy and create a family tree to pass down. Collect photos and interview relatives and friends with a recording that you can use as a podcast, blog, article, or just to keep personal.

2. **Embrace Change with Positivity:** Adopt a mindset that views challenges as opportunities for growth. This outlook can transform your life's toughest moments into lessons of strength. Be a joiner and reach out to new groups, making new connections and friends to help you embrace change.

3. **Clear Your Space:** Consistent meditation is recommended as a method to purify our mental space, ultimately boosting our resilience and inner strength over time.

4. **Regularly Engage in Self-reflection:** Use positive affirmations to reinforce your self-worth and resilience. I invite you to write down the person you see in the mirror, and who you want to be.

- On your steamy bathroom mirror, visualize your future self as Napoleon Hill taught, to act like you have already won that deal or the applause on stage after you presented that keynote speech. You may be pleasantly surprised to see how your vision evolves.

- For example, "I am beautiful. I am smart. I am witty. I am philanthropic. I am a giver. I am a great daughter. I am a fabulous mother. I am kind. I am a #1 bestselling author. I am a world renowned keynote motivational and business paid speaker. I am a successful business owner and employer for multi-million-dollar businesses. I invest in other businesses. I donate thousands of dollars to charity every year. I am a philanthropic volunteer. I am traveling the world with my children and grandchildren."

5. **Expressing Gratitude:** Develop a positive mindset, such as daily gratitude practices and cognitive reframing techniques—these are beautiful ways to make it second nature. Every morning, I say a prayer of gratitude and trust in the process and belief in my Creator. I list off all of the things and people I am grateful for, and sometimes it's the basic needs like the air we breathe, our legs and arms and voice.

Once you start with personal affirmations and gratitude, you will see how your inner beliefs, dreams and purpose come through. Now, it is time for you to find your purpose, dedicate your daily steps to overcoming life's challenges, anxieties and depression and become the strong, resilient bamboo you are meant to be.

As an event and retreat expert, business coach and networking guru, who survives and thrives through the camel humps of my life, I implement these recommendations, and they provide me with the strength and resilience required to persevere.

You never know what door opens when another closes. Transitioning from event consulting to business and life coaching is something I never envisioned. This evolution in my career helps others achieve their business and personal dreams, which feeds my soul. We have to let go of those who are weighing us down so we can make room for those waiting to lift us up.

When I released those who did not stand by me when I needed it most, I was able to focus my time on those who believed in me and showed support, and spend more time with my parents before my dad passed away.

We can all learn from those who endured unimaginable situations like the Holocaust, 9/11, military life, moving frequently, life altering divorces, death of loved ones and other life (or death) events. It's not about what happens in our lifetime, but how we rise up and find ways to be ready for action to lift ourselves and others up, and keep on going with purpose, giving back and making the best of our lives.

"The warrior, like bamboo, is ever ready for action." Be ready to grow, adapt, and thrive with unwavering trust and integrity.

Be like bamboo.

SAMARA BETH SCHWARTZ

About Samara Beth: Samara Beth is a highly accomplished 10X certified business coach, nationally recognized award-winning global event producer, destination manager, speaker, networking queen, entrepreneur and bestselling author with a career spanning over thirty years.

As the founder of Samara Beth & Co., she has transformed venues into spectacular retreats and events, earning a reputation for excellence and creativity. Samara Beth's journey, marked by resilience and adaptability, includes living in thirteen cities and thirty homes, mostly as a military and expat spouse. Her experiences have shaped her expertise in building supportive communities and navigating life's challenges with grace and determination.

Known for her contagious high energy, Samara Beth empowers audiences with her inspiring stories and practical insights. She has been recognized as 'Volunteer of the Year' and continues to inspire others through her writing and speaking engagements, making a significant impact on those around her.

Contact Samara Beth at *sb@samarabethandco.com* and check out *SamaraBethandCo.com* to read more about how SB&Co. can help you.

Author's Website: *www.SamaraBethandCo.com*

Book Series Website: *www.TheBookOfHumanEmpowerment.com*

SHAWN MARSHALL

YOU CAN'T UN-HEAR YOUR INNER TRUTH

At the start of 2017, I had hit the pinnacle of my fitness career in San Diego. I built my dream business that paid me well and had given me freedom of time. I was happy. I built a community, and my clients loved their results. I had become successful at my childhood dream!

Everything about life made sense to me—until one summer morning when it didn't make any sense at all. I suddenly had no sense of purpose.

It was a normal morning. My clients had left after a hard workout, and I stayed behind to clean up. That's when it hit me: it wasn't a "normal" morning. I felt all alone, bored, and even sad. I heard a faint but clear voice inside say to me, "This isn't it."

I knew instantly what it meant. But I pretended I didn't.

That message was too raw, real, potent, and direct. It stirred up fear, doubt, and uncertainty so I just kept on moving about my morning as if I didn't hear it at all.

But, I'd later learn that you can't un-hear the truth.

I had developed such an identity being a fitness guy that I didn't believe in myself enough to do anything different. And so, I ignored my inner wisdom and kept pretending to be a fitness guy—when, in reality, a bigger dream had entered my awareness.

I stayed in fitness for another four years while my happiness slowly dwindled.

You see, I had been life coaching on the side (for free) for a decade at a leadership academy, and had fallen in love with helping people reinvent their lives. I found myself trying to help my fitness clients transform their marriages—after, for example, they came to me because they wanted to lose fifteen pounds to look good for a weekend getaway on the beach in Mexico. Never mind that they would gain the weight back after the trip and repeat that same cycle over and over!

How satisfying was that? I became bored to tears!

I was trying to "fit" life coaching into a fitness program. And, in reality, the vision that was brewing inside me needed a bigger container that my fitness program just couldn't hold.

After four years of repressing my bigger vision of empowering my clients, helping them find their purpose, become happy and build their dreams, I found myself burnt out and rudderless.

It took the Covid-19 pandemic (and some awesome mentors) to help me find the courage to simply let go of what I had built in order to go all in on the bigger vision that had shown up.

During 2020 and 2021, I sat back and watched the world fight over just about everything: Vaccines, Black Lives Matter, abortion, Trump vs Biden, and much more.

It frustrated me to see people turning on one another.

But it was that same frustration that ultimately showed me a new purpose.

I created an interview series where I interviewed doctors who were on the Covid front lines, famous authors and spiritual leaders like Neale Donald Walsh and John Gray (author of *Men Are From Mars*), and it was during an interview with Dan Brule (Tony Robbins' Breath Coach) that my new purpose became crystal clear to me.

I suddenly knew that if people had a greater sense of purpose, along with emotional intelligence, the fighting wouldn't be happening to the degree that it was, and the world would be a much happier and peaceful place for us all.

And it was those two skills, helping people find purpose and developing their emotional intelligence, that I had been honing over the last decade at the leadership academy.

By the start of the pandemic, I had clocked in more than 50,000 hours of coaching people and realized that I had been training to help people navigate these challenging times we were all facing.

Suddenly, my purpose was clear.

I closed my fitness business a week later and started over from scratch to build a coaching company that would help people navigate uncertain times, find their purpose, and, ultimately, live a happy life.

At the same time that I walked away from fitness, I moved from San Diego to Denver and rented a huge and expensive loft overlooking downtown.

While my lifestyle wasn't cheap and I had very real problems to solve like, "How will I pay the rent?" my purpose had become so powerful that I couldn't NOT follow it, and so I bet all that I had on it!

I was so committed to my new path that I replaced a net six-figure income in the first 90 days of starting my coaching company, Reinvent Yourself Vibes. I more than doubled that in the second year.

It wasn't because I was focused on money, but because my purpose had grabbed hold of me. There was no other option but success.

If you are considering making a big change in your life too, here are a couple things I've learned about purpose that may help you:

1. The word purpose can be confusing and even daunting. Let go of the energy you have around the word purpose. Nobody can define purpose for you; rather, you get to define it for yourself.

2. To discover your purpose, you must trust your inner wisdom, which can be any or all of the following: God, your intuition, your heart, your gut, or simply your inner wisdom.

Step one toward trusting your inner wisdom? Practice quieting your mind and do it consistently.

If your life has become a never-ending checklist and you wear a "Busy badge" with honor, you will never hear your inner wisdom, and your life will not change.

Turn off your phone and TV. Get off the couch. Get outside in nature. Do things you love to do that you stopped doing long ago. Exercise. Meditate. Hike. Journal. Have intentional quiet time where you simply sit with yourself and think.

These practices will help you remove the "noise" from your life and tap into an inner wisdom that was always inside you and always guiding you. You simply can't hear it when you are so busy.

Once you have tapped into your inner wisdom, interact with it by asking questions.

Ask yourself these questions:

- What would make me happy?
- What would I do if I could do anything I wanted and had no limitations?
- Where do I feel called to serve?

- What problems can I solve easily for others?
- Who am I without my current identity?

Here's the kicker: your answers must come from you. You may get ideas from others, but your clarity and commitment to your purpose must come from you.

I'll share one final tip as you continue your journey to your next level of purpose.

In order to step fully into your purpose, you must become a master at letting go—letting go of your past, your identity, your fears, your beliefs, and your old habits. Those may have served you in the past, but you must become a new version of yourself to move forward, and it will require you to let go.

At the time of this book, I'm just three years into my bigger calling. I'm totally amazed to be coaching two politicians, one of whom is currently running for office; high level business owners; and ambitious moms, dads, and even retirees who all share the same thing in common: a desire to learn, grow, serve, and stretch themselves to be and do more with their lives.

I know that you, too, are being called forward and it's my wish for you to trust your inner wisdom. Take the big leap, and be a YES to your next level of reinvention, purpose, and happiness.

Cheers!

SHAWN MARSHALL

About Shawn Marshall: Shawn Marshall is a life-long entrepreneur, who, by ten-years-old, was knocking on doors with a lawnmower in the summer, a rake in the fall, and a shovel in the winter, because when his parents said, "No, we won't buy video games for your Nintendo, but we will show you how to make your own money," he took that advice to heart and ran with it.

Aside from a four-year stint as a Navigator in the Navy, his entire life he has lived in accordance with a purpose.

Shawn cares deeply about helping people live happy, fulfilling, and purposeful lives. He runs a successful coaching company called Reinvent Yourself Vibes, where he coaches people from all walks of life: Moms and dads who are seeking purpose, business owners running multi-million dollar companies, and highly influential leaders in politics and real estate all looking to reconnect to their hearts.

Author's Website: *www.ReinventYourselfVibes.com*

Book Series Website: *www.TheBookOfHumanEmpowerment.com*

STEPH SHINABERY

EMPOWERMENT THROUGH MENTORSHIP

Mentorship has long been essential in my personal and professional lives, yet, as I navigate this journey, I realize its evolution and role in empowering others. Where once mentors served solely as sources of advice to their mentees, mentoring is increasingly shifting into dynamic reciprocal relationships that benefit both parties involved.

Looking back over my mentors—Steve, my aunt, and my high school basketball coach—all mentors in my eyes, I see they shared qualities like authenticity, vulnerability, and genuine connections, which I consider even more critical given today's rapidly morphing world!

In previous chapters in this series, I have described mentors who saw something special in me but couldn't see for myself, investing their time, energy, and wisdom to facilitate my growth. Over time, however, as my experience deepened, I became acutely aware that mentorship involved guidance, alignment, authenticity, and mutual growth. Therefore, in this chapter of my mentorship journey, I investigate its changing form today and its effect on me.

Authenticity

One of the defining trends of modern mentorship is an increased emphasis on authenticity. While social media and digital communications may lead to superficial interactions, authentic mentoring provides real and meaningful relationships. Being true to yourself—accepting strengths and weaknesses while encouraging others to do likewise—and inviting all parties involved (mentoring participants and mentors) into fully participatory interactions that encourage mutuality between one person and another is what people value most in mentorship relationships! It takes presence for mentoring relationships!

Dr. Wayne Dyer once said, "You only ever stay where you are by your choice alone." I find great comfort in this sentiment and adopt it as my approach to mentorship. Being authentic means recognizing our freedom from society or past experiences that put roles or expectations upon us. Breaking free is the cornerstone of success in mentorship relationships!

My journey to authenticity has not always been easy; at times, expressing myself freely without fearing judgment or rejection was difficult. With mentors' guidance and example as my guideposts, I learned the power of being true to oneself to create impactful mentorship relationships. By being authentic individuals, we create an atmosphere where others feel safe expressing themselves freely without judgment from outside sources. Mutual authenticity forms lasting bonds beyond traditional mentorship relationships.

Acceptance

Modern mentorship has evolved with an increased emphasis on alignment. In the past, mentorship often consisted of authoritarian arrangements wherein experts taught their protégées their craft; modern mentoring seeks to build partnerships based upon shared values, goals, and visions, which helps ensure both professionally and personally beneficial relationships are fostered between mentors and protégées.

My relationship with Steve taught me the power of alignment. Not only was he a professional advice provider, but we also established win-win situations where both parties gained equally from our shared growth over time.

My Genius Code Academy highlights the value of mentorship that aligns with one's values and personal journey. Aligning with one's values can create synergies that facilitate growth while expanding horizons for discovery.

Today's mentorship has undergone significant changes to make it into what it is today. It is no longer an unbalanced trust; instead, it operates like a two-way street where both parties learn, grow, and benefit equally. This mutuality makes mentorship an impactful form of relationship building; exchanging experiences can enrich both sides.

Mentorship has taught me as much from my mentees as it has from me. Their fresh perspectives, creative ideas, and energetic enthusiasm inspired and challenged my thinking about bringing about change! Mutual learning makes mentorship such an enjoyable experience—it's not simply imparting knowledge; mentorship means growing together!

A friend came to me with an outstanding project idea that perfectly aligned with Genius Code Academy values, yet, as I worked together with her, I soon discovered I was learning just as much from her as from me—her enthusiasm and creativity inspired my approach to work more meaningfully and gave me a renewed sense of purpose. This experience reinforced once again that mentorship should be seen as mutually beneficial, with both parties having something valuable to contribute.

Living Authentically

As mentors, we must live lives that reflect who we are. Our mentees rely on us not just for advice but as role models when faced with life's obstacles and difficulties. Being authentic means accepting ourselves even when that may prove challenging. Being open about struggles or vulnerabilities while teaching students that it's okay to make mistakes is a hallmark of authentic mentors.

Dr. Wayne Dyer often highlighted the value of living authentically; according to him, by doing so, we can inspire others to follow in our footsteps and embrace authenticity as part of their everyday lives. I take Dr. Wayne Dyer's words seriously when mentoring, striving to live authentically while realizing my example can make an immense difference for those within my sphere of influence.

One of the key lessons I have learned as a mentor is that authenticity breeds authenticity. By showing up as authentic versions of ourselves, we create an environment in which others feel safe expressing themselves openly as well, forging stronger ties between students and mentors that exceed traditional mentoring and building stronger bonds of mutual respect, trust, and growth for both parties involved.

Harnessing Vulnerability

Vulnerability is another integral aspect of modern mentorship, although once considered undesirable. Gone are the days when mentors were seen as unwavering figures who always knew all the answers; now, vulnerability is seen as an asset. Creating safe spaces where mentors are willing to show weakness allows mentees the freedom and space they need for personal expression and growth.

As part of my mentorship journey, I've come to recognize that the power of vulnerability is not weakness—instead, it provides a remarkable platform for connection and growth. Sharing struggles and challenges helps mentees see they're not alone on their journey while opening up more about themselves fully, creating deeper bonds of friendship, mutual respect, and greater mutual understanding between us all.

Digital innovation has revolutionized how we view mentoring. While traditional face-to-face mentoring remains highly beneficial, digital communications channels now enable new forms of connecting across continents, time zones, and cultural borders thanks to technological innovations like Zoom.

Digital mentorship has enabled me to expand my reach, connecting with individuals who share my values and vision. Thanks to online platforms, I've mentored individuals all around the globe by helping unlock their potential and achieve their goals; this digital approach to mentorship has broadened my scope while broadening my perspective from different experiences and viewpoints.

Digital mentorship presents its own distinct challenges. Forming authentic, meaningful connections may prove more challenging when communication occurs solely via text and video calls, making establishing lasting mentorship relationships in this space challenging. To address these hurdles, I strive to develop intentional interactions between myself and my mentees—through personalized messages, virtual workshops, or one-on-one video sessions—prioritizing authenticity and vulnerability as part of creating powerful digital mentoring relationships that transcend virtual borders.

Mentorship's most rewarding aspects lie in its potential to have an immense ripple effect far beyond any single relationship. When we invest in others, they, in turn, become mentors themselves—spreading the knowledge, wisdom, and support they've received into communities across society, creating growth through empowerment and positive transformation. Mentoring leaves a legacy of growth behind it all.

At Genius Code Academy, I've witnessed this transformation firsthand. Many of my mentees use the tools and insights acquired to assist others on their journeys, truly showing its transformative powers that extend far beyond individual aid to create positive change throughout society! Mentorship truly has incredible transforming potential!

Dr. Wayne Dyer once observed, "Our lives are the sum total of choices we've made; as mentors, we wield immense influence over these decisions—not only those our mentees make themselves but also the various actions their choices affect." By living authentically, accepting vulnerability, and cultivating alignment, we can leave behind an impactful legacy of mentorship to empower future generations.

As my mentorship journey unfolds, I am more committed than ever to embracing modern mentorship principles and revolution. Mentorship goes well beyond simply offering advice: it requires building authentic connections between mentors and mentees, encouraging mutual growth, and leaving an indelible mark on society overall. Mentorship allows us to live our truth while helping empower others on their path toward empowerment.

Mentorship is not an endpoint but a journey toward continuous personal and professional development. Mentors journey alongside their mentees on this path together, providing support during highs and lows, successes or challenges encountered along the way, and moments of clarity or confusion experienced along this journey. A journey such as this requires openness, curiosity, and dedication toward our own development and those we mentor.

As I've explored mentorship further, I have come to recognize its greatest effectiveness when we show up fully, authentically, and vulnerable. Acknowledging our imperfections and sharing stories that ring true for others—creating space where everyone feels seen, heard, and valued. True transformation can happen when relationships go beyond superficial surface levels to inspire people to discover their inner power and take steps toward realizing it.

Mentorship is about passing on what we learn to others, leaving an impactful legacy for communities, industries, and societies as a whole.

Empowerment through mentorship encourages me to enjoy each step along my mentorship journey, just like dancing requires enjoying each step along its path—not as an endpoint but as an enjoyable process of growth, connection, and mutual empowerment for both parties involved.

I encourage you to embrace the mentorship revolution in your own life. Seek mentors whose values and vision align with yours or become mentors yourself for others. Live authentically while giving freely; together, we can transform mentorship into a powerful force for positive change!

STEPH SHINABERY

About Steph Shinabery: Steph Shinabery is The World's Best Possibility Coach, and a Nurse Anesthesiologist, Artist, Speaker, and the Founder of Genius Code Academy.

After spending much of her life in a career that lacked the inspiration and fulfillment she knew was available to her, she began a journey to answer the question: "What is it I truly desire?"

Her journey led to the creation of the Genius Identity Code™, a process for unlocking your gift, purpose and path, and helping people see, believe and execute their unique genius to achieve miraculous outcomes.

Steph works with creative experts, entrepreneurs and coaches to help them embrace their authenticity and create a life that gets them excited to jump out of bed every day!

You can find her talk, "Wake Up Your Genius Machine," on Amazon Prime Video's *Speak Up: Empower Your Ideas, Season 4.*

Author's Website: *www.StephShinabery.com*

Book Series Website: *www.TheBookOfHumanEmpowerment.com*

VESNA MATIC

HOW OUR EXPERIENCES SHAPE OUR MISSION

How did you find your life's purpose? What an interesting and intriguing question. There are countless paths that lead to our purpose. Sometimes a person finds their purpose and meaning in life because of the struggles and hardships they faced and overcame. Other times, it can come very easily and effortlessly to an individual appearing as second nature. No matter how a person arrives at their purpose, the underlying fact is that this purpose speaks to the individual and they cannot imagine doing anything else in their life.

What is essential to understand is that we all have a purpose in life. So often we measure ourselves by what other individuals are doing or what they have. Comparing ourselves to others does not serve anyone, as it can lead to feelings of worthlessness and not measuring up to society's standards. We are all unique human beings. There is no one else in the world exactly like you. Sure, we can share similar values, interests, experiences, backgrounds, etc., but nonetheless, there is no one else quite like you. Just think, there are over 7.9 billion people on this planet and no one else is the same. This is a miracle!

There are people who had a drug or alcohol addiction that took them to the darkest precipice in their life, and once they got to the other side, they decided to help others. People who were sexually, physically, and/or mentally abused have made their life's calling assisting individuals going through the same traumas.

Having a family member, or the person themselves, being diagnosed with a serious illness and later deciding to go into the medical profession. Wanting to be a parent and raising happy, well-adjusted children because the person did not come from such a home. These are just a few examples of how our experiences influence us.

When I mentioned earlier that sometimes a person's mission is innate and appears second nature to them, I believe that one explanation for this phenomenon is through the concepts of reincarnation and karma. I passionately believe in reincarnation and that we keep coming back because there are things we want to learn, experience as well as accomplish on earth. If you believe in both karma and reincarnation, you can see how what we do carries forward from one lifetime to the next.

So often I hear people say they believe in reincarnation and karma as well, but they do not look at the full meaning behind these principles and how they work together. Karma is about cause and effect. What that means is whatever we do, or do not do, will have an impact. The phrase "what goes around comes around" is an extremely popular one which explains it in a simplified manner. Sometimes karma circles back to us instantaneously, other times it may take months, years, or even other lifetimes. This karma then has an influence on our future reincarnation(s). For this reason, it is important to be mindful of our actions.

A funny story about reincarnation is that several years ago, there were a few of us sitting together engaged in a lively discussion when the topic of past lives came up. One of the women in the group stated she was a famous queen in a former life. This struck me as very comical since other people claimed fame for being this very queen. Let us face it, only one person could have been this individual. It is ironic so many individuals want to be someone famous or important in history, whether that be a ruler, nobility etc. No one wants to dabble with the idea that they were a servant to the king or queen, street sweeper, or "commoner."

The lesson here is that we have done many things, and held various positions, in our lifetimes and each life has taught us something. If you follow me, then from this culmination of past lives are born the aspirations for our present life.

Even though I believe in reincarnation, what is important to remember is that living this life to the fullest is of the utmost importance. There are some who say that the 'average' person meets and affects approximately 10,000 people in their life! Can you imagine? Think of all the people you touch in your everyday life.

So, you never know how just smiling at someone can brighten their day. Perhaps the words of encouragement you gave to someone stopped them from hurting themselves. Maybe your actions inspired someone to stand up for what they believe in or reexamine their life.

Whatever your life's purpose, what is most important is that you do it with love, take pride in it and do your absolute best as this life is the focus. Speaking your truth, doing no harm, and helping one another is everyone's purpose.

We are all important. As human beings we want to know that we matter. This world would not be the same without you. Your life holds meaning and purpose. YOU MATTER!

Here are some ideas to help you find your path in life. Meditation is always a wonderful practice. Find a quiet spot and asking the question, "What is my purpose?" before you begin your meditation. Pay attention to your dreams, particularly if you have a reoccurring dream, as this can be a past life rising to the surface. Journaling can help prompt ideas to flow. Let your mind wander and think about what you love to do, no holds barred. Follow your heart!

A little bit about me: Both of my parents came from Yugoslavia, but it has hence broken up into separate countries. My father was born in Bosnia & Hercegovina and my mother came from a very small village in Slovenia. My father attended the Serbian Orthodox church, and my mother was Catholic. It was decided amongst themselves that my brother and I were to be raised in the Catholic faith.

For this reason, I went to Catholic elementary school from kindergarten through eighth grade. The start of my school day began by attending Catholic mass at 7:30am, followed by classes at 8:00am, Monday through Friday, and Mass on Sunday.

There were so many things that did not make sense to me regarding religion. Why would only those individuals who were baptized Catholic go to heaven? Where did everyone else go when they died? If I went to my father's church, why did that "not count" as going to Mass and I still had to go to Catholic mass that Sunday? Due to these and many other unanswered questions, my journey began of learning and exploring other traditions and religions.

Now, I describe and identify myself as being spiritual. I believe it is not important what we call the higher power. It can be God, Universe, Energy, Great Spirit, Allah, etc. We, as human beings, get caught up in the word and the desire to be the one chosen faith, but our prayers and thoughts go to the same source.

I am fortunate to say that I have traveled to many places in the world (Tibet, Bhutan, Peru, Thailand, Morocco, Iceland to name a few) as well as lived in Yugoslavia. Visiting these other lands has broadened my appreciation of the diversity of other cultures. I believe it is imperative for all people to travel, because then we can experience the nuances but also see that we all want the same things: food on the table, a roof over our head, to feel safe and secure, but, most of all, be free and happy.

I am truly blessed as there was no question what I wanted to do in my life. Spirituality has always been at my core and led me to being of service through my various counseling methods and taking people on spiritual journeys around the world.

VESNA MATIC

About Vesna Matic: Vesna Matic is an LMLP, licensed Master's level psychologist. She has developed several pathways for personal therapy that integrate the science of mental health and the dimension of the human spirit to address the full spectrum of the human experience. This includes individual sessions, ceremonies as well as plant medicines.

In an adventurous exploration of multi-level healing, Vesna has taken her diverse spiritual experiences to offer clients international tours to ancient and sacred sites around the world. These journeys spark deep emotional healing and inspire new and expansive motivation to live life with great purpose and joy for those who seek the full connection of body, mind, and spirit.

Author's Website: *www.VisionsForLife.org*

Book Series Website: *www.TheBookOfInfluence.com*

WILLIAM BLAKE

PURPOSE DRIVEN THROUGH YOUR ONE WORD WHY

"The two most important days in your life are the day you are born and the day you find out why."
~ **Mark Twain**

Purpose is what drives us to do amazing things. Without it, life can feel pretty dull. In this chapter, I'm going to share how I found my purpose, the methods that worked for me, and how you can uncover your own passion and purpose. We'll break down what purpose really is, talk about intrinsic versus extrinsic purpose, and look at practical ways to make it a part of your mindset. If you're struggling to find your purpose, this chapter aims to give you some clarity and guidance.

Understanding & Defining Purpose

When I started my self-development journey, I had no clue what my purpose was. I knew I wanted to help people and loved speaking, but I hadn't nailed down exactly what I was meant to do. Over time, I learned that purpose isn't just one thing; we have different purposes that come from our experiences.

For example, when I'm speaking, my purpose is to share my light with others. When I teach at church, it's to share my Savior's love. Even in a crisis, like a house fire, my purpose would be to save my family because I love them. Our purposes are varied and shaped by our lives.

Purpose is different from goals and desires. Desires are things we want, like pizza or winning a game. Goals are desires we plan out, like a checklist for achieving something. But purpose is deeper—it's the "why" behind our goals and desires.

Simon Sinek, in his book, *Start With Why*, says the most successful people and companies begin with their "Why." He explains it like this: desires are the "What," goals are the "How," and purpose is the "Why." Companies like Apple started with their "why" and have thrived because of it. Meanwhile, companies like Dell, which started with their "what," often struggle when they try to branch out.

To find your purpose, you need to do some self-reflection. Think about what you love to do, who you care about, what you can't stand, and who annoys you. This helps you see the deeper reasons behind your preferences. For me, I realized my love for various activities came from my appreciation for creativity and seeing joy in others. That's how I identified my purpose with the word, "LIGHT," representing my desire to bring positivity and realization to others.

Here's a simple exercise to find your purpose: grab a notebook and answer these questions:

- What do you like to do, watch, or listen to?
- Who are the people you love?
- What are the things you hate?
- Who are the people you dislike?

Next, jot down 1-3 words next to each answer explaining why they're on your list. Look for common themes and create two lists: one for positive words and one for their opposites. Sleep on it and revisit them the next day to find your "One Word Why."

This exercise is powerful because your "One Word Why" is a constant purpose that's driven you and will keep driving you. It helps you understand your deeper motivations and align your actions with your core values. People I've worked with have identified words like Heart,

Value, Love, Respect, Persistence, and Drive as their guiding principles. Your word is uniquely yours and defines your purpose.

Intrinsic vs. Extrinsic Purpose

Now that we've talked about purpose, let's dive into intrinsic and extrinsic purpose. Throughout my journey, I realized many of my desires came from external influences, not from within. At various times, I wanted to be a chef, a vet, a game developer, a garage sale flipper, a speaker, a teacher, an author, a father, a business owner, a soccer player, and a content designer. Surprisingly, only a few of these aspirations were truly mine.

We often think external influences are our own desires. But a lot of our beliefs and wants come from our surroundings and past experiences. Our views on big topics like religion, politics, business, and education, and even small habits like finishing food on our plates, usually come from external sources.

To figure out if a desire is truly yours, think about where it came from. Reflect on what you want and identify where those ideas first popped up. Ask yourself: Who introduced this idea to me? Who inspired me? This helps you see if your desires come from within or are influenced by others. For instance, my desire to flip garage sales came from a Gary Vee video, and my interest in being a chef stemmed from watching "MasterChef." But my wish to be an author came from a deep desire to hold and read my own book.

To dig deeper into your intrinsic purpose, try the "7 Levels Deep" exercise from Dean Graziosi. Start by identifying one thing that would make you feel successful if you achieved it. Then, ask yourself, "Why is this important?" Write down your answer and repeat the question seven times, digging deeper each time. The first few answers will be surface level, but as you keep going, you'll uncover more profound reasons from your heart. This works best with a partner who can push you to be introspective, but you can also do it alone.

When I first did this, I started with wanting financial independence. My initial reason was to provide for my family. As I kept going, I found deeper reasons, finally realizing I wanted to control my life. This process was powerful and helped me create the life I wanted.

By understanding the difference between intrinsic and extrinsic purposes, you can better align your actions with your true passions and values, leading to a more fulfilling and purpose-driven life.

The Role of Mindset in Achieving Purpose

Your mindset is key in shaping your life and achieving your purpose. It's the lens through which you see the world and the foundation of your attitudes and behaviors. A growth mindset—believing that abilities and intelligence can be developed with effort—can transform how you handle challenges, setbacks, and opportunities.

On the other hand, a fixed mindset—believing abilities are static—can hold you back and stop you from reaching your potential. By cultivating a growth mindset, you open yourself up to continuous learning and improvement, which is essential for living a purpose-driven life.

Three Tips to Change Your Mindset

1. **Improve Self-Talk**: How you talk to yourself shapes your mindset and well-being. Positive self-talk can boost your confidence and reinforce a growth mindset. Replace thoughts like "I can't do this" with "I am capable and can learn to do this." Make a list of affirmations that resonate with you and repeat them daily. By improving your internal dialogue, you can foster a more optimistic and resilient mindset.

2. **Surround Yourself with Growth-Minded People:** The people around you influence your mindset and motivation. Seek out those who encourage your growth and share a positive outlook. Join communities or groups that align with your values, or spend more time with friends and family who uplift you. Be mindful of the media you consume—choose books, podcasts, and content that motivate and educate you, fostering a positive environment.

3. **Embrace Failure as Learning:** Adopt a growth mindset by viewing failure as a learning opportunity. Embrace the concept of failing fast and failing forward—quickly recognize mistakes, learn from them, and move forward with newfound knowledge. Reflect on past failures and identify their lessons. Ask yourself, "What did this teach me?" and "How can I apply this lesson moving forward?" Reframing failure this way builds resilience and keeps you progressing towards your purpose.

By improving self-talk, surrounding yourself with growth-minded people, and embracing failure as learning, you can shift your mindset to support your purpose. Cultivating a growth mindset is ongoing, but with consistent effort, you can transform how you think and live.

Finding your purpose and cultivating the right mindset are transformative steps towards a fulfilling and meaningful life. By understanding what truly drives you and developing a growth mindset, you can navigate life's challenges with confidence and resilience.

Remember, purpose comes from within. Through exercises like finding your "One Word Why" and digging deep with "7 Levels Deep," you can uncover your true motivations and desires.

As you embark on this journey, keep these mindset tips in mind: Improve the way you speak to yourself, surround yourself with positivity and growth-minded people, and embrace failure as a learning opportunity. These strategies will help you stay focused and motivated, enabling you to live in alignment with your purpose.

Take the first step today. Reflect on your inner motivations, apply the exercises, and integrate these mindset tips into your daily life. With commitment and persistence, you can transform your mindset and discover a purpose that brings you joy and fulfillment.

WILLIAM BLAKE

About William Blake: William is a speaker and motivator. He focuses on the skill sets of learning, listening, and observing to help people access new avenues of success and solutions. What might seem like regular everyday skills that most overlook, William teaches people how to find creative ways of accessing those skills.

William Blake is a stalwart professional in the world of organization, strategy, and methods. Being diagnosed with Dyslexia at a young age and struggling with reading and speaking, William is an example that through perseverance, any challenge can become a superpower.

William spearheads a dynamic coaching and speaking venture, empowering dyslexics to harness their unique strengths and embrace a world of boundless possibilities. He is also one of the chapter team leaders and corporate associates at Champion Circle Professional Association founded by Speaker Jon Kovach Jr.

From speaking to youth to being a camp counselor at Idaho Diabetes Youth Programs, William loves volunteering and helping children and teens believe in themselves and their unlimited potential. And of most importance to William is his love for his family. With his wife, he is dedicated to raising his daughters in a world of greatness, happiness, and unlimited belief.

Author's website: *www.WilliamBlakeLight.com*

Book Series Website: *www.TheBookOfHumanEmpowerment.com*

"The very best way to empower the world is by empowering ourselves with confidence, leadership, and determination."

- Erik Swanson -

HABITUDE WARRIOR & INTEGRITY PUBLISHING EDITORIAL TEAM

Habitude Warrior International and Integrity Publishing take great pride in our editorial team who put their sweat, tears, and heart into each and every project and national bestseller! Thank you team!

JON KOVACH JR.
Team Manager

Jon Kovach Jr. strives to assist every author and every team member in the process of self-development for ultimate success.

PAT MINTON
VP of Operations

Pat Minton has been with the Habitude Warrior International team for over 20 years getting her start with Brian Tracy & Erik Swanson.

JILLIAN KOVACH
Editorial Manager

Jillian is a vital team member of Habitude Warrior & Integrity Publishing bringing her expertise managing our Editorial Department.

FATIMA HURD
Editorial Team & Photographer

Fatima is our Professional Photographer for Habitude Warrior as well as one of our members on the Proofing Department team.

LAUREN COBB
Editorial Team Member

Lauren Cobb is part of our Proofing Department for Habitude Warrior & Integrity Publishing as well as one of our authors.

To inquire about joining our team please send us an email to Team@HabitudeWarrior.com

Habitude Warrior Mastermind

Join a team of
AWESOME
Entrepreneurs, Coaches, Business Owners, and Leaders to support you in your journey of success!

Be one of my personal guests for a session!
www.MastermindGuestPass.com

www.ingramcontent.com/pod-product-compliance
Lightning Source LLC
Chambersburg PA
CBHW051258120626
46547CB00015B/1994